B. M. Attridge
6 October 1992.

Councillors and tenants:
local authority housing
in English cities, 1919–1939

Themes
in Urban
History

General editor: Derek Fraser

Councillors and tenants: local authority housing in English cities, 1919–1939

edited by M. J. DAUNTON

Leicester University Press   1984

First published in 1984 by Leicester University Press

Copyright © Leicester University Press 1984

Designed by Arthur Lockwood
Phototypeset in Linotron Times, printed and bound
in Great Britain at The Pitman Press, Bath

British Library Cataloguing in Publication Data
  Councillors and tenants. – (Themes in urban history)
  1. Public housing – England – History – 20th century
  I. Daunton, M. J.   II. Series
  363.5′8   HD7288.78.G7
  ISBN 0–7185–1223–5

FOREWORD

Urban history is an expanding field of study, sustained by a considerable volume of research. The purpose of this series, originally conceived by the late Jim Dyos, is to open a new channel for the dissemination of the findings of a careful selection from that research, providing a conspectus of new knowledge on specific themes.

For each volume in the series, each of the contributors is invited to present the core of his work: the essays, originating in theses but now specially written for this volume, are combined under the control of the editor, who writes an introduction setting out the significance of the material being presented in the light of developments in that or a cognate field.

It is hoped that in this way the fruits of recent work may be made widely available, both to assist further exploration and to contribute to the teaching of urban history.

In this, the sixth volume of the series, Martin Daunton takes us for the first time wholly beyond the First World War, a virtually uncharted sea for the urban historian. Through detailed case-studies in three very different urban contexts, this volume demonstrates how urban municipal housing became the focus of important political, social, economic and architectural decisions and developments. Much evidence of the outcome of those inter-war developments remains with us in the fabric of the modern English city.

Derek Fraser
University of Bradford

CONTENTS

LIST OF ILLUSTRATIONS

LIST OF TABLES

LIST OF ABBREVIATIONS

Note Places of publication are given only for works published outside the United Kingdom. In abbreviating less frequently cited periodical titles, commonly accepted abbreviations such as *J.* for *Journal*, *Rev.* for *Review* have been used; other abbreviations are listed below.

BABTE	Bristol Association of Building Trades Employers
BCM	Bristol Council Minutes
BCRO	Bristol City Records Office
BHCM	Bristol Housing Committee Minutes
BO	*Bristol Observer*
BTM	*Bristol Times and Mirror*
CCRO	Cleveland County Record Office
CDC	Chester-le-Street District Council Offices
DCRO	Durham County Record Office
DDC	Derwentside District Council Offices
EcHR	*Economic History Review*
GLS	Local Studies Section, Gateshead Central Library
HBC	Hartlepool Borough Council Offices
LCC	Leeds City Council
LM	*Leeds Mercury*
LWC	*Leeds Weekly Citizen*
MOH	Medical Officer of Health
PRO	Public Record Office
RIBA	Royal Institute of British Architects
RO	Record Office
SLS	Local Studies Section, Sunderland Central Library
STLS	Local Studies Section, South Tyneside Central Library
TPI	Town Planning Institute
T&WCRO	Tyne and Wear County Record Office
WDP	*Western Daily Press*
WHR	Reference Section, West Hartlepool Central Library
YEN	*Yorkshire Evening News*
YEP	*Yorkshire Evening Post*
YO	*Yorkshire Observer*
YP	*Yorkshire Post*

NOTES ON THE CONTRIBUTORS

M. J. DAUNTON is Lecturer in Economic History at University College London, and is the author of *Coal Metropolis: Cardiff 1870–1914*, *House and Home in the Victorian City: Working Class Housing 1850–1914* and articles on urban and labour history. He is currently completing the official history of the Post Office.

MADGE DRESSER is a Senior Lecturer in Social History at Bristol Polytechnic where she teaches on the M.A. in historical studies and on the humanities and social sciences undergraduate honours degree.

ROBERT FINNIGAN took a first degree in history and geography in the School of Social Sciences at the University of Bradford and then carried out postgraduate research into housing policy in inter-war Leeds, for which he was awarded an M.Phil. in 1981. In 1980 his essay 'Housing policy in Leeds between the wars' appeared in *Housing, Social Policy and the State*, edited by J. Melling. At present he works as a Research Assistant at Leeds University and also lectures part-time at Leeds Polytechnic.

ROBERT RYDER was born in Brighton in 1953. He was educated at Brighton, Hove & Sussex Grammar School and read Modern History from 1972 to 1975 at Durham University. He then spent a full-time year in Durham researching the history of local authority housing. His contribution to this volume has been drawn from the resulting M.Phil thesis (presented in 1979). Since 1976 Bob Ryder has worked for the Department of the Environment in London and Leeds. (Any views expressed in his contribution to this book are, of course, his own and not those of the Department.)

Introduction

M.J. DAUNTON

Introduction

M.J. DAUNTON

'The real housing problem of today', remarked Professor William Smart in 1904, 'narrows itself down to this: how far the experience gained points in the direction of the municipality itself building and owning houses for certain of the poorer classes.'[1] Theorists and politicians alike gave different answers. In 1905, Lettice Fisher was adamant that 'the majority of thinkers will agree that the main task of providing house accommodation must be left to private enterprise, and that the most important duty of local authorities is to induce the private builder . . . to do his work in the best possible manner.'[2] The limitation of public activity to the regulation of private enterprise was also the guiding principle of J.S. Nettlefold, the dominant figure on Birmingham's Housing Committee. Indeed, he argued that 'every house built by the local authority stops at least four being built by other people, which means that municipal house building will eventually decrease rather than increase the supply of houses in proportion to demand.'[3] A.C. Pigou, however, was less adamant, and was 'inclined to rank housing with education and insurance, in regard to which subsidies are already provided, rather than with food and clothing, in regard to which such subsidies are not, and so far as present indications go, cannot in general be provided.'[4] At the other extreme, Alderman W. Thompson of Richmond saw a dynamic role for public housing. 'If local authorities were to build largely themselves', he argued, 'they would be able to assist in meeting the demand for more house room; to provide an effective check where necessary on exorbitant rents; to set up a standard of a decent sanitary home that a working man might reasonably expect.'[5] On this interpretation, the local authority was the guarantor of both quantity and quality in the housing market.

The emphasis in the history of council housing has been very much upon this question of the changing definition of policy and the correct role of public initiative. Surprisingly little has been written as yet about the manner in which councillors functioned in their new guise of builders and landlords, once the local authorities had, for whatever reasons, become the major suppliers of new working-class accommodation. Historians have attempted to explain how speculative builders before 1914 determined the scale of the private building programme; there has been comparatively little attention paid to the process by which local authorities after 1919 determined the scale of the public building programme. Recently, research has been directed towards the techniques used by private landlords before 1914 to select tenants, determine rent levels, secure payment, and remove defaulters;[6] there has been less concern for the patterns of landlord-tenant relations which emerged in the public sector after 1919. It is precisely these neglected topics which are considered by the contributors to this volume. Their concern is directed away from the causes of public involvement in the housing market and the development of national policy which have dominated the historiography of council housing, towards the manner in which individual local authorities grappled with the immediate problems which arose from their entry into the market. But why did local authorities enter the housing market on a large scale after the First World War? It is necessary to comment upon this debate, for the timing and nature of the process which impelled councils into the provision of housing did in part control the manner in which the new role was perceived.

The formulation of national policy

The coming of the council house remains controversial. Had the private housing market undergone a structural crisis by 1914 so that state intervention was a necessity for the continued provision of working-class housing? Or could it be argued that the private market was functioning in a satisfactory manner up to the First World War, so that the crisis in the housing market came not from within, but from the external distortions of state intervention during the war? In other words, did the failure of the market induce state intervention, or did state intervention induce the failure of the market?

Many historians have simply assumed that private enterprise could not in normal conditions supply decent accommodation to the lowest income levels. Economic growth might be intimately associated with low housing standards. Bad housing conditions on this view were an integral part of Victorian capitalism, reflecting a skewed distribution of income and the absence of effective demand from those most in need. 'Slums', argued H.J. Dyos, 'helped to underpin Victorian prosperity.' The capital which could have improved housing conditions was invested elsewhere and not distributed in higher wages. The payment of higher wages would have increased the cost of commodity exports and reduced capital exports, both of which would have threatened Britain's trading position. 'One of the real costs of industrial expansion was the making of slums.' On such a view, bad housing was not an unfortunate side-effect of economic growth, which would in time make available the resources of its ultimate solution. Growth and slums were of necessity cause and effect.[7]

Such an interpretation of the economics of working-class housing means that the development of housing policy is analysed in terms of the gradual and inevitable acceptance of state intervention to replace private initiative.[8] The form of public involvement is taken for granted: council housing at subsidized rents. The development of policy is read in the light of the dawning of such a realization, rather than in terms of the motivations and concerns of the time. A.S. Wohl can thus find in the debates of the 1880s on housing in London, 'a new awareness, a new era' of municipal socialism and central government subsidies.[9] The housing policies of the late nineteenth century are seen as precursors of twentieth-century council housing. J.N. Tarn's study of the philanthropic housing movement is based upon the assumption that it is 'in the end, the account of how council housing, as we understand it, was born out of that curious Victorian private enterprise housing movement.'[10] Public involvement in the bye-law era of the late nineteenth century to remove the worst slums and to control standards of new construction had only exacerbated the problem by reducing the stock of cheap property, increasing costs, lessening 'the profitable inducements to build more cottages, besides necessitating higher rents.'[11] The manifest failure of both philanthropic activity and the public regulation of private enterprise led, in this view, inexorably to public provision of subsidized accommodation. The lesson of history in this interpretation is that housing policy required 'a full programme of social welfare benefits'; the problem to be explained by the historian is the slow acceptance of public responsibility for housing provision.[12]

The search for the origins of the dominant form of new working-class accommodation *after* the First World War distorts the interpretation of housing policy *before* the war. Subsidized public housing was in fact alien to the whole approach of the philanthropic housing movement, an understanding of which demands the analysis of the response of a particular social group to the specific social and economic structures of London in the second half of the nineteenth century.[13] The ideological framework of the late nineteenth and early twentieth centuries was dominated by concepts which have since been relegated to the margin of concern. The housing debate of the 1880s was informed less by a new awareness of municipal socialism and central government subsidies, than by the land question. The assumption of most historians is that the housing problem was an aspect of the division of the national income between capital and labour; but to many contemporaries it was an aspect of the land question. It was possible to argue that rents exceeded the ability of the tenants to pay because of the high cost of urban land. The solution to the housing problem was on this interpretation not to subsidize rents, but to reduce the charge for land, whether by the reduction in the cost of transport to make a wider area available for residential use, or by the imposition of taxes on the increase in site values, which would remove the incentive to hoard land. This would solve both the housing problem and the crisis in local government finance which had arisen from the slow growth of rateable value at a time of mounting public expenditure. This interpretation came to the forefront of Liberal ideology in the 1880s, and reached its climax in Lloyd George's land campaign in the years leading to the First World War. It was a view which sought to unite capital and labour against land, suggesting that the interests of both tenants and landlords were opposed to the providers of the building sites. The Conservative approach was different. The argument developed by the Conservatives was that land and houses *taken together* were overtaxed in relation to other sources of income; the solution to the crisis in local government finance was therefore to shift taxation away from rates levied on real property towards other forms of income and central government grants-in-aid. The Liberals could reject the policy of Exchequer grants as a dole in aid of land which was designed to protect the owners of the ground from a reasonable contribution to the cost of urban services. It followed that many Liberals would be wary of central government subsidies to house building, which seemed to distract attention both from a solution to the financial problem by the taxation of land, and from a solution to the housing problem by reducing the price of sites.[14]

The debate over the land question provided the context for 'the first attempt in Parliament to secure state aid for housing'. It is perhaps not surprising that the

Housing of the Working Classes Bills of 1912 and 1913 were the product of the Unionist Social Reform Committee, for they formed an alternative strategy to the Liberal land campaign. Sir Arthur Griffith-Boscawen informed the Commons that 'we propose boldly . . . state aid for housing to spread the burden over the broader shoulders of the taxpayers. That is absolutely necessary and important because in no other way can you get this housing work carried out.' The finance should come from central taxes rather than local rates. This was to deny the Liberal prescription on taxation, that the burden should be shifted to land. 'Land Taxers led the opposition to the Bill; they had their own solution to urban problems.' The Conservative pamphlet *The History of Housing Reform* of 1913 was categoric in its advocacy of public housing supported by central funds. 'If a certain number of houses are not built at a non-economic rent, the present housing evil is irremediable and the problem must be given up in despair. If on the other hand, those houses are to be built, it seems clear from experience that some state encouragement to Local Authorities will have to be given.'[15]

The Report of the Liberal Land Enquiry Committee of 1914 adopted a different approach. The unsatisfactory housing conditions arose from an inability to pay an economic rent for a sanitary dwelling, but the solution was not to provide subsidized houses at uneconomic rents, for this would eliminate the profit of the builder and thus delay the solution of the problem by ordinary market forces. Rather, minimum wage legislation and the destruction of casual employment would allow the payment of an economic rent, whilst the cost of development could be reduced by the use of cheap suburban land on garden-city lines. Public utility societies were encouraged rather than local authorities.[16] There was, then, no single pre-ordained housing policy in the years just before 1914. There was a trenchant debate over the approach to be adopted which is missed if the end result of subsidized council housing is taken for granted.

It is therefore necessary to explain why the particular solution of subsidized council housing was ultimately adopted, for the circumstances might in part determine the manner in which local authorities adopted their role of builder and landlord. It should be stressed that the reliance on council housing to the exclusion of other approaches to the housing of the working classes is a peculiarity of Britain amongst western capitalist economies. As the *Report of the Committee on Housing in Greater London, 1965*, states, 'Elsewhere the direct financial assistance which government provides for house building and the controls which it exercises over the distribution of housing have been spread through a wider variety of institutions and sectors, and meet a wider variety of needs.' The building of private rented housing has been encouraged, within a comprehensive system of regulation. Public initiative has not everywhere driven out private rented housing which may rather be incorporated into government policy. There was no inevitability about the demise of the private landlord as the main provider of new working-class housing. It was possible to mitigate the worst faults of the private sector by strict regulations alongside tax incentives and cheap loans.[17] The interesting historical question becomes why the private landlord was rejected as a crucial component of state policy in Britain, rather than incorporated as one element amongst a range of approaches.

Whilst rents have in many countries been an important issue, landlords themselves have seldom attracted the political interest focused upon them in Britain. 'In countries where the rights and wrongs of the private landlord have not been the subject of such prolonged and embittered political conflict it has been possible to establish more productive and responsible relationships between government and the various interests and groups concerned.'[18] The dominance of policy after the First World War by council housing rested in part upon the political and social isolation of the private landlord. In the debate over the land question and local taxation, landlords did have a justifiable grievance that, with the mounting burden of rates in the late nineteenth and early twentieth centuries, they were bearing an undue incidence of taxation. But they had no real voice within either the Conservative or Liberal approaches to local taxation, and they were left in a politically isolated position. The Conservative doctrine of central government subsidies grew out of the demands of agriculture for relief, whilst the Liberal policy stood for industrial, mercantile and finance capital against the landed interest. Urban house capital stood between the two, agreeing with the 'Conservative complaint about finance-and-mercantile capital's immunity from the poor rates, and with the Liberal outrage at the landowners' evasion of the municipal burden.' In any case, Conservative policy was developing in a manner which would involve the sacrifice of the small house owner. The aim was to safeguard the owners of large estates and capitals, by creating a protective 'rampart' of small proprietors. This role could not be fulfilled by private landlords, who were politically unpopular and so might bring other classes of property into disrepute. The rampart was rather to be constructed by encouraging the growth of owner-occupation and a 'property-owning democracy'.[19]

The sense of isolation was intensified by the fact that urban property was a characteristic investment of the petty bourgeoisie. The small businesses of the lower middle class were highly vulnerable, and surpluses were accordingly placed in secure and local outlets. 'Petty bourgeois property was localised and immobile, with clear ideological consequences.' In the mid-nineteenth century it was possible for ratepayers to mobilize on a local political stage, but by the end of the century the scope for local action was reduced, with the increased importance of other groupings on local councils; the emergence of a local bureaucracy; and the need to fulfil the requirements imposed by central government. But the lower middle class, unlike its counterpart in Germany, was unable to develop a national political presence in order to protect its interests. Dr Crossick has suggested why this should be the case. Industrial capitalism evolved more gradually in Britain, so that the polarization of large and small capital was less stark. There was 'no traditional ideology of a pre-industrial petty bourgeois kind around which discontented groups could focus', so that 'there was no distinctive consciousness in relation to industrial and commercial capital.' Neither was there a strong class of small rural property owners to provide a base. The shop-keeper radicalism of the early nineteenth century had little rationale by the later years of the century; its denunciation of monopoly and privilege had become identified with the ideology of laissez faire and free trade. Whereas in Germany the petty bourgeoisie urged state protection of the small man against large-scale business, in Britain the lower middle class remained tied to an ideology of laissez faire, which could be used to defend industrial concentration as a rational market response. There was a failure to develop a distinctive political voice which would move beyond a merely negative denunciation of municipal socialism, to a positive demand for state protection of private landlords.[20]

The result was that the private landlord was not to be an integral component of housing policy. This helps to explain the general nature of public intervention, within the specific context of the disruptions of the First World War and reconstruction. It is not enough to talk about a generalized inability of the private market to supply housing, for this says nothing about the precise timing and circumstances of intervention which might determine the outcome. The existence of slums at all periods can hardly be denied, but that does not say anything about the exact point at which it was felt that the private market had broken down. The war provided the timing and specific context for the emergence of local authorities as large-scale builders and landlords.[21] It was the speed and scale of the post-war housing programme which forced the government to rely on local authorities as the agents for executing a national policy.

The Liberal Land Enquiry Committee at the time, and Dr Offer more recently, have observed the existence of a general, deep-seated, structural crisis in the housing market of Edwardian England. The cost of providing houses rose with higher interest rates, increased building costs, more stringent bye-laws, and a mounting burden of rates. However, landlords were unable to obtain appreciably higher rents to cover increased costs because real wages were stagnant, and effective demand was further reduced by a slackening of the birth rate and a lower level of migration to the towns. Property values fell steeply in London, and this collapse 'marked a decline in the attractions of housing as an investment.'[22] A specific example of this Edwardian crisis is provided by County Durham. The coal companies in the north-east supplied miners with either a rent-free house or a rent allowance. The cost of supplying houses increased, whilst the rent allowance was fixed at an historic figure. The owners had every reason to stop building and to substitute a rent allowance. This rejection of the traditional method of supplying accommodation in the Great Northern coalfield created tension in the housing market before 1914.[23]

It may, however, be argued that the Edwardian housing market faced less a permanent structural crisis than a cycle whose upturn was prevented by the war. Building was not uniformly depressed, and 'the exceptions include some of the most important industrial areas in the country.'[24] The capital value of housing had fallen before,[25] and it could be argued that as the level of empty houses was reduced, rents would recover, and investment would be stimulated. Whether this would have happened in the absence of the First World War cannot be known, but the process does presuppose the unfettered operation of the laws of the market. It could be suggested that an unwillingness to permit such an outcome converted the cyclical downturn into a permanent structural change in the market. In the early years of the twentieth century, the perception of social problems changed, and housing formed part of this process.[26] Housing became a political issue so that free market economics could not be allowed unfettered operation. Housing was a commodity with a dual economic nature: it was a good supplied under commercial considerations of profit; it was also a vital investment for the production of commodities in general. An adequate housing stock is an obvious necessity for securing a labour force, whilst the standard of housing accommodation is a significant determinant of labour productivity. The supply of housing might therefore be controlled by considerations other than its own commercial viability. A tension might emerge between the two approaches to housing. Once it was accepted that housing should be viewed as a prerequisite for an efficient economy and a stable society, the private landlord was in a precarious position, for his performance was not being assessed in terms of its own commercial viability. Criteria of 'national efficiency' and social welfare produced controls and regulations which disturbed the market relationship between the effective demand of working-class tenants and the cost of supplying accommodation. The profit expectations of the landlords were given a lower priority than the raising of environmental standards and the protection of tenants' rights.[27]

Private landlords were on the periphery of the economic and political structures. This was apparent before the First World War from the failure to redress their grievances concerning the burden of local taxation and the reduction in their power of repossession of property.[28] This was confirmed by the imposition of rent control in 1915, which introduced a whole new range of distortions and disruptions, but which also reflected a number of pre-war trends. The divide between pre-war structural crisis and wartime destruction of the private market is in fact misleading, for the attitude adopted by the government during the war reflected the pre-war perception of the limited claims of landlords upon the state. The crucial rent strike of 1915 on Clydeside which inspired the introduction of rent controls grew out of a deep-seated pre-war tension in landlord-tenant relations in Scotland, and was not simply the result of wartime distortions.[29] The Increase of Rent and Mortgage Interest (War Restrictions) Act of 1915 indicated the willingness of the government to sacrifice the interests of the landlords in a manner which was not thought desirable for other forms of property. Higher priority was given to tenants' rights and to the maintenance of production of other commodities. It was the specific context of wartime rent control which was to determine in large part the development of council housing after the war. The precise point at which the private market was considered to have broken down was of considerable moment. What, when, was the outcome of the introduction of rent controls in 1915?

Public housing in a controlled market

Once rent controls were imposed in 1915, a new set of distortions were introduced into the housing market, which helps to explain the context for the large-scale programme of council housing after the war. The Act of 1915 was designed to prevent the imposition of scarcity rents. It provided that the rents of all houses whose rateable value did not exceed £35 in London, £30 in Scotland, and £26 elsewhere, should not be increased above the 'standard rent', defined as the rent paid on 3 August 1914. Control on rents necessitated control on mortgages. The rise in interest rates brought about by war finance created a danger that mortgages would be called in to gain a higher return. House owners would not be able to compete for funds at the higher rates, in view of the restrictions on their income. The Act of 1915 therefore laid down that mortgages were not to be called in and the interest not to be increased. The Act was to apply for the duration of the war and six months afterwards.[30]

The Act of 1915 resulted in a redistribution of income from landlords and mortgagees towards tenants. Although owners had fewer losses from unlet property and arrears, the increased cost of repairs and management eroded profit margins. Mortgagees had been unable to recall their money and obtain the higher rate of return earned by other investors; retrieval of the principal by transferring the mortgage would result in a large capital loss. These two classes suffered an erosion of their income, and the result was a gain by the tenants. The share of labour in the gross national product rose from 55.3 per cent in 1910–14 to 67.4 per cent in 1921–4, and one element in the redistribution was the fall in the share of rent from 11.0 to 6.8 per cent.[31] Private landlords and mortgagees were one of the few sectors of property sacrificed by the government during the war. The political isolation of landlords was clear before the war with the erosion of their legal power over tenants and the deterioration of their fiscal position; it was confirmed by the Act of 1915; and the development of policy between the wars did little to rectify their grievances. Rather, policy relied upon the provision of rented property by local authorities, or building for owner-occupation by the private market.

At the end of the war, the government faced a serious dilemma. If the Act of 1915 were allowed to expire six months after the end of the war, rents would certainly rise. This would in many cases be justified by the general inflation, but the opportunity to exact scarcity rents would exist at a time of extreme dislocation. A failure to increase rents would present equally serious problems. 'A commercial rent could not be obtained on new houses in competition with similar existing houses built at a lower cost and restricted in rent. Private capital would therefore be attracted to other investments offering better and more secure prospects.' Rent controls were necessary because the shortage of houses permitted the imposition of scarcity rents; but the existence of rent controls hindered the provision of new houses to end the shortage. 'You will not get the houses until the Act is removed, and, therefore, unless the Act is removed the necessity for the Act remains.'[32]

It was considered impossible to remove the restrictions, for the housing shortage and consequent ability to impose scarcity rents was greater in 1918 than in 1915. Rent control was therefore continued by the Increase of Rent and Mortgage Interest (Restrictions) Act of 1919. Rents could be increased by 10 per cent and mortgagees could charge an additional $\frac{1}{2}$ per cent, up to a maximum of 5 per cent per annum. It was, however, admitted that a 35 per cent increase in rents was required to place owners in as good a position as in 1914. At the same time, rent control was extended to all houses with a rateable value of up to £70 in London, £60 in Scotland, and £52 elsewhere. The Increase of Rent and Mortgage Interest (Restrictions) Act of 1920 again increased these limits to £105, £90 and £78. Rents could now be raised to 40 per cent above the standard rent, and mortgage interest could be increased by 1 per cent up to a maximum of $6\frac{1}{2}$ per cent per annum. Post-war inflation meant that landlords were still not restored to their pre-war position. It was felt that rents could only gradually rise to meet the general price level, in order to avoid disturbance and to keep rents within limits which public opinion considered to be equitable. Rent strikes at Coventry and Woolwich suggested the dangers which might result at a time of great anxiety about stability during demobilization. The Act of 1920 was to remain in force until June 1923, by which time it was hoped 'that it will be possible to allow the ordinary economic forces to operate, and to fix the economic balance.' Since private enterprise could not be expected to remove the housing shortage unaided, the only way to return to 'ordinary economic forces' was for the state to intervene in order to subsidize both the private and the public sector until the shortages caused by the war were removed. At this point, rent and mortgage controls could be removed and the housing market could 'be again established on an economic footing'.[33]

The post-war programme of house building was thus seen as a finite emergency measure to deal with wartime shortages before the restoration of a free market. But matters did not work out so simply, for the housing programme was cut before the shortage was removed. The 'Addison' Housing Act of 1919 promised 500,000 houses. In fact, local authorities completed 170,090 while a further 39,186 were built by subsidized private enterprise. 'The crusade had fizzled out after achieving only just over two-fifths of its target.'[34] This interpretation of subsidized public housing views it as a short-term response to the distortions of rent control, as an attempt to bridge the gulf between controlled rents and current market rents. Such an approach contradicts the recent analysis of Mark Swenarton. The view stressed here is that council housing was a temporary *ad hoc* response to post-war price distortions; the view stressed by Dr Swenarton is that council housing was 'an *ad hoc* response to an immediate political crisis.' The government seized upon housing as an antidote to revolution. The new houses had to be of a design superior to anything supplied in the past, in order to show that aspirations could be met under the existing order, and to 'provide visible proof of the irrelevance of revolution.' Dr Swenarton argues that the Act was essentially a 'political creation', stressing that 'both Cabinet and Parliament accepted the housing programme of 1919 as the necessary price of social stability, the unavoidable premium of the "insurance against revolution".'[35] The government was indeed aware of the ideological purposes of house provision and design, but the argument must be kept in perspective. The remarks of Dr Melling on the provision of housing by employers are apposite. 'Housing', he claims, 'was simply too costly and the workers too well organised to use accommodation as a manipulative or coercive instrument against a workforce.' But whilst housing was not supplied primarily to discipline the workforce, the fact that employers might in some circumstances be compelled to provide accommodation by other considerations, such as isolation from existing centres of population, meant that it could be used to fulfil certain managerial objectives.[36] The same remarks surely apply to public intervention. The motivation for council housing lay within the housing market; but once the state was compelled to provide accommodation, it could then be used as a device to legitimize the existing organization of society.

The housing programme was abandoned in July 1921. Dr Swenarton explains the change in policy in terms of the erosion of the power of labour with the end of the post-war boom. 'The "insurance against revolution" was no longer needed.' Treasury demands for retrenchment, which had been ignored when something worse threatened, could now be heeded, and the programme was cut in terms of both quality and quantity.[37] This is to stress political and ideological rather than economic explanations. More emphasis should perhaps be placed upon the desire of the government to deflate in order to return to the gold standard, and upon the extreme difficulty of building 500,000 houses at a time of economic dislocation after the war which upset the initial assumptions about the cost of the scheme. The finance of the Addison programme resulted in 'liquidity problems', both for the local authorities and for the contractors who built the majority of the houses. This is well shown by the contributors to this volume. Local authorities had to raise money on the open market. Local Bonds could be issued to attract small investors within the area, but many issues were failures, and in the whole of England and Wales this method raised only £17m up to 31 March 1921. In Bristol, less than half the anticipated £800,000 was raised; in Stanley, only £600 was secured to cover schemes costing £250,000. By contrast, £35m was raised nationally by issuing stock, and £15m from mortgage loans. The difficulties of raising money were to force many local authorities to postpone their housing schemes. This was to remain a particularly important issue in County Durham, where economic depression, low rateable values and high rates promised poor security for investors. The rate base of towns in County Durham was weaker than the more prosperous and socially mixed cities such as Leeds and Bristol, which produced a serious problem of housing finance throughout the inter-war period. But it was not only the local authorities which experienced liquidity problems; so did the contractors who needed to finance their operations, and the builders' merchants who wished to restock after the war. Dr Marriner has concluded that 'despite the government's public protestations of willingness to take all the steps necessary to ensure that the campaign for building "Homes fit for Heroes" reached its target, the government was not prepared to adopt any measures at all to assist contractors to overcome what was, for many firms, the most intractable problem of all. Failure to raise sufficient cash meant insolvency for contractors and contributed to the serious shortfall in the supply of houses.'[38]

There were also serious shortages of real resources. Controls on building were removed at the end of 1918, and local authority schemes had to compete for scarce resources at inflated prices. Although in 1919 local authorities were given powers to limit luxury building, there was no effective control over building, and costs rose from an estimated £600 per house in 1918, to £1,200 a house in 1920. Skilled labour was in short supply, and the unions were able to resist dilution and to use their strong bargaining position to gain additional allowances. Builders could form cartels in order to limit the impact of competitive tenders, as appears clearly in Madge Dresser's analysis of negotiations between the Housing Committee and the Bristol Association of Building Trade Employers. The case-studies of County Durham and Bristol provide abundant evidence of the problems of local authorities in fulfilling their targets under the Housing Act of 1919.[39]

Contracts issued to April 1921

1	Built by builders' federations and speculative builders for sale to local authorities		17,500
2	Direct labour	8,800	
	Office of Works	5,200	15,500
	Guilds	1,500	
3	New building techniques		20,000
			53,000
All contracts			160,000

Source: M. Swenarton, *Homes Fit for Heroes. The Politics and Architecture of Early State Housing in Britain* (1981), p. 128.

There was indeed a contradiction between the need to produce houses and the opposition of powerful interests to the transfer of scarce resources to building. There were three possible solutions to the dilemma, which are apparent in the contributions of Madge Dresser and Robert Ryder. The first possibility was 'finding a substitute for the local authorities as building agents.' This could be done by replacing the local authority by private builders. The Housing (Additional Powers) Act of 1919 subsidized builders to construct for the private market. Local authorities also purchased houses erected by speculative builders, and reached agreements with builders' federations to distribute contracts among their members at an agreed price. The second solution was 'organising the building process without the building contractor.' This could be achieved by using the Office of Works, the government's building department, as an agent of the local authority. The Office of Works built 5,314 houses of 170,090 completed by the local authorities under the Act of 1919. Another means of replacing the contractor, which was debated in Bristol, was to use building guilds, which were quasi-syndicalist groups of workers. The third option was 'expanding the resources available for housing by the use of additional labour and new methods of building.' It was hoped that by eliminating bricks and bricklayers it would be possible to lessen the shortage of both materials and labour. New building techniques were accordingly recommended, and particularly the Dorlonco steel-frame system which was used in 250 houses in Bristol. However, none of these strategies could adequately overcome the fact that the building programme coincided both with the strains of conversion from a war economy and with an inflationary boom.[40]

The failure to remove the housing shortage after the war made it inexpedient to end rent controls. In 1923, the dilemma was again apparent: the rent level of old houses was below the commercial rent for new property; an adequate supply of housing was needed before restrictions could be removed; but the supply would not be forthcoming until the controls were abolished. The Onslow Committee of 1923 remarked that

> we cannot but conclude that the Rent Restriction Acts, although their necessity in the past may not be challenged, have had an adverse effect on the provision of new houses. They have helped to prolong the shortage of accommodation which rendered them necessary, so that if the country is ever to get back to the position whereby the bulk of its houses is to be provided by private enterprise, the sooner all restrictions can be removed the better.

However, an immediate end to restriction was ruled out, and a period of transition to 'freedom of contract between landlord and tenant' was proposed, during which the housing shortage would be removed by the joint efforts of private and public enterprise. The Rent and Mortgage Interest Restrictions Act of 1923 reaffirmed the controls contained in the legislation of 1920 for a further two years; the powers were extended after 1925 for successive short periods. A cautious element of deregulation was introduced. Control was shifted from the *house* to the *tenancy*, by providing for decontrol whenever the landlord came into possession. By the end of 1928, 6 per cent of working-class houses were decontrolled, and by the middle of 1930, 11 per cent. The combined rents and rates of controlled houses were 50 per cent higher than in 1914, whereas in decontrolled houses they were between 85 and 90 per cent above pre-war levels.[41]

Rent control was a poorly focused redistribution device which had serious consequences for the housing market. Consumers' real income increased at the end of the war, whilst the price of housing was fixed. Tenants could therefore afford more space, so that rent controls in effect increased the shortage of housing. The establishment of maximum prices without the imposition of rationing resulted in part of the demand at the fixed price going unsatisfied. But investment would not be attracted to supply the houses which were demanded, for the rate of return was depressed. Instead, investors moved to areas of the economy where prices were not fixed. The housing market was in disequilibrium. Demand exceeded the supply at controlled rents, and there was no incentive for private enterprise to close the gap. The assertion that rents must be controlled until the shortage disappeared implied permanent controls, unless one of two things occurred: either incomes must fall back to the level of 1914; or massive subsidies were required to remove the shortage. In the early 1920s, there was an attempt by employers to win back some of the gains made by workers in the post-war boom, and weekly real wages of fully employed workers were eroded between 1921 and 1923. Thereafter, real wages increased for those in employment, and demand did not return to the level of 1914. The alternative strategy in bringing the market back into equilibrium was to build housing – whether council or private – which was subsidized in order to increase the supply at non-economic rents. Once the shortage was removed, then controls could be safely disbanded. However, the experience of the Housing Acts of 1919 suggested that subsidies on the requisite scale were unrealistic. The housing market as a result remained in disequilibrium and controls persisted. The consequences were complex. The real income of landlords was reduced, but tenants did not gain the full extent of the benefit of controlled rents, for part of the gain was dissipated in bidding up other prices. Tenants could afford more space, but they could not necessarily obtain it. The benefits to the tenants were randomly distributed. Rent-controlled houses were used less efficiently than if rents had risen with prices and income. The incentive to 'ration' accommodation was reduced, so that small families might remain in large houses. The unsatisfied demand was squeezed out into alternatives such as furnished accommodation and houses for sale, whose price was thus increased. Whilst tenants as a whole benefited at the expense of landlords and mortgagees, these groups were amongst the lower levels of wealth holders and might, indeed, be less wealthy than their tenants. Identical houses might have controlled and uncontrolled rents, but there was no guarantee that the poorest tenant rented the cheapest house. The conclusion reached on American experience after the Second World War might well be applied to Britain after the First World War:

> This transfer has been an indiscriminate one, made without regard to the income position of individual tenants and landlords nor without much attention to the relative economic status of tenants and landlords as a group. . . . The income transfer that is involved in rent control is not one that can be justified on the usual grounds used for supporting progressive income tax or free public education. It has . . . no justification except the political one that there are more tenants than landlords.[42]

There are two possible resolutions of the dilemma of rent controls which had become a cause as well as a consequence of housing shortages. Both denied a continuing role to private landlords in the provision of new working-class accommodation, but gave a different emphasis to the contribution of council housing. The Conservative view of public intervention was made clear by Neville Chamberlain's Housing Act of 1923. The subsidy was available for only two years, at the end of which it was assumed that the shortages would be over. In other words, the Act complemented the Rent and Mortgage Interest Restrictions Act of 1923, for rent controls were also to continue until 1925, when it was believed that market rents and free enterprise could return.

It was assumed that only remedies of an emergency type were needed. Consistently with this attitude, a deliberate attempt was made to prevent the permanent establishment of the local authorities as suppliers of working-class houses in general. The main Act of 1919 had opened the door for the treatment of the provision of working-class houses as a sort of social service. The door was now closed as far as possible by a clause that only allowed local authorities to build houses themselves if they succeeded in convincing the Minister of Health that it would be better if they did so, than if they left it to private enterprise. . . . The local authorities were to be merely 'also rans'.[43]

The alternative approach was explained by J.S. Whybrew of the National Labour Housing Association in 1920. Rent control should be made permanent, with Rent Courts to establish fair rents. In his view, private enterprise would not return to provide working-class housing, so that state initiative should be the normal, rather than the emergency, method of supply. The provision of housing by local authorities was not a temporary expedient to remove the wartime shortage, designed to allow current controlled rents and market rents to come into line. Rents should be determined by 'moral' rather than political economy, by criteria of justice rather than by what the market would bear.[44] When Labour came to power in 1924, the role of the local authorities in providing working-class housing as a matter of course was reaffirmed. A long-term housing programme was established, by extending the Chamberlain subsidy to 1939 and introducing the new, more generous, 'Wheatley' subsidy to cover the same period.[45]

In the early 1930s, the Conservative approach to public housing was reasserted. The Labour government in 1930 had introduced a new subsidy which was specifically designed for slum clearance rather than 'general purposes' or additional building. This 'Greenwood' subsidy was to augment rather than replace the existing Wheatley subsidy.[46] However, by the Housing (Financial Provisions) Act of 1933, the Wheatley subsidy was terminated on all houses for which plans had not been approved by the end of 1932. Public housing for general needs was to end, and attention in future was to concentrate upon slum clearance. There was, in other words, a return to a sanitary policy of public housing. The argument of the Report on Local Expenditure of 1932 was that the fall in building costs and interest rates allowed lower rents and so made a general subsidy unnecessary.[47] The policy of the government was

to concentrate public effort on the clearance and improvement of slum conditions, and to rely in the main on competitive private enterprise to provide a new supply of accommodation for the working-classes – the provision of private enterprise to be supplemented where necessary by means of unsubsidised building by the local authorities.[48]

This view of the proper role of council housing was associated with a change in Conservative policy towards rent control. The Committee on Rent Restriction Acts of 1931 divided the housing market into three classes. In Class A, houses inhabited by the middle class, private building for owner-occupation had removed the shortage, so that rents could be decontrolled. In Class B houses, occupied by artisans and the lower middle class, the shortage was being reduced and decontrol could continue as before on vacant possession. In Class C, 'the real working-class house', the position was different. Private enterprise had not returned, and few houses and been decontrolled. The logic of earlier committees was rejected. Rent control was no longer hampering building, which was proceeding at an unprecedented rate for owner-occupation. Rent control had encouraged a change in the nature of the market supplied, but was not preventing construction for the more affluent working-class and the middle class who could now buy rather than rent. This was a trend which the Conservatives wished to encourage, but it was unlikely that such a strategy could work for the provision of Class C houses. Neither was it anticipated that the decontrol of Class C property would result in the reappearance of private landlords on a large scale. Whilst shortage had preceded control, it was not now anticipated that increased production would follow decontrol. Rents in Class C houses should therefore remain under control. This view was incorporated in the Rent Restriction Act of 1933 which complemented the Housing (Financial Provisions) Act of the same year. Rent controls and general purpose council housing were no longer needed for Classes A and B, where private building for owner-occupation was adequately meeting demand. But at the bottom of the market in Class C houses, it was unlikely that private enterprise would return. Rent controls and the replacement of slums by local authority housing were required.[49]

Rent control in Britain, 1931

	percentage of houses			
class	controlled	decontrolled	new	total not controlled
A	44.2	26.7	29.2	55.8
B	60.0	8.9	31.1	40.0
C	78.1	11.2	10.7	21.9
Total	69.1	12.7	18.2	30.9

Source: P.P. 1932–3 xxi, *Rent and Mortgage Interest Restrictions. Statistics of Houses. Memorandum by the Minister of Health and Secretary of State for Scotland.*

Conservative policy had been modified since 1923 when the complete abandonment of rent control and the return of private enterprise to all sectors of the market had been anticipated. In the 1930s there was instead an acceptance of a dual housing market. The boom in private building for owner-occupation was relied upon for the prosperous working-class and middle-class market.[50] Free enterprise could be restored, but in a different guise from the rental market of the period before the war. The 'rampart' strategy was paramount for this sector of the market, but was inappropriate at the bottom end. Rent control was now accepted as a permanent feature of that sector, but the burden imposed upon private landlords was not to be compensated by tax relief or subsidy. Private landlords were not to be incorporated into government policy. Rather, tenants at the bottom of the market would rely upon 'filtering up' into accommodation vacated by suburban owner-occupiers; or local authority replacement of slum property at subsidized rents; or local authority building without subsidy at economic rents. In the 1920s, council housing was viewed by the Conservatives as a finite temporary measure to remove shortages in order to end controls over the housing market. By the 1930s, this had changed: controls were seen as a permanent feature of part of the market where private enterprise would not reappear; council initiative had a precisely limited role. Whereas Conservative policy changed, the Labour party had a different approach of commitment to controlled 'fair' rents and council involvement as the normal means of supplying new working-class housing. Implementation of this policy had to wait until 1945. What must be stressed is that housing acts and rent acts were complementary in the inter-war period: the role of council building was determined by the assessment of the need for control in the housing market.

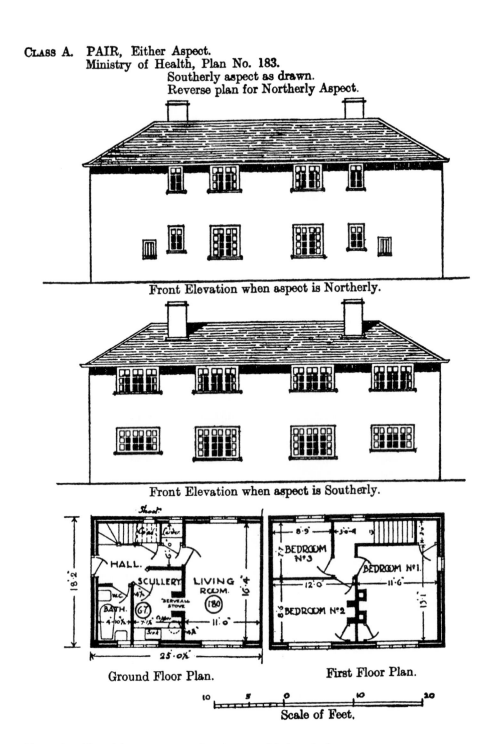

CLASS A. PAIR, Either Aspect.
Ministry of Health, Plan No. 183.
Southerly aspect as drawn.
Reverse plan for Northerly Aspect.

Front Elevation when aspect is Northerly.

Front Elevation when aspect is Southerly.

Ground Floor Plan.

First Floor Plan.

Scale of Feet.

Figure 1.   Class A houses: non-parlour houses with three bedrooms.

CLASS A. PAIR, Northerly Aspect.
Ministry of Health, Plan No. 165.

Front Elevation.

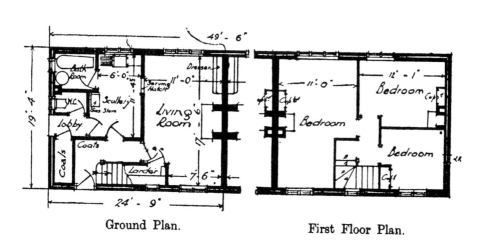

Ground Plan.   First Floor Plan.

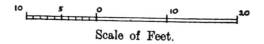

Scale of Feet.

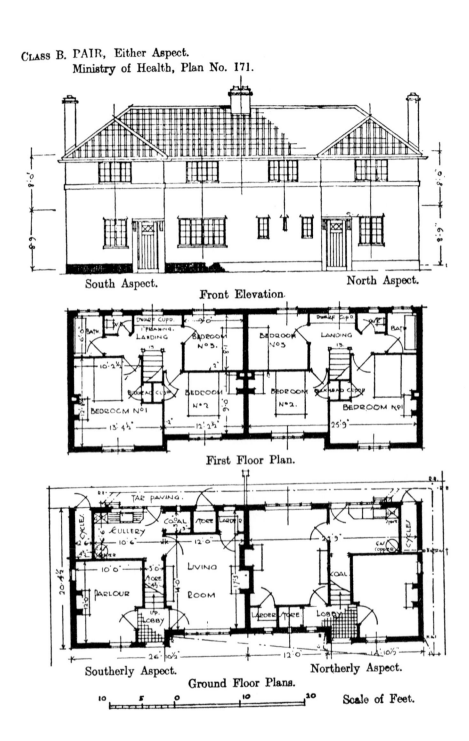

CLASS B. PAIR, Either Aspect.
Ministry of Health, Plan No. 171.

South Aspect.   North Aspect.

Front Elevation.

First Floor Plan.

Ground Floor Plans.

Southerly Aspect.   Northerly Aspect.

Scale of Feet.

Figure 2.   Class B houses: parlour houses with three bedrooms.

18

CLASS B. PAIR, Either Aspect.
Ministry of Health, Plan No. 150.

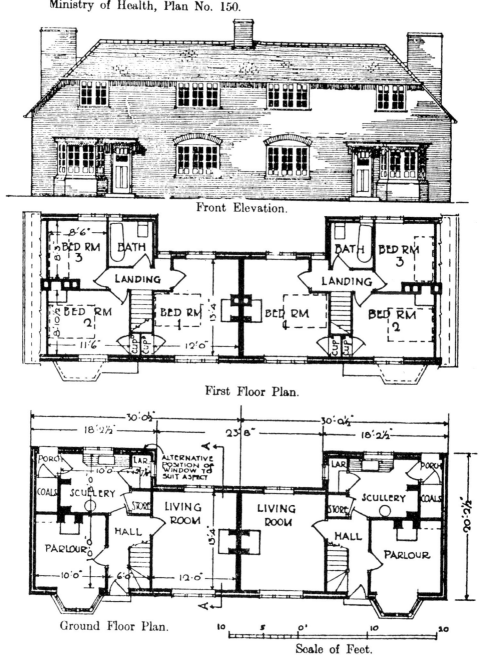

Front Elevation.

First Floor Plan.

Ground Floor Plan.

Scale of Feet.

This analysis of the changing basis of housing policy between the wars is necessary in order to provide the context for the case-studies which follow. The great merit of these studies is to suggest that an understanding of the trends in national policy is not enough. Activity at the local level cannot be understood merely as a direct response to directives from the centre. It is the tensions which arose from the local implementation of national policy which form one of the most significant themes of the contributions to this volume. The historiography of council housing is dominated by concern with the formulation of policy at the centre; the importance of these studies is that attention is directed towards the process by which local authorities decided on their response and determined the scale of their house-building programme. The changing balance of power between central and local government from Edwin Chadwick and the public health movement onwards has been an abiding topic in urban history. This volume extends the debate both in time and theme.

Robert Ryder's essay articulates the theme in the most explicit manner, for it provided a major focus of his thesis. Whereas Madge Dresser and Robert Finnigan considered the local response to national legislation, Ryder went a stage further by utilizing the correspondence between the local authorities in County Durham and the Ministry of Health. The formulation of policy did not end with the passing of an Act, for it had to be administered by the permanent officials at Whitehall and the elected councillors in the localities. The civil servants might be perturbed by the financial weakness of local authorities in a depressed area such as County Durham, and by the different perception of housing policy which had developed in Labour-controlled councils. The result at the most extreme might be the removal of housing policy from the political control of local elected bodies by, for example, the creation of the North Eastern Housing Association in 1936. Whilst Robert Ryder pays more explicit attention to this subject of local-central relations, it also emerges in the studies of Bristol and Leeds that local considerations explain divergences in the level of activity under the various subsidies. The political complexion of the local authority might be out of phase with that of the national government. The Conservatives in Leeds could therefore fail to take full advantage of the generous Wheatley subsidy provided by the Labour government. In Bristol, private builders were more active than in County Durham, and the Chamberlain subsidy was used more extensively by private enterprise. The scale of the house-building programme of any council would depend upon the dominant political party; the level of activity of private builders; and the financial viability of the local authority. Financial weakness might prevent a Labour council from building when it wished; financial strength might not result in building by a Conservative authority. The depressed, financially suspect, Labour-dominated local authorities of County Durham were forced to a different assessment of the house-building programme from the more prosperous, financially secure, Conservative-dominated Council of Leeds. This volume will have served an important service if it directs attention towards these patterns of local implementation of national policy. All too often in the past, the analysis has ended at the point at which the Act was placed on the statute book, rather than at the point at which the Council decided to build.

The council as landlord

The emphasis in the history of council housing upon the formulation of national policy not only neglects the process by which individual local authorities determined the scale of their building programme; it also ignores the fundamental question of how the Council should act as landlord. The analysis should stop neither with the passing of the Act, nor with the building of the house, but must also consider the continuing relationship between landlord and tenant. This provides another major area of interest in the three case-studies presented here. Historians have only recently turned their attention to the nature of landlord-tenant relations before the First World War, and have as yet not considered the impact of rent control and security of tenure upon the private sector between the wars. Essentially, all landlords – whether private or public, within a free or regulated market – have to consider the same range of issues. These include the determination of rent levels, the selection of tenants, the attitude towards sub-letting and lodgers, the treatment of arrears, the repair and maintenance of the property. A number of techniques could be used to carry out the common tasks. A private landlord might decide to undertake all the tasks in person; he might prefer to use a rent collector to visit the houses whilst retaining control of the decisions on the management of the property; or he might pass the whole business over to an agent so that there was a clear division between ownership and control.[51] Local authorities had to undertake the same range of tasks, and had to develop the machinery to manage their estates and control their tenants.

Private landlords between the wars faced an erosion of their position in comparison with their tenants. E. J. Churchman of the National Federation of Property Owners and Ratepayers demanded in 1937 that 'we want freedom to deal with our own, if we choose, in the same way as the butcher, the baker and the grocer does.'[52] Changes in the law of landlord and tenant shifted the balance of power towards the tenants, although shortages at the bottom of the market might create countervailing forces. The outcome for landlord-tenant relations demands close inspection. But if the position of private landlords had changed since 1914, even more striking was the emergence of public landlords. Robert Ryder remarks that 'the Council often had to face a dilemma which did not exist for the private landlord.' Councils could not act upon purely commercial considerations. They had to provide for tenants 'least eligible in the eyes of the private owner', and they might well view housing as an aspect of social policy. But this led to dangers of a mounting deficit on the housing account. A major theme of council housing was precisely the 'difficulty of reconciling estate management with social policy', and this is well shown by the contributors to the present volume.

The first task facing councillors was the determination of rent levels. This was a much more complex matter for local authorities than it had been for private landlords whose concern was simply to maximize their net income. In the public sector, the formulation of a coherent strategy on rent levels was a major issue throughout the inter-war period. This is considered by each contributor. There were, essentially, two related problems. One was the redistribution of income between areas, which was particularly important for a depressed region such as County Durham. The second was the redistribution of income between families, which was of particular concern in Leeds in the 1930s.

The Act of 1919 specified that any loss in excess of a 1d. rate would be borne by the Treasury. The subsidy was therefore redistributive between areas. Regions which were prosperous or which did not have a serious housing problem would be paying to assist regions which were depressed or with poor housing. The subsidy was also redistributive between families, for the rent to be charged took into account the ability of the tenants to pay. In the first instance, rents were to be established by existing controlled rents rather than by building costs. By March 1927, it was expected that economic rents could be charged, calculated on the basis of two-thirds of the cost of building the house, which was the level to which costs were expected to fall after the post-war peak. However, tenants who could not afford this rent were to be charged whatever seemed appropriate. There was, therefore, a distinction between initial non-economic rents, and eventual economic rents, in each case modified by the individual circumstances of the tenant. It was expected that the subsidy could be reduced as the gap between controlled and uncontrolled rents was removed by the restoration of the free market in housing.[53] The assumption proved to be false, for the housing shortage remained, and rents in the private sector were held below economic levels. In County Durham, the minimum rents recommended by the Ministry of Health were at least double the prevailing level in the free market. The result was that the rents of houses built under the Act of 1919 were to fall rather than rise. This generated tension between local and central government. Since the financial burden of low rent levels would be borne by the national taxpayer rather than by the local ratepayer, there was every incentive for the local authority to reduce rents, and for the Ministry to oppose reductions. Generally, rents fell from the minimum levels specified by the Ministry of Health, on the basis of what working-class families could afford rather than on the recovery of an economic return. The subsidy of 1919 was, therefore, 'progressive with need', concentrated upon those areas which most required assistance, and varying rent levels by ability to pay.[54]

Subsequent legislation was, by contrast, regressive in character, both in respect to families and regions. The subsidy to be paid by the national government was fixed rather than open-ended as in 1919. The result was that a depressed area with a low rateable value and a high rate poundage might be forced to stop building whereas a prosperous area with a buoyant rateable value and a lower rate poundage might be able to continue building. The subsidy from central government would therefore be concentrated on those areas which were least in need of assistance. This consideration was of particular importance in the case of County Durham, where the rateable value was low, the rate poundage high, the economy depressed, and housing conditions poor. This depressed area was taxing itself to order to finance housing, rather than receiving assistance from more prosperous areas in the country. The subsidies were also regressive between families. The Act of 1924 laid down that rents were to be determined by the controlled rents of similar pre-war houses. This would establish the average rent charged by the local authority, around which the rent of individual houses could vary as much as desired. But the rules of 1924, unlike those of 1919, did not explicitly sanction differential rents according to the ability of the tenant to pay. Although such a course of action was not prohibited, the legal position was uncertain. Since lower rents for some tenants would imply either higher rents from other tenants or an increased contribution from ratepayers, the incentive for local authorities to act was reduced; it was different when any shortfall was made good by the national taxpayer. The principles upon which the rents of individual houses were to be determined were vague, and the question of who was to benefit from the subsidy uncertain. The extent to which the subsidy was regressive or progressive between families depended on local policy. There was a tendency for subsidies to go to the more affluent families who could afford to pay the balance of rent which was not covered by the subsidy. The poorer the family, the less the chance of its receiving a subsidized house.[55]

Local authorities were encouraged in the early 1930s to make the subsidies operate in a more progressive manner. The aim was that those who could afford it should pay an economic rent, so that the rents of the less prosperous families could be reduced. But whereas in the early 1920s, local authorities had been willing to operate on progressive principles at the expense of the national taxpayer, they were less enthusiastic in the 1930s when such a policy was at the expense of the local ratepayer.[56] The introduction of schemes of differential rent rebates in order to reduce the regressive nature of subsidies involved complex political issues of redistribution between council tenants, and between council tenants and other ratepayers. The schemes were for the most part limited to slum clearance tenants of the 1930s, which minimized the potential conflict. The real problem would arise where the tenants of general purpose council housing were brought into the scheme. The depth of feeling was shown in Birmingham in 1939 when between 6,000 and 8,000 council tenants staged a rent strike for 13 weeks, with the result that the rebate scheme was postponed. There was a reluctance on the part of tenants to be means-tested, with the prospect of higher rents, in order to subsidize poorer tenants from slum clearances.[57] Robert Finnigan explains the operation of the rent rebate scheme in Leeds. The problem of dealing with slum clearance tenants was peculiarly acute in the city, for Leeds had, in relative terms, the largest clearance programme in the country. The issue which faced the Council was how the tenants from the slums were to pay. Where the clearance schemes were small, it was possible to limit rebates to these tenants without creating an intolerable burden on the rates, but the scale of clearances in Leeds meant that the rebate scheme was extended to existing tenants in general purpose housing, whose rents might be raised in order to finance the rebates to the poorer tenants.

In 1938, there were 112 rebate schemes in England and Wales, mostly limited to slum clearance tenants. They took a number of forms. One possibility was a table which specified the rent payable by families with various incomes and numbers of children. This was adopted in Barking. More usual were schemes which established a standard rent, from which rebates were granted according to various criteria. This could be done by allowing a deduction from the standard rent according to the extent to which income fell below a fixed scale. This was the most common form of rebate. In Stoke, for example, the standard rent was paid when the income was £3 or above; where the income was £2 10s. to £3, a rebate was allowed of 1s. for each child in excess of two; where the weekly income was £2 to £2 10s., a rebate was allowed of 1s. for each child up to the first three, after which 2s. was allowed for each additional child; where the weekly income was less than £2, the minimum rent was paid. Alternatively, the rebate could be based upon rent as a fixed proportion of income, as in Carlisle where 20 per cent of the family income was to be spent on rent, less 6d. a week for each child of school age. In Oldham, the rebate was calculated on the basis of the weekly income per head. Where the weekly income per head was above 12s. after adjustments had been made for essential expenditure, then no rebate was allowed, but where it was less than 12s., a rebate of 3d. was allowed for every 6d. by which it fell short. The scheme at Leeds was based upon another principle, that of the subsistence scale. The income which remained after subsistence needs had been deducted was calculated. In some towns, the whole balance was payable in rent, but in Leeds only a proportion was paid.[58]

These rent rebate schemes might make subsidies more progressive only between families within a particular local authority area, and even then they were somewhat limited. Leeds had one of the few comprehensive schemes. What the schemes could not do was make subsidies progressive between areas. In depressed districts such as County Durham, there were few tenants who could afford an economic rent, which meant that there were also few houses which could be let at low rents.[59] A reduction in the general rent level could in this case come only from the rates, which in County Durham entailed the redistribution of income from working-class families in private rented houses, who might be worse off than those in the council houses who were receiving the subsidy. Increased contributions from the rates could lead, as Ryder indicates, to hostility towards the subsidizing of 'the wages of a particular few at the expense of the rest of the mining community.' The problem was that tenants might well not be able to afford the rents of their council houses, and the Medical Officer of Health of Stockton found that the death rate on the council estate exceeded the death rate in the slums as a result of dietary deficiencies. The local authorities in these depressed areas of the north-east faced a serious dilemma. High rents would impose hardships on the tenants, but lower rents would strain the over-stretched local tax base, resulting in an inability to continue building in the future. This could mean that the regions most in need of housing at low rents were unable to build during the period of low costs in the 1930s, whereas the more prosperous districts of the Midlands and South could take advantage of the situation.[60] Subsidies were not necessarily concentrated on those who needed them on a national basis. The problems of rent policy in the public sector had not been solved by 1939. Anomalies and a random redistribution of income characterized both the private rental market and the local authority sector.

Local authorities had to select the tenants to live in the new houses which had been built. The priority in the early 1920s was initially given to ex-servicemen, but this gave way to criteria of housing need. There was, however, still a concern to ensure that tenants were 'desirable' and could pay the rent. This appeared clearly in the 'Instructions to Enquiry Officers' issued by West Hartlepool Council in 1932. The enquiry officers were to inspect the rent book, establish whether any rates were outstanding, determine the income, and inspect the applicant's house. Selection became more difficult with the large-scale slum clearance schemes of the 1930s. The problem of inability to pay could be met to some extent by the use of rent subsidies, but this still left the problem of 'undesirable' tenants. A frequent response was to allocate the less respectable to 'problem' estates. Tenants were vetted, and as a result 'the social structure of the council estate is affected by housing management'.[61] The most important issues which arose once the tenants were installed were sub-letting and rent arrears. Arrears were a particularly serious problem in County Durham, especially after the coal dispute of 1926. Sub-letting could be seen as one solution to the tenants' problem of finding the rent, and some councils did grant half-tenancies with separate rent books. On the whole, however, councils were more hostile than private landlords to sub-letting, which was opposed on the grounds that it contributed to overcrowding, increased dilapidations, and reduced the ability to control the property.

In order to deal with these questions of estate management, councils had to develop an administrative machinery. Allocation might be left to the Council or Housing Committee, but it was usual for a formal bureaucracy to develop. This is analysed by Madge Dresser in the case of Bristol. The task of management could be organized in a variety of ways.[62] At the simplest, a rent collector could visit each house weekly in order to receive the rent, as his sole responsibility. A further stage was to use the rent collector to report back any requests by the tenants for repairs.

Some councils gave more initiative to the officers who visited the tenants. The 'comprehensive' housing assistant collected rents, received requests for repairs, supervised the general appearance of the estate, and handled simple tenancy matters such as applications for transfer. The 'intensive' system added welfare work to these responsibilities, on the lines pioneered by Octavia Hill's lady rent collectors. This was the method adopted in Bristol where a Lady House Visitor was employed. However, her concern for welfare was isolated from the technical and financial aspects, rather than integrated with them. On the whole, it would appear that councils in the 1920s and 1930s relied upon the simpler methods of rent collecting, and viewed house management as a technical rather than a social question. Instead, tenants were informed of the social behaviour which was required of them by the Council through the issue of handbooks, the exclusion of publicans, and the encouragement of gardening.

The social relationships arising from the ownership and occupancy of housing are second in importance only to the relationships arising from employment. The emergence of mass council housing and the changing legal position of private landlords resulted in far-reaching changes in landlord-tenant relations in the inter-war period. One imperative task for urban historians is to turn their attention to the changes in the private sector as landlords adjusted to the distortions of rent control and the improved security of tenure. How did the pattern of ownership change? How were the tasks of selecting tenants, recovering arrears and maintaining the property viewed in the changed circumstances of the 1920s and 1930s? Did the techniques of management change with a greater reliance upon agents rather than personal control? The essays in the present volume mark an important advance in our understanding of the emerging pattern of relationships in the public sector. The contribution to urban history is twofold. On the one hand, there is the analysis of urban administration and politics as local authorities added another function to their range of tasks. Housing became and remained one of the crucial elements of local politics.[63] On the other hand, there is the significant change in urban life as tenants came to face a public, politically accountable bureaucracy concerned with social policy as well as financial returns, in place of private landlords operating on commercial principles. The tenants of council houses were experiencing a physical change in their social life as they moved to suburban estates constructed on garden city principles; they were also experiencing a less apparent but no less significant change in the social relationships which arose from the ownership and management of property.

Domestic space and society

Dr R.J. Morris has recently pointed to the need of historians 'to come to terms with housing as a physical form. . . . Any study of housing and the relationships which cluster around housing (production and consumption) must examine the fundamental material base of social life.'[64] This will surely provide a central concern of urban historians in the future. The initial focus of urban history was the production of houses, which resulted in a concern for the determinants of the building cycle and the process of development of building estates. More recently, attention has turned towards landlord-tenant relations, viewing the house as an item of consumption which created social relationships between buyer and seller. The argument needs, however, to go a stage further to consider the interplay between the physical environment and the social life it contained. Council housing obviously changed the nature of the relationship between the provider and user of the accommodation, by substituting a public body for a private individual, with all that that entailed. But more than this, council housing implied a fundamental change in the physical setting of social life. This is an important element in the contributions to this volume, particularly in the essays of Madge Dresser and Robert Finnigan.

The point has been made by Mark Swenarton that historians have dealt with politics, society and economy but have ignored design, whilst design historians have ignored everything else. Both disciplines are therefore implying 'that design and society are not involved in a single process but are separate and distinct.' It is important to integrate design and society for two reasons. One is that the layout of housing, both internal and external, reflects various social expectations in the minds of those supplying the property. This might be unconscious and implicit in the case of private housing before 1914, but in the case of public housing between the wars might be conscious and explicit. Design could be intended to modify social behaviour, and was not simply the outcome of a value-free or socially neutral technical exercise. The second reason is that design is not simply accepted by the users, but is rather interpreted. The social expectations of those providing an amenity might well differ from the expectations of its users. Indeed, 'the meaning and use of domestic space are not intrinsic to a set of physical characteristics.' Social and physical space might be congruent, but they might also be in tension.[65] It is necessary therefore to analyse both the process of design, with its interplay between technical considerations, financial necessity and social assumptions, and the manner in which the physical space which resulted was interpreted in practice by those who lived on the new estates. This must be a crucial element in any appreciation of public intervention in the housing market in the twentieth century, whether it be the suburban garden-city estates of the 1920s and 1930s, the high-rise blocks of the 1960s, or the rehabilitation of the 1980s.

The tenants who left the working-class districts which had been built on bye-law principles before 1914 for council houses were experiencing two changes in their physical environment. One was in the external or public space. A high-density grid-iron layout gave way to development on low-density, garden-suburb principles. The second was in the internal layout of the private space of the house. Council housing created a relatively standardized house-form which eroded the regional diversity in bye-law housing. The diversity which existed before the First World War appears clearly in the towns covered in the present volume. The north-east of England had the highest level of overcrowding of English provincial towns. In Gateshead, for example, 33.7 per cent of the population lived in overcrowded conditions in 1911. The houses were predominantly small, with 59.5 per cent having three rooms or less in 1911. In Sunderland, the pattern was similar, with 32.6 per cent of the population living in overcrowded conditions, and 62.0 per cent of the houses having three rooms or less. In Leeds, the position was somewhat better. In 1911, 11.0 per cent of the population lived in overcrowded conditions, and 36.9 per cent of the houses in the city had three rooms or less. Housing conditions in Bristol were, on these measures, more favourable. The level of overcrowding was 4.8 per cent of the population, and the proportion of houses with three rooms or less 24.1 per cent. The diversity was not, however, simply in house size and level of overcrowding. The architectural style also varied. In County Durham, there were three major house forms. One was, as the name implies, confined to a narrow strip along the Tyne. This was the Tyneside flat. At first sight, these flats appeared to follow the common English style of two-storeyed terraced houses. However, on closer inspection it was apparent that where there would normally be one front door leading to a two-storey house, on Tyneside there were two front doors leading to separate flats on the ground and first floors (fig. 3b). The flats built in the late nineteenth century and early twentieth century usually had three rooms on the ground floor and four on the first floor. In Gateshead in 1911, 62.5 per cent of the population lived in flats, although the aggregate figure for the urban districts of England and Wales was only 3.7 per cent. Although the level of overcrowding and house size was broadly similar in Sunderland, the architectural style was very different. The characteristic working-class house in Sunderland was built in single-storeyed terraces (fig. 3a). Elsewhere in the county, the normal house-type was the two-storeyed terraced cottage. Leeds, of course, was dominated by another regional style: the back-to-back house (fig. 4b and c). Whereas the Tyneside flat divided the space under one roof horizontally, the back-to-back house divided the space vertically. These houses usually had three or four rooms. The three-roomed houses had a kitchen and scullery on the ground floor with two bedrooms above. The four-roomed houses had an additional room either by placing another bedroom in the attic, or by removing the scullery to the basement in order to create two habitable rooms on the ground floor. In Bristol, the house style followed the standard pattern of the Midlands and South. This was a two-storeyed through house with a back addition (fig. 4a). These houses invariably had three bedrooms on the first floor, and either two or three habitable rooms and a scullery on the ground floor. Housing conditions and styles varied widely across the country at the outbreak of war.[66]

This regional diversity was not apparent in the council houses built between the wars. A number of standard national house-types emerged, which departed from the pre-war vernacular styles to which the council tenants had been accustomed in their previous accommodation. A few councils, including Leeds, did experiment with cottage flats which were similar to the pre-war Tyneside flats, and in Bristol there was a short flirtation with the provision of single-storey 'chalets'. On the whole, however, local authorities followed one of two national forms which were unlike any of the pre-war bye-law property. These were known as A3 and B3 houses. 'A' houses did not have a parlour, whereas 'B' houses did. The number referred to the number of bedrooms. The Ministry of Health prepared numerous 'type-plans' which local councils could follow (see figs. 1 and 2). Most bye-law housing had been the width of one room, with a greater depth. This led to restrictions on light and air, particularly where there was a back addition. The aim in council houses was to abolish back projections and to move to an internal layout which was less narrow and deep. This would allow more light and air into the house, and was associated with a greater attention to the aspect of the house, made possible by the abandonment of rigid terraces in a grid-iron layout.[67] This might well be an admirable ambition, but the perceptions of the architects might well clash with the expectations of the residents. This was most obvious in the A3 houses where there was no parlour. The trend in working-class housing before the First World War had been to assign one room for special occasions, separate from the everyday life of the house. This parlour had a symbolic purpose which was clearly differentiated from the secular or everyday space of the kitchen. There was a strong sense of distinction between front and back, between the special and the secular space of the house.[68] A3 houses offended this definition of space. Raymond Unwin betrayed a deep insensitivity to the culture of the working-class when he remarked that

> When mankind first took to living in houses these consisted of one room; perhaps the most important fact to be remembered in designing cottages is that the cottager still lives during the day-time in one room. . . . There can be no possible doubt that until any cottage has been provided with a living-room large enough to be healthy, comfortable and convenient, it is worse than folly to take space from that living-room, where it will be used every day and every hour, to form a parlour, where it will only be used once or twice a week.[69]

A large proportion of the council houses erected between the wars were indeed non-parlour types, which meant that local authorities were flouting 'the housing *mores* of the people'. The decision that two living rooms were 'an unjustifiable luxury' ignored the cultural expectation of distinction between everyday and special use. The Mass-Observation report on housing during the Second World War concluded that 'in this respect at any rate, the new houses built between the wars have proved themselves much less in accordance with the needs of the people who live in them than the old houses of the nineteenth century.'[70]

Perhaps the major criticism of design in the 1920s and 1930s was the lack of attention given to the provision of amenities and to the development of a sense of community on the new estates. Councils were attracted to cheap land on the fringe of towns, developed on low-density lines. The estates were as a result often isolated from employment, shops and recreation facilities. The problems which resulted were only seriously considered at the end of the 1930s. In Leeds, it was not until the planning of Seacroft at the onset of the Second World War that there was any attempt to design an estate as a self-contained community. The other estates in the city were dormitory suburbs devoid of amenities. The comparison between Birmingham's estate at Kingstanding and the town of Shrewsbury was used to point the difference. Both had a population of about 30,000, but whereas Shrewsbury had 30 churches, 20 halls, and two libraries, Kingstanding had only one church and one hall. The policy in Birmingham did change, so that by 1938 the aim was to make the larger estates 'as far as possible self-contained communities'. In 1943 it was suggested that the ideal was 'neighbourhood units' around a community centre, which would be built at the same time as the houses.[71] The failure to do this in the 1920s and 1930s has been considered by some commentators to be the greatest failure of the local authority house-building programme between the wars. The housing estates at Bristol and Leeds lacked amenities for shopping and recreation. The estates were isolated from the established facilities of the central districts, further from the work-place, and with inadequate transport links. The move to the estates also disrupted old communities with their informal network of assistance and obligation, for as Robert Finnigan shows, families from one clearance area were dispersed to a number of estates. One solution, of course, was to build flats in the central districts, close to the existing facilities and work. This was attempted in Leeds at Quarry Hill.[72] Such an approach was very much an exception in provincial cities, and by 1939 the problem of adding social amenities to houses on the suburban estates had barely been tackled.

'Watling', claimed Ruth Durant in 1939, 'is not much more than a huge hotel without a roof.' This London County Council estate at Hendon in north London indicates some of the problems which might emerge. A major issue was the relationship

Figure 3.   a. Cairo Street, Sunderland (Tyne and Wear Archives, Acc 269 (C2), 1903)

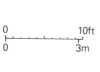

a

b. A pair of flats in Cato Street, Gateshead (Gateshead Local History Library; plan approved 5 May 1886).

b

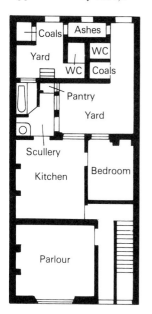

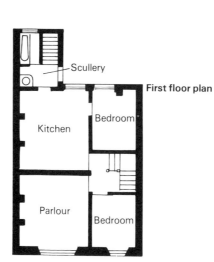

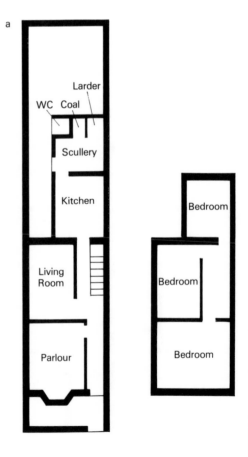

a

Larder

WC Coal

Scullery

Kitchen

Living
Room

Parlour

Bedroom

Bedroom

Bedroom

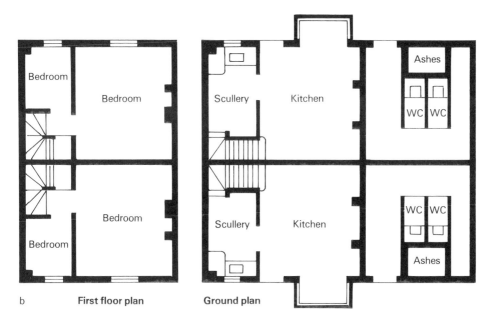

b   **First floor plan**   **Ground plan**

c

Figure 4.   a. Ruby Street, Bedminster, Bristol (Bristol Record Office, building plans, vol. 31, 1895.
b. A pair of back-to-back houses, Hawes Street, Leeds (Leeds City Archives, plan 45, bundle 4, July 1890).
c. Basement of back-to-back houses, Royal Park Terrace, Leeds (Leeds City Archives, plan 12, bundle 4, July 1890).

between the housing market and the labour market. The estate was surrounded by newly established factories and middle-class housing estates which provided little competition with the council tenants for employment. But the new factories required predominantly unskilled labour, drawn largely from the wives and children of the tenants. The chief wage-earners were more likely to work in other areas of London. In 1937, only 26.3 per cent of the tenants worked within the area, in comparison with 54.3 per cent of other residents of the estate. Sons who wished for a better job were likely to follow their fathers and work outside the area, for Watling itself had a 'blind-alley prospect'.

> Local industry furnishes Watling's youth mainly with blind-alley employment. When these boys and girls have passed their early adolescence they often have to look further afield for new work. Moreover, as unskilled labourers they would hardly be able to afford the rents on the Estate. For those young people who do learn a trade Watling provides only lodgings. They work in London, and as they get older and marry it is impossible for them to remain here even if they wish. There is hardly any accommodation for childless couples and, in any case, they are not eligible as tenants, since, as a rule, the LCC accepts only people from the London area.

The initial tenants of council housing tended to be in the younger age groups, and the movement of the young away from the estates maintained an unbalanced age structure.[73]

Rosamund Jevons and John Madge in 1946 considered the lessons of Bristol Corporation's housing policy between the wars for post-war reconstruction. 'It is perhaps inevitable', they remarked, 'that any authority which embarks for the first time on an ambitious programme of housing will make serious mistakes. Mistakes did occur in most areas between the wars, when, for the first time in our history, local authorities undertook the great social task of housing the people.' They criticized the isolation of the estates from the life of the city; the concentration of large and poor families; the sprawling, low-density development; the lack of community life and self-government; the failure to provide housing for a variety of family types; and the lack of a coherent rent policy.[74] But it would be wrong to condemn the inter-war housing estates with too much vigour. The task of the historian is to comprehend the process by which a particular design came to dominate, and how the resulting physical form related to the social life it contained. In terms of current social attitudes towards design in the 1980s, it is the high-rise blocks of the 1950s and 1960s which are held in contempt, whilst the bye-law housing, which was condemned by the adherents both of garden suburbs between the wars and of the modern movement after the Second World War, is now cherished. Cottage estates might not have returned entirely to favour, but it is Quarry Hill which has been demolished.

Conclusion

Housing tenure in Britain underwent a fundamental change between the wars. The pattern which had developed during industrialization and urbanization in the nineteenth century was overturned, and another pattern created which has persisted to the present. In 1914, the public sector accounted for less than 1 per cent of the housing stock, and owner-occupation for perhaps 10 per cent. When allowance has been made for philanthropic and employers' housing, the contribution of private landlords cannot have been less than 85 per cent of the total housing stock. By the Second World War, the position had been transformed by the rise of owner-occupation and public housing on the one hand, and the decline of the private landlord and his regulation on the other. A survey in 1939 indicated that 31.5 per cent of the houses built between the wars were owned by local authorities, a further 49.1 per cent by owner-occupiers, and only 19.4 per cent by private landlords. A large number of the houses built before 1914 had also passed into owner-occupation. In 1939, 27.1 per cent of pre-war houses were owner-occupied. The remainder of the pre-war housing stock comprised 41.3 per cent owned by private landlords with controlled rents, and 21.6 per cent with decontrolled rents. These changes taken together amounted to a remarkable tenurial revolution.[75]

Historians have scarcely started to analyse this transformation, which constitutes a crucial element in the social, economic and political history of inter-war Britain. This volume is a significant contribution to what will become a major concern for urban historians as they change the focus of their research from the Victorian and Edwardian housing market to the realignments which have taken place since 1914. The authors are indeed writing at a time when the policies they analyse are under close scrutiny. The public sector is experiencing its greatest slump since 1945. The present government is committed to reducing the size of the public sector, both through a low level of new construction and by the sale of the existing stock. Rehabilitation policies have meanwhile assumed a new importance, whilst political support for continued public housing has reached a post-war low. Historians need to take a part in this discussion on current policy, for all too often the debate is based upon a misconception of the forces which created the existing pattern of tenure. The essays in this volume therefore have an important message, both for historians who seek to explain the process by which the Victorian property market was replaced, and for policy-makers who are debating the future of the patterns which emerged in the inter-war period. The question asked in 1904 by William Smart has still not been answered.

APPENDIX: HOUSING LEGISLATION 1919–38

Housing, Town Planning &c Act, 1919 ('The Addison Act')
[9 & 10 Geo V, c 35]

This Act made it the duty of local authorities to conduct, within three months, a survey of the housing needs in their district and to submit plans for the provision of dwellings to remedy any shortage. The work was to be supervised by the Ministry of Health through a Housing Commissioner in each of eleven regions.

The financial liability of local authorities was limited to the product of one penny in the pound on the rates: the residual cost was to be borne by the Exchequer. Public utility societies were also eligible for an annual subsidy.

Housing (Additional Powers) Act, 1919
[9 & 10 Geo V, c 99]

Under this Act, houses built by private enterprise in compliance with certain building conditions were eligible for a lump-sum subsidy, which in practice was to range from £130 to £260. (The average subsidy for the 39,186 houses built was £242.)

Housing &c Act, 1923 ('The Chamberlain Act')
[13 & 14 Geo V, c 24]

Houses built by private enterprise and certified by the appropriate local authority as comp-lying with certain standards of size and amenity were to qualify for a subsidy (usually in the form of a lump sum of £75) paid by the Exchequer through the local authority. Councils were allowed to make an additional grant to private builders themselves.

If a local authority could satisfy the Ministry of Health that it was preferable for the Council to build houses itself, each house would qualify for a subsidy of £6 per annum for 20 years. The subsidy clauses of this Act were to apply only to those houses completed before October 1925, but were extended for 15 years by the Act of 1924. The subsidy was reduced in 1927 by a third for houses completed after September of that year and was finally withdrawn for houses completed after September 1929.

Housing (Financial Provisions) Act, 1924 ('The Wheatley Act')
[14 & 15 Geo V, c 35]

This Act granted local authorities a subsidy of £9 per house per year for 40 years (£12 10s. per annum in agricultural parishes) in respect of all houses complying with standards similar to those set by the 1923 Act and completed within the next 15 years. In most cases the local authority would contribute £4 10s. per annum from the rates towards each house.

Houses built by private enterprise qualified for a subsidy only if they were to be let at an approved rent.

The Exchequer subsidy was reduced in 1927 to £7 10s. and was finally withdrawn in 1933.

Housing Act, 1930 ('The Greenwood Act')
[21 & 22 Geo V, c 39]

This Act gave local authorities power to acquire 'clearance areas' of slum property (requiring total demolition) and 'improvement areas'. Before clearance began, local authorities had to provide accommodation for the people displaced.

The Exchequer subsidy was to be £2 5s. per annum for 40 years for each person rehoused in an urban district and £2 10s. per annum in an agricultural parish. There were extra allowances available where the site was particularly expensive or where rehousing involved the erection of flats. The local authority rate contribution was in most cases £3 15s. per annum per house.

Housing (Financial Provisions) Act, 1933
[23 & 24 Geo V, c 15]

This Act abolished the Wheatley subsidy for all housing schemes not approved by the Ministry of Health by December 1933.

Housing Act, 1935
[25 & 26 Geo V, c 40]

Local authorities were to conduct a detailed survey into overcrowding in their district and were empowered to declare 'redevelopment areas' where the extent of overcrowding was particu-larly serious.

The basic subsidy was up to £5 per annum for 20 years for each dwelling erected to relieve overcrowding, with extra allowances for expensive sites and the building of flats. There were elaborate conditions for the level of local rate contributions.

The Act also allowed local authorities to consolidate their accounts for housing schemes subsidized under earlier legislation, thus giving greater scope for councils to adjust the rents of individual dwellings.

Housing Act, 1936
[26 Geo V & 1 Edw VIII, c 51]

The main purpose of this Act was to consolidate the legislation already in force (principally the Acts of 1930 and 1935). Subsidy arrangements were not affected.

Housing (Financial Provisions) Act, 1938
[1 & 2 Geo VI, c 16]

This Act introduced a uniform scale of subsidy for all new schemes. The basic subsidy was to be £5 10s. per annum for 40 years for each house (£10 per annum in agricultural parishes) and a minimum of £11 per annum for flats on expensive sites. It was possible for some of the poorer urban areas (municipal boroughs and urban districts) to claim from the Exchequer an extra £1 per annum for each house: the county council would then be required to contribute a further £1 per annum. The Act also established a new scale of local authority contributions from the rates.

NOTES

1 W. Smart, 'The problem of housing', *Economic Journal*, xiv (1904), 529.
2 L. Fisher, 'The town housing problem', *Economic Journal*, xv (1905), 32.
3 J.S. Nettlefold, *A Housing Policy* (1905), 34.
4 A.C. Pigou, 'Some aspects of the housing problem', in B.S. Rowntree and A.C. Pigou, *Lectures on Housing* (1914), 66.
5 W. Thompson, *The Housing Handbook* (1903), 12.
6 See in particular D. Englander, *Landlord and Tenant in Urban Britain 1838–1918* (1983).
7 S.G. and E.O. Checkland, 'Housing policy: the formative years. A review article', *Town Planning Review*, xlvi (1975); H.J. Dyos, 'The slums of Victorian London', *Victorian Studies*, xi (1967), 27.
8 Dyos, *op. cit.*, 34; A.S. Wohl, *The Eternal Slum: Housing and Social Policy in Victorian London* (1977), xi.
9 Wohl, *op. cit.*, 249.
10 J.N. Tarn, *Five Per Cent Philanthropy. An Account of Housing in Urban Areas between 1840 and 1914* (1973), xiv.
11 Thompson, *op. cit.*, 10.
12 A.S. Wohl, 'The housing of the working-classes in London 1815–1914', in *The History of Working Class Housing. A Symposium* (1971), ed. S.D. Chapman, 43; S.G. and E.O. Checkland, *op. cit.*, 321–2.
13 See the interpretation of G. Stedman Jones, *Outcast London. A Study in the Relationship between Classes in Victorian Society* (1971).
14 D.A. Reeder, 'The politics of urban leaseholds in late Victorian Britain', *International Review of Social History*, vi (1962); A. Offer, *Property and Politics 1870–1914. Landownership, Law, Ideology and Urban Development in England* (1981).
15 Offer, *op. cit.*, 388; P. Wilding, 'Towards Exchequer subsidies for housing 1906–1914', *Social and Economic Administration*, vi (1972), 8–11; M. Swenarton, *Homes Fit for Heroes. The Politics and Architecture of Early State Housing in Britain* (1981), 33.
16 Swenarton, *op. cit.*, 41, 47; *The Land. The Report of the Land Enquiry Committee. Volume II, Urban* (1914), 97–180; B.S. Rowntree, 'How far is it possible to provide

satisfactory houses for the working classes at rents which they can afford to pay?', in Rowntree and Pigou, *op. cit.*, 3–31.

17 *Report of the Committee on Housing Greater London, 1965*, 214–15, 225. For a discussion of housing policies in other countries, see R.H. Duclaud-Williams, *The Politics of Housing in Britain and France* (1978); P.F. Wendt, *Housing Policy. The Search for Solutions. A Comparison of the United Kingdom, Sweden, West Germany and the United States since World War II* (1962); D.V. Donnison, *The Government of Housing* (1967), chapter 3.

18 *Report of the Committee on Housing in Greater London, 1965*, 218.

19 Offer, *op. cit.*, 165–8, 209–15, 221.

20 G.J. Crossick, 'The emergence of the lower middle class in Britain: a discussion', in *The Lower Middle Class in Britain 1870–1914*, ed. Crossick (1977), 41–6, and 'Urban society and the petty bourgeoisie in nineteenth-century Britain', in *The Pursuit of Urban History*, eds A. Sutcliffe and D. Fraser (1983); R.J. Morris, 'The middle class and the property cycle during the industrial revolution', in *The Search for Wealth and Stability*, ed. T. Smout (1979), 92 and 'The middle class and British towns and cities of the industrial revolution 1780–1870', in Sutcliffe and Fraser, *op. cit.*; E.P. Hennock, *Fit and Proper Persons. Ideal and Reality in Nineteenth Century Urban Government* (1973), *passim*.

21 Swenarton, *op. cit.*, 47, 136; P. Wilding, 'The Housing and Town Planning Act 1919 – a study in the making of social policy', *Journal of Social Policy*, II (1973), 32–2; L.F. Orbach, *Homes for Heroes. A Study of the Evolution of British Public Housing 1915–21* (1977), chapter 3.

22 *The Land*, 82–9, 94–6; Offer, *op. cit.*, 254, 268–72, 290–4.

23 M.J. Daunton, 'Miners' houses: South Wales and the Great Northern coalfield, 1880–1914', *International Review of Social History*, xxv (1980).

24 S.B. Saul, 'House-building in England 1890–1914', *Economic History Review*, n.s. xv (1962–3), 122–3, 134.

25 W. Fraser, 'Fluctuations of the building trade and Glasgow's house accommodation', *Proceedings of the Philosophical Society of Glasgow*, xxxix (1907–8), 27, gives the years' purchase of property in Glasgow.

26 See the pertinent comments in Donnison, *op. cit.*, 43.

27 S. Merrett, *State Housing in Britain* (1979), 279; see also Daunton, *House and Home. Working-Class Housing in the Victorian City 1850–1914* (1983).

28 On taxation, see Offer, *op. cit.*, and on the power of repossession, Englander, *op. cit.*

29 D. Englander, 'Landlord and tenant in urban Scotland: the background to the Clyde rent strikes, 1915', *Journal of Scottish Labour History*, xv (1981); Orbach, *op. cit.*, chapter 1.

30 P.P. 1918 XIII, *Ministry of Reconstruction. Report of the Committee on the Increase of Rent and Mortgage Interest (War Restrictions) Acts*.

31 *Ibid.*; C.H. Feinstein, 'Changes in the distribution of the national income in the United Kingdom since 1860', in *The Distribution of the National Income*, ed. J. Marchal and B. Ducros (1968), 117, 123, 126.

32 Public Record Office, HLG 41/24; P.P. 1918 XIII, *Committee on the Increase of Rent . . .*

33 P.P. 1918 XIII, *Committee on the Increase of Rent . . .*; P.P. 1920 XVIII, *Report of the Committee on the Increase of Rent and Mortgage Interest (War Restrictions) Acts*; Englander, *Landlord and Tenant in Urban Britain*, chapter 11.

34 S. Marriner, 'Cash and concrete. Liquidity problems in the mass production of "homes for heroes", *Business History*, xviii (1976), 152–3.

35 Swenarton, *op. cit.*, 81, 85–7, 111–13, 189, 195.

36 J. Melling, 'Employers, industrial housing and the evolution of company welfare policies in Britain's heavy industry: West Scotland 1870–1920', *International Review of Social History*, xxvi (1981).

37 Swenarton, *op. cit.*, 129, 131–2, 161.

38 Marriner, *op. cit.*, 182; Swenarton, *op. cit.*, 117–21.

39 Swenarton, *op. cit.*, 113–17; Orbach, *op. cit.*, chapters 5 and 6.

40 Swenarton, *op. cit.*, 122–9; S. Marriner, 'Sir Alfred Mond's octopus: a nationalised house-building business', *Business History*, XXI (1979), 23–44.

41 P.P. 1923 XIIii, *Final Report of the Departmental Committee on the Increase of Rent and Mortgage Interest (Restrictions) Act 1920*; PRO, HLG 41/43.

42 D. Gale Johnson, 'Rent control and the distribution of income', *American Economic Review*, XLI (1951), 569, 582; F.W. Paish, 'The economics of rent restriction', *Lloyds Bank Review* (1950); E.H. Phelps Brown and J. Wiseman, *A Course in Applied Economics* (2nd ed., 1964), 213–34; E.O. Olsen, 'An econometric analysis of rent control', *Journal of Political Economy*, LXXX (1972), 1081–100; W.D. Gampp, 'Some effects of rent control', *Southern Economic Journal*, XVI (1949–50), 425–47; PRO, HLG 41/2; P.P. 1918 XIII, *Ministry of Reconstruction. Report of the Committee on the Increase of Rent and Mortgage Interest (War Restrictions) Acts*; B.R. Mitchell and P. Deane, *Abstract of British Historical Statistics* (1962), 345.

43 M. Bowley, *Housing and the State* (1945), 37.

44 P.P. 1918 XIII, *Committee on the Increase of Rent. . .*; PRO, HLG 41/6, 41/42.

45 Bowley, *op. cit.*, 40–1.

46 *Ibid.*, 135, 137.

47 *Ibid.*, 46, 138.

48 *Report of the Departmental Committee on Housing, 1933*, quoted in Bowley, *op. cit.*, 138.

49 P.P. 1930–1 XVII, *Ministry of Health. Report of the Interdepartmental Committee on the Rent Restriction Acts*; Bowley, *op. cit.*, 140.

50 See D.H. Aldcroft and H.W. Richardson, *Building in the British Economy between the Wars* (1968).

51 Daunton, *House and Home*, chapters 6 and 7.

52 PRO, HLG 41/63.

53 Bowley, *op. cit.*, 17–18.

54 *Ibid.*, 19–20.

55 *Ibid.*, 38–9, 42–6.

56 *Ibid.*, 126–31, 136–7.

57 *Ibid.*, 125, 128–9; S. Schifferes, 'Council tenants and housing policy in the 1930s: the contradictions of state intervention', in Political Economy of Housing Workshop, *Housing and Class in Britain* (1976).

58 G. Wilson, *Rent Rebates* (3rd edn, 1939).

59 Bowley, *op. cit.*, 163; Wilson, *op. cit.*, 35.

60 Bowley, *op. cit.*, 103–13, 126–7.

61 S. Damer, 'A note on housing allocation', in *Housing and Class in Britain*; C.J. Thomas, 'Some geographical aspects of council housing in Nottingham', *East Midlands Geographer*, IV (1966).

62 See J.P. Macey and C.V. Baker, *Housing Management* (2nd edn, 1973), 281.

63 See, for example, P. Dunleavy, *The Politics of Mass Housing in Britain, 1945–75. A Study of Corporate Power and Professional Influence in the Welfare State* (1981).

64 R.J. Morris, 'Materialism and tenements', *Scottish Economic and Social History*, I (1981), 75.

65 Swenarton, *op. cit.*, 203; R.J. Lawrence, 'Domestic space and society: a cross-cultural study', *Comparative Studies in Society and History*, XXIV (1982) 104; A. Rapoport, *House Form and Culture* (1969).

66 P.P. 1908 CVII, *Report of an Enquiry by the Board of Trade into Working-Class Rents, Housing and Retail Prices*; *Census of England and Wales, 1911*. VIII, *Tenements in Administrative Counties and Urban and Rural Districts*, tables 3 and 4; Daunton, *House and Home*, chapter 3.

67 A. Sayle, *The Houses of the Workers* (1924), chapter XV compares bye-law and council housing.

68 M.J. Daunton, 'Public place and private space: the Victorian city and the working-class

household', in *The Pursuit of Urban History*, ed. A. Sutcliffe and D. Fraser (1983).

69 R. Unwin, *Cottage Plans and Common Sense* (1902), 11, 13.

70 *An Enquiry into People's Homes. A Report Prepared by Mass-Observation for the Advertising Service Guild* (1943), 104–7.

71 A. Briggs, *History of Birmingham, Volume* II, *Borough and City 1865–1938* (1952), 235, 308; A. Sutcliffe and R. Smith, *History of Birmingham,* III, *Birmingham 1939–70* (1974), 250.

72 A. Ravetz, *Model Estate. Planned Housing at Quarry Hill, Leeds* (1974).

73 R. Durant, *Watling. A Survey of Social Life on a New Housing Estate* (1939), 15 and passim; see also T. Young, *Becontree and Dagenham* (1934) and J. Madge and R. Jevons, *Housing Estates* (1946).

74 Jevons and Madge, *op. cit.*, 87–100.

75 *Ministry of Health. Report to the Minister of Health by the Departmental Committee on Valuation for Rates, 1939* (1944), 7.

Council house building
in County Durham, 1900–39:
the local implementation
of national policy

ROBERT RYDER

Council house building in County Durham, 1900–39: the local implementation of national policy

ROBERT RYDER

1 Introduction

The following chapters are drawn from the M.Phil thesis 'Council House Building in County Durham, 1900–1939: the Local Implementation of National Policy', presented to the University of Durham in 1979. The thesis has five main chapters, the first of which – on the philosophies held by housing reformers in the early twentieth century and the course of national policy up to 1939 – is not represented here. The second and third chapters of the thesis – on housing in County Durham before the First World War and the achievement of local government between the wars – have been heavily edited to produce section 2 of this paper. The final two chapters of the thesis – on the Council as builder and as landlord in the inter-war years – have also been shortened but are substantially those which appear as sections 3 and 4 below.

2 Housing in County Durham, 1900–39

There are two very good reasons for choosing County Durham as a survey area. In the first place, there is the wide range of economic activity which it encompassed during this period. The area in question is not the forlorn rump of a county left by the local government reorganization of 1974, but one which stretched from the great shipbuilding conurbations of south Tyneside and Wearside down to the engineering and steel towns of Darlington, Stockton and West Hartlepool. In the middle was the Durham coalfield, with its scores of mining settlements, a strange mixture of village life and urban industrial development; and to the south and west were wide areas of genuinely rural country. For much of the inter-war period, of course, many parts

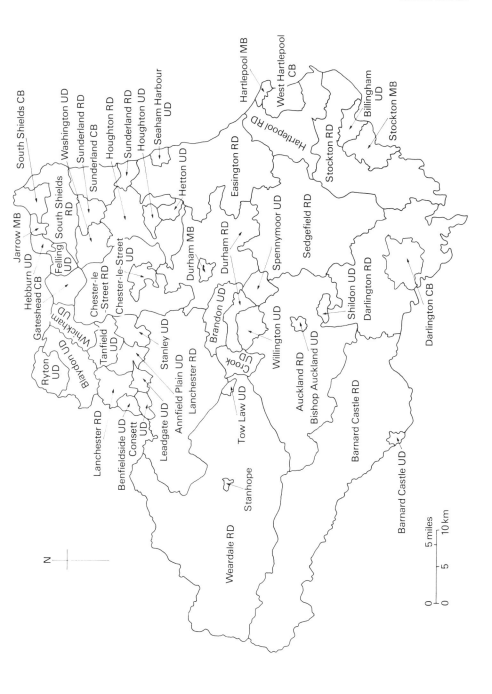

Figure 5.   Local authority areas in County Durham in the 1920s.

of the region were severely affected by depression and economic decline. By looking at the whole of a county as diverse as this, one can examine the different problems of the communities within it and the ways in which their elected councils tried to tackle them. No district and no local authority is exactly like another – so the wider the comparisons the better; and the sounder, one hopes, the generalizations.

Secondly, there is the particular historical interest of north-east England because of its chronic record of bad housing conditions – one of the least enviable traditions of the region. At the 1901 census the five county boroughs of Tyneside and Wearside were by a long way the most overcrowded towns in the whole country. And the more detailed survey carried out in the 1930s[1] confirmed that the north-east still made all the other black spots seem pale by comparison: its boroughs and its urban and rural districts dominated the overcrowding tables in their respective leagues. Against this background of abysmally poor conditions, the efforts of local government stand out much more clearly. For the other very interesting feature of County Durham in this period is that its local authorities were considerably more active than those in most of the country. By the outbreak of the Second World War, council houses made up nearly a sixth of the housing stock in County Durham, compared with less than a tenth in England and Wales as a whole. Except in a few agricultural districts, the Council had become the largest single domestic landlord.

a. The legacy of the nineteenth century

The high level of overcrowding in County Durham before 1914 can be explained, statistically at least, by the large average family size and the small average dwelling size. In 1911 family sizes were higher in Durham (an average of 4.8 persons per family) than any other English county. They were particularly high in the coalfield, but were also well above the national average in most of the large towns. At the same time, average dwelling sizes in the north-east (at 3.8 rooms per dwelling) were easily the lowest in the country. Unfortunately, as was often the case in the rented housing market, the worst conditions commanded the highest prices. It is true that wage levels were relatively good in the north-east before 1914,[2] but rents in Tyneside and Sunderland were among the highest in the country outside London and, as table 1 shows, were not much lower in parts of the coalfield.[3]

Table 1.   Rent levels in County Durham, c. 1905
Index: London (1905) = 100

industrial towns (1905)		coalfield (1903)	
Jarrow	68	South Tyneside	68
Gateshead	66		
		North-west	62
South Shields	61		
Sunderland	59		
Darlington	58	North-east	58
Stockton	54		
		Eastern	49
		Central	47
		South-west	46

Of course, these facts do not explain how the poor conditions actually arose. This is best attempted by looking separately at the four distinct areas of the county: south Tyneside and Sunderland; the southern towns of Darlington, Stockton and the Hartlepools; the Durham coalfield; and the rural areas in the south and west of the county.

The growth of the Tyne and Wear conurbations in the second half of the nineteenth century was based on the development of the coal trade and the rise of shipbuilding and marine engineering. The population growth was massive – numbers more than tripled between 1851 and the First World War. There was also an enormous increase in the housing stock, but not in line with local needs or the standards obtaining in the rest of the country. At the 1911 census over 30 per cent of the population in Sunderland and the towns of south Tyneside were living at a level of more than two persons to a room, a phenomenally high proportion compared with the national average of just under 10 per cent.

One of the reasons for the high level of overcrowding in south Tyneside was the predominance of a building form known as the Tyneside flat, which accounted for about 60 per cent of the housing stock by 1911. This is a form of two-storey terraced housing where the front doors come in pairs: inside, there is a self-contained flat on each floor (see fig. 3b above). It was almost unknown outside the North-east and even there was uncommon outside Tyneside districts. Earlier flats were usually of two rooms each, but from the 1880s the common pattern was three rooms on the lower floor and four above. The later variety undoubtedly marked an improvement in standards in its day. But the units were still too small to make much of a dent in levels of overcrowding.

The peculiarly local development of this form (similar in its way to the rise of back-to-back housing in Leeds) raises some intriguing questions, which would be a digression here.[4] The housing pattern in Sunderland holds different mysteries. Apart from the older riverside quarters to the east, where large old three-storey houses were divided into many small tenements, the characteristic working-class accommodation consisted of small terraced houses of a single storey, with a tiny yard to the rear. Like Tyneside flats, these houses offered better conditions than older property in the town, but were still too small, in comparison with standards elsewhere in England and Wales, for the size of family occupying them.

The towns in the south of the county had a much more balanced industrial development and a more conventional housing pattern. Darlington was a long-established market town, which grew into a major railway engineering centre; Stockton was an old port which expanded along with the iron and steel fortunes of Middlesbrough, and developed its own iron, shipbuilding and engineering industries; and West Hartlepool, though it began life as a coal port, also built up iron and steel works and some shipbuilding and marine engineering. Whereas along the Tyne and Wear there were strong physical and industrial pressures to impose a high-density housing pattern, the southern towns were more fortunate. The greater industrial diversity of Stockton and West Hartlepool allowed them to develop hinterland where there were few obstacles to new building; and Darlington was even better placed, expanding its industry and its housing stock outwards in concentric rings. The result in these boroughs was a pattern of terraced housing similar to that in most other industrial towns. Overcrowding, though still higher than the national average, was less than half the level of the Tyne and Wear towns; and rents, too, were considerably lower.

The principal feature of the housing pattern in the Durham coalfield was the 'free house' system. It meant simply that certain categories of miners, mainly family men who worked below the surface, were given free occupation of a house built and owned by the coal company. If there were not enough free houses to go around, the unlucky miners who qualified for this benefit were given – if they could produce a rent book – a weekly rent allowance, which at 2s.–2s. 6d. per week was only about half the rent they were likely to have to pay. The system was barely known outside the north-east – a Royal Commission in 1925 found that almost all of the existing 68,000 free colliery houses in England and Wales were in Durham and Northumberland.[5] The system affected the vast majority of families whose livelihood depended on the pit: the coalowners' figures indicate that in 1903 fewer than 10 per cent of their employees who were householders did not receive some aid from the system, either in the form of free accommodation or of rent allowance.[6]

The effect of the free house system was to encourage a low overall standard of housing. It was more economical for a miner to live in free accommodation than to have the inadequate rent allowance: the Land Enquiry Committee thought 'the most serious evil is that there are always applications from men living in "rented" houses for the tenancy of a free colliery house, however old and worn-out it may be.'[7] As coalowners would rather have sunk their investment in colliery workings than in housing, it is hardly surprising that most free houses were small and cheaply built. The same low standards were also adopted by the private builders operating in the mining districts of the county: there was no incentive for private enterprise to build to a higher standard than that of the colliery houses. In every broad area of the coalfield (except the south and south-west) the average level of overcrowding in 1911, in terms of 'more than two persons to a room', was between 30 and 36 per cent. This was as high as in the Tyne and Wear towns and therefore among the very worst in the country. And the indications are that rents in the northern half of the coalfield were not far behind those in the conurbations.[8]

The best housing conditions in the county were in the agricultural districts stretching around Darlington, Stockton and the Hartlepools, from which they drew their prosperity: overcrowding there was only 11 to 12 per cent in 1911. Conditions in the rural areas to the west were not so good. Industries like lead-mining in Weardale and Teesdale, textiles and dyeing in Barnard Castle, and iron works at Tow Law, had collapsed by the late nineteenth century. The result was stagnation both in population levels and in the housing stock.

b. House-building activity, 1900–14
At first sight the building record of County Durham between 1901 and 1911 appears quite creditable. Over the whole county the housing stock increased at a higher rate than the number of families: by 21.1 per cent as against 17.5 per cent. But this pattern was by no means uniform throughout the county, nor did it apply to the last few years before the First World War. The areas where the housing supply exceeded the new demand (and could thus help to relieve the overall shortage) were chiefly the towns of Darlington, Stockton and West Hartlepool, and some of those on south Tyneside. But in the local authority areas on the coalfield the increase in families – a very high 37.4 per cent overall – far exceeded a 28.6 per cent increase in the housing stock. Furthermore, in the north-east generally there was a cyclical decline in the level of building activity from 1903 which continued beyond 1911.[9]

In the coalfield districts the failure of the housing supply to keep pace even with the increase in families between 1901 and 1911 was largely due to the inertia of the coal companies, who were finding it much more economical to pay more miners the weekly rent allowance (a fairly small and static sum) than to sink capital in the expensive and unrewarding business of house building. Whereas the number of miners they employed grew by 45,528 (46.1 per cent) between the censuses of 1901 and 1911, the stock of colliery houses increased between 1903 and 1913 by only 7,869 (19.2 per cent).[10] This meant that there were approximately 400 colliery houses per thousand miners in 1901, but little more than 300 per thousand by 1913. The gap was nowhere near filled by private builders and in several mining districts a crisis was developing.

It is not surprising, therefore, that what council house building there was before the First World War took place in the coalfield. (There was, in fact, one scheme in Sunderland, opened in 1903; but this was a slum clearance measure taken to deal with a particularly unhealthy dockland site.[11]) The coalfield was the area where there was an increasing shortfall in housing supply and therefore the most pressure on councils to use their powers under the Housing Act of 1890 to build houses for the working classes. Among the miners themselves there was a background of social housing provision from about the turn of the century in the example of 'aged miners' homes', which were small terraced bungalows built from union funds for retired members. Even so, the fact that council schemes threatened to be a charge on the ratepayers at large meant that councillors had to be fairly committed before embarking on house-building initiatives. It is interesting, therefore, that the districts which did get schemes going before the war were generally ones where the Independent Labour Party had obtained a majority, or a fairly large proportion of seats, on the Council. Conversely, the I.L.P. made very little headway in the councils on industrial south Tyneside; and housing initiatives, even when broached in these councils, were always voted down.[12]

The number of dwellings erected by local authorities in Durham, before the war brought building to a halt, was between 650 and 700. The councils which got schemes off the ground were Sunderland (the slum clearance scheme mentioned above) Stanley, Annfield Plain, Seaham Harbour, Houghton-le-Spring, Chester-le-Street, and the rural districts of Sunderland, Easington, Sedgefield and Chester-le-Street.[13] Their work represented a quarter of 1 per cent of the total housing stock of the county at that time. In absolute terms, therefore, the contribution that council schemes made towards the housing needs of the county before the First World War was very small. Nonetheless, the efforts of those councils which did succeed in getting a scheme off the ground were remarkable. At a time when there was no great national campaign for council housing and no provision for an Exchequer subsidy, when locally there were often powerful vested interests and prejudices to overcome, it demanded considerable initiative and determination to win support for a housing scheme and to carry it through. After the First World War, however, this field of action was magnified enormously and the obligations of local government, in terms of its responsibilities as builder and landlord, grew on a scale unimagined before 1914.

c. The achievements of local government in the inter-war period
The total number of houses built between the wars by local authorities in County Durham was about 60,000.[14] When this figure is translated into a form comparable with the rest of England and Wales, it can be seen that the overall level of council

activity was relatively high (see fig. 6). Measured against the size of population and the existing housing stock, the level of building in Durham was about 50 per cent greater than in the rest of the country. It can also be seen that this high level of local authority activity within County Durham contrasted with a low level of private building over the same period. Even with the inclusion of housing association dwellings, the rate of private house building in the county represented little more than half of that in the rest of England and Wales.

About 7,000 council houses were erected in County Durham under the Addison Act, 4,000 under the Chamberlain Act, 17,000 under the Wheatley Act, and 32,000 under the acts of 1930 and 1935. When compared with the national figures, the distribution of council housing activity in Durham shows a reasonable similarity in respect of the Addison, Chamberlain and Wheatley schemes, up to about 1927–8. There was a trough of council activity in the late 1920s, which was most severe in mining districts (where the effects of the coal dispute and the close grip of the Ministry of Health in 1926–8 meant that few houses came to be completed in 1928–30) but was also noticeable in the larger towns. In the latter case this may have been due to the general effect of cuts in the Chamberlain and Wheatley subsidies in 1927, which produced a fall in council building on a national scale. Under the Housing Acts of 1930 and 1935, however, the level of building activity was very much higher in County Durham – more than twice as high as in the rest of England and Wales. This was determined to a great extent by the concentration of overcrowded and slum property in the county, but other factors – the more favourable subsidy arrangements, for example, and the growing domination of local government in Durham by the Labour party – must also have played a part.

The level of council activity in the various districts of County Durham over the period 1919–38 is shown, together with details of private building, in table 2.[15] One of the most striking features to emerge from this summary is the high level of local authority building in the more viable areas of the coalfield (broadly, groups A, B and C in the table) where the councils were about twice as active as average local authorities in the rest of England and Wales. Council activity was considerably lower in the more depressed mining districts (mainly those in group D) and very low in the small towns and agricultural villages in the west (group G). The main urban centres have been divided into two groups – the Tyne and Wear area (group E) and Darlington, North Teesside and the Hartlepools (group F). The level of council building was generally higher in the Tyne and Wear area, although not as high on the whole as in the more active coalfield districts. The Tyneside districts of Felling, Hebburn and Jarrow did, however, match the coalfield level – Felling being the most active local authority in the county, in terms of council houses per thousand population.

In the private house-building sector, one can see that the balance between the Tyne and Wear area and the southern towns was the reverse of that in the council sector. Private building was particularly high in Darlington and in Billingham – the large development in the latter between 1927 and 1930, coinciding with major industrial expansion, making it the district of greatest private activity. On the coalfield itself there was a wide variation in private building between different districts. The greatest activity was in the Easington district, where mining prospects were the brightest. The lowest levels of private building were in the south-western parts of the county, where even the low figures that obtain are inflated in some cases (for example, Shildon, Crook and Willington) by housing association activity under the Acts of 1930 and 1935.

These different levels and patterns of building activity must be seen, of course, in the context of demographic movements over the period and the levels of over-crowding and unfitness of property. Population growth in the 1920s was very slow in the county as a whole (only 0.5 per cent increase between 1921 and 1931) but the falling birth rate meant that the increase in private families (14.7 per cent), and thus the need for additional houses, was still quite large. On top of this requirement was the need for extra housing to reduce the high level of overcrowding (more than three times higher than in England and Wales as a whole) that existed in 1921. By the time of the 1931 census, councils and private builders together had added 37,000 houses over the decade, but this was 9,000 fewer than the number of new families created and led to an increase of 25 per cent in the number of families obliged to share accommodation. Nevertheless, the fortuitous effect of the falling birth rate on family size (which in County Durham fell from an average of 4.61 in 1921 to 4.04 in 1931) brought about a significant improvement in the general level of overcrowding (from 29.5 to 20.3 per cent). In some districts, like Brandon, Crook and Shildon, the combination of a fairly modest Addison Act council estate, a larger than average drop in family size and a high rate of emigration, served to cut overcrowding by more than half between 1921 and 1931. In other districts, however, like the Tyne and Wear towns, which in fact had a considerably higher rate of both local authority and private building, demographic movements were less obliging and the improvement in over-crowding was less spectacular.

Unfortunately, there is no comparable census information about family size and overcrowding for the 1930s,[16] but the picture indicated by the national registration in

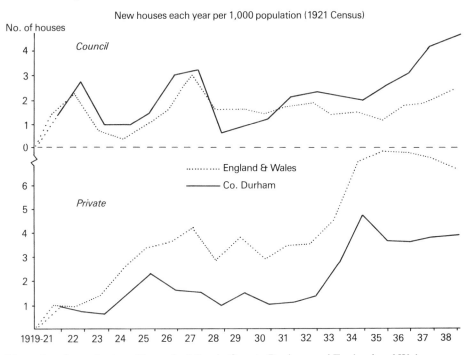

Figure 6.   Annual rates of house building in County Durham and England and Wales, 1919–38.

Table 2. *Level of council and private house-building activity in County Durham, 1919–38 [By districts as constituted in 1938]*

		number of houses built 1919–38		houses (1919–38) per thousand registered population in 1939		council housing (1919–38) as % of total 1921 stock	council housing as % of total house-building 1919–38
		council	private	council	private		
Ⓐ	Ryton	641	517	47.0	37.9		55.4
	Blaydon	1,442	1,057	48.3	35.4		57.7
	Whickham	1,320	1,375	61.7	64.2		49.0
	Consett	1,650	1,560	43.7	41.3		51.4
	Stanley	2,366	785	48.3	16.0		75.1
	Lanchester RDC	1,159	1,022	71.4	63.0		53.1
		8,578	6,316	51.1	37.6	25.1	57.5
Ⓑ	Chester-le-Street	1,294	1,181	73.9	67.4		52.3
	Chester-le-Street RDC	2,534	1,060	61.0	25.5		70.5
	Washington	890	251	52.5	14.8		78.0
	Houghton	1,959	768	69.6	27.3		71.8
	Hetton	1,177	312	61.8	16.4		79.0
	Sunderland RDC	1,162	282	48.9	11.9		80.5
		9,016	3,854	61.4	26.2	27.7	70.1
Ⓒ	Easington RDC	4,008	6,090	49.1	74.6		39.7
	Seaham	2,021	589	79.2	23.1		77.4
		6,029	6,679	56.3	62.4	36.6	47.4
Ⓓ	Brandon	618	65	31.2	3.3		90.5
	Durham	754	940	40.9	51.0		44.5
	Durham RDC	2,502	540	75.1	16.2		82.2
	Crook & Willington	909	276	31.0	9.4		76.7
	Spennymoor	74	524	4.1	28.8		12.4
	Bishop Auckland	209	615	5.8	17.0		25.4
	Shildon	197	149	13.9	10.5		56.9
	Sedgefield RDC	1,320	970	37.0	27.2		57.6
		6,583	4,079	32.1	19.9	13.6	61.7
Ⓔ	Gateshead	3,104	3,774	30.5	37.1		45.1
	Felling	2,340	433	100.0	18.5		84.4
	Hebburn	1,268	578	59.9	27.3		68.7
	Jarrow	1,640	118	61.0	4.4		93.3
	South Shields	4,415	3,097	45.8	32.1		58.8
	Boldon	725	1,790	47.0	115.9		28.8
	Sunderland	5,502	5,642	33.2	34.0		49.4
		18,994	15,432	42.1	34.2	18.7	55.2
Ⓕ	Darlington	978	6,954	12.6	89.7		12.3
	Darlington RDC	72	520	7.3	52.5		12.2
	Stockton	3,393	3,339	50.9	50.1		50.4
	Stockton RDC	54	327	6.8	41.3		14.2
	Billingham	1,271	2,773	62.8	137.1		31.4

Table 2 (contd)

	number of houses built 1919–38		houses (1919–38) per thousand registered population in 1939		council housing (1919–38) as % of total 1921 stock	council housing as % of total house-building 1919–38
	council	private	council	private		
West Hartlepool	1,501	4,010	23.4	62.4		27.2
Hartlepool	514	278	33.1	17.9		64.9
	7,783	18,201	29.7	69.5	15.3	30.0
Ⓖ Tow Law	—	103	—	31.8		—
Barnard Castle	79	207	16.6	43.5		27.6
Barnard Castle RDC	59	177	3.1	9.4		25.0
Weardale RDC	44	121	4.0	11.1		26.7
	182	608	4.8	16.1	2.5	23.0
County Durham	57,165	55,169	41.5	40.0	19.6	50.9
Rest of England & Wales	1.018m	2.756m	26.2	71.0	13.2	27.0

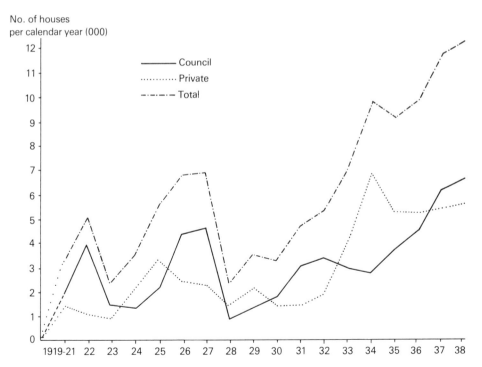

Figure 7. Annual rate of local authority and private house building in County Durham, 1919–38.

1939 is one of overall population decline. This seems to have been particularly heavy in the Tyne and Wear area and in most parts of the coalfield. Given that the level of both local authority and private house building was much higher in the 1930s in County Durham than in the 1920s (and even allowing for the greater number of demolitions after 1930) it is likely that overcrowding was further reduced by a substantial margin. If this was the case, then much was again due to a combination of local government activity and wider population movements.

Overall, it is fair to conclude that local government was instrumental in achieving a dramatic improvement in the quantity and quality of the county's housing stock. The areas in which conditions had been worst – south Tyneside, Sunderland and the coalfield – were those where the improvement was most emphatic. The greater part of this overall improvement was due, particularly in the coalfield, to a high level of activity by local authorities. Conditions in Darlington, north Teesside and the Hartlepools had been much better to begin with, but there had again been a marked improvement. In this case the greater credit belonged to private enterprise, whose building activity – at least by the standards of County Durham – overshadowed that of the local authority sector. By national standards, however, the contribution made by private enterprise was generally low and in some districts negligible. Just why private enterprise was so inactive is a difficult question. The economic depression affecting many districts, the difficulty of building new houses to let at a profitable rent, and the poor market for building for sale to owner-occupiers, were undoubtedly factors. But the intervention of local authorities in the housing market was not: the comparatively low level of activity in the private sector was evident even in the 1920s when the rate of council house building was no higher in County Durham than in the rest of England and Wales. Even when the rate of council building increased in Durham in the 1930s, it did not prevent a relative boom taking place in the private sector. The achievement of local authorities in many districts of County Durham in the inter-war period appears very much, therefore, to have been in making good a substantial part of the deficiency both in the quality of working-class housing, for which private enterprise had previously been responsible, and in the quantity, which even between the wars the private sector was unable to correct.

d. Constraints on local authority action

A major influence on house-building policy locally was the political composition of the Council itself. It was, of course, almost impossible for a local authority to escape completely from involvement in house building: the Acts of 1919, 1930 and 1935 imposed clear obligations to prepare schemes for additional and replacement housing, whatever the Council's own feelings were. If only for this reason, it is misleading to assume that only Labour councillors were personally committed to direct local government involvement in house building. In the county boroughs of Darlington, West Hartlepool, Sunderland and South Shields, which for much of the period were not under Labour control, the level of council building was fairly high, and certainly in keeping with local needs. Yet when South Shields fell to Labour and Gateshead was regained by the socialists in the later 1930s, the Councils' direct involvement in house building was actually reduced, for the task of building and running new estates was largely handed over to the independent North Eastern Housing Association.

On the whole, however, it is true that councils under Labour control displayed greater enthusiasm for intervention in local housing provision. Sometimes this was seen in an acceleration of council house building once Labour had obtained a majority: this was the case in Blaydon after 1925[17] and in Jarrow after 1935,[18] when the socialists won control for the first time. In some of the earlier Labour strongholds the rate of council house building was fairly high throughout the period: for example, in Felling (where by 1935 the Council was composed of 19 Labour men, a communist and a 'progressive')[19] and in Stanley (where by 1934 every councillor was a socialist).[20] To analyse the movements of political control in the local authorities of the county between the wars would require a lengthy study in itself. But the outline is fairly clear: there was overall a remorseless – though occasionally interrupted – shift towards Labour control, so that in 1936, as a ratepayers' paper reported gloomily, '28 out of 40 Councils in County Durham [were] in the hands of the Labour Party.'[21] The Labour councils were chiefly in the Tyneside area and the coalfield, where the level of local authority housebuilding was highest; the non-Labour councils were mainly in the towns and agricultural districts in the south of the county, where the level of activity (as well as the level of housing shortage) was considerably lower.

The other major influence on the level of building was that of the Ministry of Health, which was responsible ultimately for deciding whether the proposals for a council scheme should proceed or not. Except in the early stages of the Addison scheme, when it sometimes chivvied councils which it felt were not doing enough, the Ministry's influence upon the level of building was largely either passive or negative: it did not initiate, but either rubber-stamped proposals already drawn up by a local authority or turned them down. This was one reason for its general unpopularity among local authorities.

A major cause of disagreement, however, and one that was of particular importance in the North-east, was the coal dispute of 1926 and its effect on local government finance. The effects in mining districts which concerned the Ministry most were the enormous increase in rent arrears, which made existing schemes vastly uneconomic, the rise in local rate levels and the threat to the long-term industrial prospects of the area. The result was that the Ministry was liable to reject out of hand any request for further housing provision made by a local authority seriously affected by the dispute or its aftermath. This was a complete reversal of the philosophy ruling at the outset of the Addison scheme, when the main consideration was the housing need of a district rather than its resources or its economic prospects.

e. Alternatives to council house building

Before examining in detail the problems which local authorities in County Durham encountered between the wars in their role as builders and landlords, it will be useful to mention briefly the forms of action which some councils took as an alternative to assuming the full responsibility of house building and estate management themselves. In some cases the alternatives were deployed by councils with the clear intention of relieving pressure on their own resources. In others the action was taken as a supplement to direct local government involvement, or simply to make the most effective use locally of policies determined by central government.

The main involvement which councils experienced in contributing to building projects other than their own was the option provided in the 1923 Act to supplement the Exchequer subsidy with a contribution from local rates. This option allowed a local authority the active role of stimulating private enterprise in the district. At least ten local authorities in County Durham made it their policy to encourage private builders with a bonus from the rates.[22] In most cases the Exchequer subsidy of £75 (the capitalized value of annual payments of £6 over 20 years) was augmented by a contribution from the rates of £25, although Stockton and Leadgate offered less than that and Easington more.[23] In West Hartlepool the rate contribution was administered with a view to improved town planning: the amount paid on top of the Exchequer grant of £75 varied with the density of the development, so that the full bonus of £25 was only given if the overall density was less than 20 houses per acre.[24] Whatever the variations in cash and conditions imposed by councils, the logic behind adding to the ratepayers' burden was basically the same. As the Easington Clerk reported to his councillors, 'it is infinitely to the advantage of the Ratepayers to encourage Private Enterprise to build their own houses': if private builders were not tempted into action, the cost to ratepayers of the Council erecting an equivalent number of houses would be much greater.[25] The local authorities which adopted this practice were therefore staking limited amounts in an attempt to avoid larger debts later on. In the Easington district the stake was in fact quite large – about £56,000 in rate-borne contributions by April 1927 – but the policy was rewarded by a level of private building much higher than in most coalfield districts.[26]

The possibility of encouraging private builders to ease the councils' burden faded in the later 1920s as the Chamberlain subsidy was phased out. There was, of course, a revival of unassisted private building in the 1930s, which helped to relieve the housing shortage generally, but this could not reduce the obligations imposed on local authorities by the Acts of 1930 and 1935. However, the opportunity to divest themselves of rehousing responsibilities became available to local authorities in County Durham from 1936, in the shape of the North-Eastern Housing Association (NEHA). This body was founded as a limited company through the Commissioner for the 'Special Areas', who was 'guided by the fact that, while the need for better housing in the North Eastern Area is exceptionally acute, the payment of the contribution out of the rates in respect of the new houses will involve a number of Local Authorities in this area in grave financial difficulties.'[27] The North Eastern Housing Association was designed to spare local authorities the expense of building houses under the 1930 and 1935 Acts: after the Council had designated and dealt with its unhealthy and overcrowded areas, it could call on the NEHA to build and maintain the replacement housing. The association could do this economically because, in addition to receiving the usual Exchequer subsidies for the houses it built, it was given a further grant by central government equivalent to the standard contributions that the local authority would have been expected to make from the rates. Pressure on the local ratepayers – and thus on the Council itself – was reduced at the expense of the taxpayer at large. The main disadvantage, from the Council's point of view, was that it lost to an independent organization its complete local control over building and estate management policies in the non-commercial housing sector.

The association was given a mixed reception by local authorities in County Durham. Sixteen councils refused to co-operate with it at all, and the 19 that did were not always willing parties.[28] The resentment arose not from the government's aim to spare the local ratepayer, but the way in which it was carried out: while the NEHA was not in itself undesirable, even some of the councils which co-operated with the association thought that it would have been preferable for the subsidy in lieu of rates to be paid direct to local authorities for them to do the job. The national government's action was not the calculated menace that many believed, but it followed the trend, which was discernible in its unemployment assistance policy and the first attempts at regional policy in the 1930s, of attempting to ease contentious matters of social policy out of the arena of national and local politics.

Of the 7,500 association houses which had been completed, or were under contract or out to tender by July 1938, 28 per cent were in Sunderland, 16 per cent in Gateshead, 12 per cent in Easington rural district, 9 per cent in South Shields and 8 per cent in the Hartlepools.[29] By the end of 1939 the NEHA had completed about 7,600 houses,[30] although some of these were in Wallsend, north of the Tyne, and in four local authority areas in Cumberland. The association estimated that by its building these houses, instead of local government, it had saved ratepayers over £$\frac{1}{2}$ million.[31]

The third main option that a council could pursue in order to reduce its own direct involvement in housing matters was to sell the houses it had already built, thus ending its responsibilities as a landlord. The chief exponents of the selling policy were the county boroughs of South Shields and West Hartlepool, the latter having disposed of about 340 houses (30 per cent of its total stock) by 1939.[32] Although the practice worked quite smoothly in West Hartlepool, the South Shields Council found the advantages much smaller than it had hoped: by 1930 it had bought back a third of the 174 houses it had previously sold, and was finding difficulty in disposing of them again.[33] Similar problems were experienced by Houghton UDC, one of the few mining districts to experiment with council house sales: the buyers were often unable to keep up with mortgage repayments or just wanted 'to be relieved of their liability' and move to rented accommodation elsewhere. The Council was forced to repossess or repurchase many of the houses and to put them back on the rented market.[34]

3 The Council as builder

Although most councils would have been familiar before the First World War with the procedures involved in getting a building project of some sort off the ground, the responsibilities imposed by inter-war housing schemes were of a quite new order. As we saw in the previous section, local authorities in County Durham were responsible for building about 60,000 houses between the wars – about a sixth of the total number of houses standing in the county in 1939. This section looks at the physical processes involved in this: the raising and servicing of loan capital, the purchase of large tracts of land, the supervision of valuable building contracts, and the direct employment of building labour. Finally, there is the question of how the Council, through its control of the planning and design of large new housing estates, could now exercise a major influence on the physical environment of its district.

a. Finance
All inter-war council housing schemes made a loss and the loss was borne by public funds. The subsidy was a mixture of Exchequer and local rate contributions which varied according to the terms of the particular Housing Act under which the scheme was built. While subsidies payable by the Exchequer were (with the exception of the Addison scheme) on a fixed scale of annual payments prescribed by statute, local authorities could limit their own financial liability by means of the building and estate management policies which they adopted. For example, by using direct labour to build housing estates and by paring down the standards of design and amenity which were incorporated, councils could reduce construction costs. Similarly, net running costs could be kept down by charging the maximum rents allowed by the Ministry of Health and by taking whatever measures were necessary to ensure that the amounts due were actually collected from the tenants.[35] As we saw in the previous section, a

few councils tried to reduce both capital and current liabilities at a stroke by selling as many of their houses as possible to private buyers. But though such policies could keep demands upon local rates down to a minimum, it was almost impossible for councils to avoid the burden entirely. In most districts of County Durham it grew steadily during the inter-war period.

The first burden which local authorities had to face was the raising of loan finance to cover the full capital cost of each housing scheme. Before land could be purchased and construction could begin, the Council had to seek the approval of the Ministry of Health to the raising of a loan to cover the estimated capital cost of the project. So although the Ministry's decision was in effect to allow or to refuse the building of houses, it was actually delivered in terms of an agreement or a refusal to sanction the Council's borrowing of the necessary funds. If the Ministry's sanction could be obtained, the Council would then attempt to raise a loan on the security of its power to levy local rates.

Loans could be obtained either in the public or private sector. The main source of funds in the former was the Public Works Loans Board, which usually lent to local authorities at slightly less than the market rate. The PWLB would only agree to lend if the local authority's application had been recommended to it by the Ministry of Health. This second stage of ministry approval was not always forthcoming: larger districts (with a rateable value of over £200,000) were often debarred and the remainder had to convince the Ministry that they were unable to raise sufficient money in the open market. Even when a council's application had been officially recommended, the PWLB had to satisfy itself that the loan would be a secure investment of its funds: districts in which the rate in the pound was already high, or where inefficiency was suspected, were liable to have their applications turned down. The only other means of raising loans in the public sector was by borrowing from other local authorities. This was unusual and only happened where a council's own scheme had fallen through and it was decided, in effect, to transfer any loans which had been raised to another council in a position to make use of the capital. One of the very few examples recorded in County Durham was a loan of £40,000 to Easington RDC by the borough of Kingston-upon-Thames in 1922.[36]

The sources of private loans were much more varied, but they may be divided basically between corporate bodies and individual members of the public. A major attempt to tap the latter source was made during the Addison scheme. In order to reduce the competition for loans in the open market, local authorities were instructed to issue housing bonds for sale to the public and to campaign for subscriptions. Despite appeals which often went so far as to urge that housing bonds were not only a safe investment but also an insurance against bolshevism, the response of the public was not very gratifying. Certainly, the results in County Durham were hardly worth the effort involved. After several months of appeals the councillors of Stanley managed to raise only £600 against 1919 Act schemes which were to cost over £250,000,[37] while in South Shields only £7,865 could be raised against schemes costing more than £500,000.[38] Once the Addison scheme had been brought to an end, no serious attempts were made to attract the investment of the small saver. For the rest of the inter-war period loans from individuals for housing purposes were rare, but one notable example is a loan of £30,000 made to Easington RDC in 1926 by George Bernard Shaw.[39]

Loans from financial institutions and other corporate investors constituted the major part of local authorities' borrowing in the private sector. The most orthodox source of loans was the local clearing or savings bank branch. But the local bank manager was not always disposed to lend to the Council, or he might insist on hedging the transaction with certain conditions. For example, in 1927 the Stanhope Council found that their own bankers (Barclays) were unwilling to grant a long-term loan for housing purposes and others (the Midland) would only agree on the now familiar condition that the whole of the Council's current account business would be transferred to them.[40] A second major source of institutional capital was insurance companies and friendly societies wishing to obtain a steady rate of return through long-term lending to the public sector. Two good examples of this type of investment are the loan of £38,000 made to the Jarrow council in 1922 by the Hearts of Oak Benefit Society[41] and the loan of £51,000 made to Sedgefield RDC by the Prudential Assurance Company in 1926.[42] These loans were exceptionally large – the majority from such institutions did not exceed £10,000 at a time. Another source of private institutional loans consisted of bodies whose desire for a sound investment was accompanied by a concern to help ameliorate housing conditions in the area. Such, one may assume, was the concern of the East Pontop Coal Company in lending £2,000 to Annfield Plain UDC in 1920[43] and of the Derbyshire Miners' Association in lending £40,000 to Easington RDC in 1925.[44]

Given this wide range of sources from which local authorities could borrow capital, it might be imagined that the initial financing of housing projects was a fairly simple matter. In fact, in County Durham it was only the first in a series of serious obstacles on which a council's schemes could founder. The basic problem was that most local government districts in Durham not only lacked residents able to make substantial private loans, but were also without the potential to attract the investment of financial institutions based elsewhere in the country. No self-interested body would readily wish to invest in economically crippled areas such as Brandon, the Auckland coalfield and (later) Jarrow, where there were few industrial prospects and where the high level of both local rates and rent arrears gave poor promise of security for a loan. If an investor particularly wanted to lend to local government, he could find far more financially attractive areas than County Durham – unless, perhaps, the local authorities there were willing to pay a higher rate of interest.

The difficulty of attracting private loans to the area was pressed home to local authorities in Durham by the Ministry of Health's policy in the later 1920s of refusing to recommend the Public Works Loans Board to provide the capital for new schemes unless the councils could themselves raise private loans to cover a proportion of the total cost.[45] The theory behind this policy was that if local authorities in Durham were forced to seek loans in the open market they would quickly come to appreciate that existing schemes should be managed more efficiently and that plans for future schemes would have to be more modest. The effect of the policy on the housing programme in County Durham was disastrous. The coal dispute of 1926 had caused the level of rates and rent arrears to soar and had reduced the already limited attraction which the area held for investors. When the Hetton Council was told by the Ministry to raise privately the money for any new schemes, there came the despairing reply that it was 'useless to advertise for loans.'[46] The result in Hetton, and in nearly all mining districts, was that the rate of council house building slumped dramatically in the years 1928 to 1930. The adverse effect of the Ministry's policy was thus felt with most force by the areas in most need of help.

Even when the Ministry of Health did recommend the Public Works Loans Board to make a loan to a local authority, there remained, though to a much lesser extent than in dealings with the private sector, the problem of security. Before they agreed to make a loan, the PWLB commissioners had to satisfy themselves that the financial circumstances of the council concerned were sufficiently healthy. It appeared (though even the Ministry of Health itself did not have any official information) that the commissioners worked by a rule of thumb that precluded lending to local authority areas in which the annual rate in the pound already exceeded 23s.[47] Twenty-three councils in County Durham crossed this barrier in the inter-war period, on a total of 51 occasions.[48] A refusal by the PWLB might also have been influenced by any suspicion of maladministration raised by the annual reports of the district auditor or by any apparent sign of incompetence, such as the insolvency of the Brandon Council in 1928 which led to its bankers withholding an annual repayment of previous debts to the commissioners[49] or the suspension of the Board of Guardians at Chester-le-Street and temporary rule by a Ministry of Health inspector in 1927–8.[50] Nevertheless, apart from this brief period in the late 1920s, the Public Works Loans Board was the source of loans most heavily used by local authorities in County Durham between the wars.

Once the raising of building capital had been achieved, the most important financial aspect of a council housing scheme was the net cost to the local community. Many variables affected the annual reckoning. Some went to determine the capital cost of the scheme and others the level of income to be off-set against the annual repayments of capital and interest. Some could be influenced by the policies of a local authority. It was up to the Council to decide whether to undertake an ambitious house-building programme or whether to do as little as possible, to decide how far to strive for savings by economies in the building process and how far to seek high receipts of rent. Other factors were in the hands of market forces and government policy.

The market was responsible for wide variations during the inter-war period in the cost of building a council house. Construction costs were twice as high in the summer of 1920 as they were ten years later. Similarly, the rate of interest payable on new loans was only half in the mid-1930s what it had been for loans sealed in 1920. Thus, when it came to calculating the annual loss on a 1919 Act housing scheme, the effect of high building costs was exaggerated by the more onerous terms of borrowing.

Government policy determined the level of Exchequer subsidy which councils could off-set against annual repayment of housing loans. The size of subsidy varied considerably between the different Housing Acts. At one extreme, the Addison Act of 1919 provided for the total annual loss on a council's housing schemes – less the contribution of a penny rate – to be borne by the Exchequer. At the other extreme, council houses built for 'general needs' (as opposed to slum replacement) after the 1933 Act received no Exchequer subsidy at all. In between these extremes were the Chamberlain subsidy (1923 Act) of £6 per council house per year for 20 years, the Wheatley subsidy (1924 Act) of £9 for 40 years and the Greenwood subsidy (1930 Act) of £2 5s. for 40 years for each person rehoused. Thus a council's rate contribution could also vary considerably. For example, the ratepayers of Brandon only had to find 8s. 8d. per year for each of their Addison Act houses;[51] but had the building of these houses been delayed for some reason and carried out under the Wheatley Act, the annual cost to ratepayers would have been at least £4 10s. per house, or more than ten times as much as it actually was. Unfortunately, statistics are not available to allow a satisfactory analysis to be made of the overall cost, falling separately to the Exchequer and to local rates, of housing in County Durham under the different inter-war Acts. But it is clear that the proportion of total annual expenditure on council housing borne by the local authorities themselves grew steadily over the inter-war period.

The final factor to be considered in assessing the cost of a housing scheme to the ratepayers of a district is the capacity of that district to bear the debts of its council. The key to the question is the rateable value of the area: a district with a high rateable value would obviously have less difficulty in bearing the cost of a given number of council houses than would a district of the same population but with a low rateable value. An underlying weakness of the local rating system is that while working-class districts have the greatest need of expenditure on social services, they are also the districts with the least capacity for bearing such expenditure on the rates. For example, housing conditions in the Tyneside district of Felling were very much worse than in Darlington,[52] and the ratepayers of the former had by the financial year 1939–40 to pay a very high 2s. in the pound towards housing schemes; while the ratepayers of Darlington paid only 2d. in the pound.[53] Whereas in Felling the burden of a 2s. rate for housing was visited upon a predominantly working-class community in the heart of a depressed area,[54] a rate of the same order in Darlington, even if it had been necessary, would have made a far less crushing demand on most members of the community.

This was the vicious circle built into the logic of the local rating system – and it meant that any national policy for social services which assigned financial liability to the local rates often worked against the communities which it set out to help most. This anomaly can be seen on a wider scale by comparing County Durham with the rest of the country, for the level of rate poundage in the county as a whole was consistently higher in the inter-war period than in any other county in England. In the financial year 1938–9, for example, when the average rate in the rest of England was about 12s. in the pound, the figure for the administrative county of Durham was £1 2d.[55]

The only social policy between the wars which attempted on a significant scale to short-circuit the injustices of the local rating system was the Housing Act of 1919. The size of a local authority's approved programme under the Addison Act was roughly in proportion to the needs of the district (as expressed in its 'survey of housing needs') and the cost to its ratepayers was roughly in proportion to their resources (as a fixed percentage of the rateable value of the district each year). The balance of the cost of an Addison scheme was met out of Exchequer funds, raised more equitably by taxation spread over the whole country. (This principle – the attempt to equalize local needs and resources – has been recognized over the last 20 years in the system of rate support grant to local authorities.) But all other inter-war schemes were based on a system of flat-rate subsidies which rarely took account of the problems of the poorer local government areas. From this general criticism one can exempt in some measure the Housing Act of 1930. By offering subsidies calculated on the number of slum-dwellers rehoused, it tended to encourage action in the areas where it was most needed and, because these subsidies were fairly generous and coincided with a period of favourable building costs, it meant that such action was not unduly burdensome to local ratepayers. This is borne out by the high level of activity under this Act in County Durham in the 1930s.

By the standards operating since 1945, the proportion of local authorities' total rate income spent on housing was not particularly high. In the 1930s most districts earmarked between 2 and 3 per cent of their total rate income for housing purposes. Nevertheless, local government expenditure on housing grew considerably over the inter-war period. This is illustrated by the example of two county boroughs, South Shields and West Hartlepool. From the financial year 1921–2 expenditure in both towns grew from the starting point of a penny rate (about £500 and £300 per annum respectively) by an average of about 10 per cent per year up to 1939 (to about £3,200 and £1,600 per annum). The expenditure actually grew in two stages, in the late 1920s and from the mid-1930s. There was a more stable period in the early 1930s which followed a slackening of the building programme in the late 1920s and the gradual recovery of rent arrears accrued in those years.[56] The most important feature, however, is that despite the policy decisions mentioned at the beginning of this section by which local authorities could reduce the cost of their housing liabilities – and both South Shields and West Hartlepool adopted such policies, the former in striving to reduce rent arrears, the latter in using direct labour and promoting extensive council house sales – the trend of rate-borne expenditure was always upward.

b. Land
The inter-war council housing programme involved an enormous increase in the amount of land owned by local government. Exact figures are not available, but by 1939 councils in County Durham had probably purchased more than 6,500 acres of land – about ten square miles.[57] All of this land was purchased freehold, since Ministry of Health policy refused to countenance leasehold. The overall cost to public funds was in the order of £1½ million.[58]

Most of the land acquired for council housing lay outside the limits of existing built-up areas. The significance of this in social and planning terms is examined later on, but it is worth noting here the fairly obvious point that building sites were generally easier and cheaper to come by the further they were from existing urban centres. Nevertheless, some local authorities found it very difficult to find any suitable land at all within their own district boundaries. Jarrow was particularly hard-pressed and had to buy the 19 acres it needed for its 1919 Act scheme in the adjoining South Shields rural district.[59] A major disadvantage in such a case was the loss to the developing council of the subsequent rate income from its own property.

Jarrow's land problem arose mainly from its unrealistic boundaries, which were eventually extended in the local government revisions of 1936. A far more serious problem, however, and one which mere administrative changes could not solve, was the extent of disused mine workings under much of the county. In many areas of the coalfield the settling of old workings and consequent subsidence of streets and foundations occurred frequently. Councils in these districts were only permitted by the Ministry of Health to raise loans to buy new tracts of land if professional advisers (usually the District Valuer in consultation with a mineral valuer) were prepared to rule out the danger of serious subsidence. Very often such assurances could not be given: more than one council must have wondered 'whether it would be at all possible to secure a site in the District which would be absolutely stable and free from the effects of pit-workings.'[60]

As a result of the unreliable sub-soil in much of the county, there were often unwelcome delays in the start of council housing schemes. An unfortunate aspect of this problem was that those districts where mining had been intense were often those where the need for new housing was high. As the Housing Commissioner for the North-east reported to the Ministry of Health in 1921, 'it has been the case in County Durham that where houses are urgently required, sites have been difficult to obtain.' In Tanfield, where 37 per cent of the population in 1921 were living more than two to a room, the official estimate was that over 600 new houses were needed – yet the Council was able to build only 24 under the 1919 Act because of the shortage of suitable land. Out of more than 30 acres in which the Council had expressed interest only three acres were found to be sufficiently free from the risk of subsidence.[61] On the whole, housing schemes in many districts would have started more quickly if the risk of subsidence had not been so widespread. It is likely that this factor prevented a greater number of houses being built. It certainly added to the cost of some estates and affected the location of many others.

The landowners with whom councils did business fell into four distinct groups: there were the coal companies (of which there were over 50 at the end of the First World War), the church authorities (the Dean and Chapter of Durham and the Ecclesiastical Commissioners), the owners of large estates (like the Marquis of Londonderry and the Earl of Durham) and a host of smaller private landowners. Most conveyances were of between 5 and 15 acres at a time, but this varied according to local circumstances: in some Tyneside towns, for example, land ownership was quite fragmented and the few large sites were hard to come by, whereas in many coalfield districts the land belonged to a few major owners and was available in fairly large tracts. There were a few very big purchases: the acquisition of some 207 acres of outlying farmland by the borough of Darlington was one such case.[62] At the other end of the scale, councils sometimes had to bid for a few hundred square feet of land which would otherwise have blocked access to a larger site.[63]

Even within a particular district the price of land for council housing development could vary considerably. Few sites cost less than £100 per acre and few more than £300, with prices generally being lower in rural and coalfield districts than in the urban boroughs. The range can be illustrated by two extreme examples. The mining district of Brandon was able to buy all the building land it needed on sites virtually detached from the existing built-up areas. In all, the Council bought 64 acres of farmland at prices between £54 and £76 per acre.[64] The borough of Darlington, on the other hand, had to pay £1,600 per acre for a small site in the centre of the town, where roads and main sewers were already made up.[65] The wide range of prices payable within a single district is illustrated by the example of Gateshead. The Council bought $11\frac{1}{2}$ acres at Sheriff Hill for only £160 per acre, but had to pay nearly £550 per acre for 17 acres at Bensham and £1,280 per acre for a small site in a built-up area closer to the town centre.[66]

An important factor influencing the price of land, apart from its location, was the negotiating power of the vendor. A price was usually fixed by agreement, although from 1919 a local authority could use effective powers of compulsory purchase. The fact that the Council could fall back on such powers weakened the bargaining position of the vendor, who knew that ultimately he could be forced to part with his land at a price determined by the District Valuer. The process of negotiating a purchase was frequently handed over to this official by local authorities, on the grounds that his expertise and authority to fix a compulsory figure would expedite the transaction. It was unusual for the District Valuer not to be called in at some stage of the proceedings, if only because in most cases the Ministry of Health, before giving a council sanction to raise a loan, required his assurance that the agreed price was a fair one.

There can be no doubt that without the threat of compulsory purchase held in reserve councils in County Durham would often have had to pay considerably more for building land than the official valuation price. There were a few instances of generosity on the part of landowners – notably the Consett Iron Company, which offered land to several councils at the bargain price of £50 per acre.[67] But the general trend is shown by the prices asked by less public-spirited local landowners before the secondary legislation of 1919 came into force. For example, the Blaydon Council had to pay the Earl of Strathmore £605 per acre early in 1919 for land at Rowlands Gill. The local Labour Representation Committee could justifiably complain to the Local Government Board that this was 'a monstrous price',[68] for land in the district was obtainable for only £100 to £200 per acre once the procedure for compulsory purchase had been established. Similarly, the Easington housing committee was offered agricultural land in 1918 by various owners at prices in several cases as high as £400 and £700 per acre.[69] The sites in question were eventually acquired, under threat of compulsory purchase, for £50 to £100 per acre.[70]

This problem was not confined to the coalfield districts. Darlington was faced in 1919 with two owners of farmland, one asking £450 per acre and the other waiting for 'a tempting offer':[71] the eventual price was slightly over £100 per acre.[72] Nor was the Church above trying its luck with local councils. For instance, 'a suggestion of profiteering' was made when the Ecclesiastical Commissioners asked nearly £600 per acre for land in the Sunderland rural district valued at half the price.[73] Some aristocratic landowners did not lag far behind. Lord Boyne, for example, sought a price from Auckland RDC related to the density of the proposed development – £80 per acre for eight houses to the acre, and £120 for twelve houses. The official valuation was only £36 per acre.[74] In most of these cases under the Addison scheme the threat of compulsory purchase enabled local authorities to acquire building land at a reasonable price. Speculative offers continued to come the way of councils throughout the inter-war period, but the authorities soon developed the knack of dealing with them.

Nevertheless, a high proportion of the building land purchased by councils in this period was in fact acquired in the early days under the Addison Act. Because they were required by the Ministry of Health in 1919 to make good the housing shortage in their districts within a limited period, many local authorities hastened to buy sufficient land to meet the whole of the foreseeable requirement. So when in 1921 the Addison scheme was brought to a halt, most councils owned considerably more land than was needed for the houses they had built or had obtained the Ministry's sanction to build. Some local authorities, like Darlington and the coalfield district of Brandon, found that they had no need to buy any more land before 1939 than they had acquired under the 1919 Act. In other districts, like Felling-on-Tyne, 1919 Act purchases might represent about 40 per cent of the Council's whole inter-war estate.

As councils were nearly always in possession of more land than they were able to use for housing schemes actually approved by the Ministry of Health, they had to decide how best to use their potential building sites in the meantime. Often this was simply a matter of allowing the continuation of an agricultural tenancy until building was ready to begin. This was hardly a profitable arrangement: agricultural rents recovered by the Easington Council, for example, were on average less than 1 per cent per annum of the purchase price paid.[75] But it was preferable to the alternative of dispossessing a tenant farmer prematurely: if a council sought to take over the land at short notice it could face a heavy claim for loss of crops.[76]

When a council's surplus 1919 Act land was eventually taken over for building under a subsequent Act, accounting transfers were made to credit the Addison scheme and debit the later scheme with the current value of the land. This was sound accounting practice, but because the transferred land usually adjoined a completed 1919 Act housing estate its market value was considerably enhanced. This meant that the 1919 Act programme (which was financed predominantly from the

Exchequer) made a 'profit' at the expense of later schemes (which all imposed a relatively greater burden on the ratepayer than the 1919 Act scheme). In effect, therefore, such accounting transfers helped the Ministry of Health to reduce the embarrassing proportions of its recurring liability under the Addison scheme.

If local authority land became genuinely surplus (that is, if the Council had completely abandoned its own housing plans) or if the Council decided that there were advantages in encouraging private builders, attempts were made to sell plots to any interested parties. Again, this often resulted in a profit being made by whichever housing account was involved, especially where the surplus land adjoined an existing council estate. The price fixed by the District Valuer for such plots could be as much as ten times more than that originally paid by the council. For example, Stanley UDC sold several plots to private builders for between £1,700 and £2,000 per acre from an estate which it had bought by compulsory purchase for £200 per acre.[77] Occasionally a council might sell the whole of an unwanted site to private builders. One of the few examples is the borough of Stockton, which decided in 1938 that its land at Newham Grange was not needed for municipal purposes: streets and sewers were made up and 230 individual plots were offered for sale.[78] Disposal of land sometimes fitted into a wider pattern of town planning. At one end of the scale, land in Darlington was sold by the Council for the building of a corner shop; at the other extreme, over 40 acres in the same borough were sold off for factory development.[79] The terms of disposal were not without the occasional irony: the Council of the depressed mining district of Brandon was obliged under the Ministry's rules to sell land for a badly-needed estate of aged miners' homes at a valuation nearly ten times higher than the original price;[80] less seriously, the Jarrow Council, having bought land from the Dean and Chapter of Durham at £200 per acre, moved in a mysterious way to sell the Roman Catholic authorities a building plot for a church on the site at £1,800 per acre.[81]

c. Building
Although many local authorities were already familiar with the practice of appointing architects, dealing with tenders and managing the administrative aspects of particular building projects, the sheer size of housing schemes between the wars generated a far heavier burden of responsibility. The change in scale for, say, a rural district council – previously accustomed to the occasional letting of contracts for the building of a public convenience or washhouse but faced in 1919 with the prospect of having to supervise housing development over several hundred acres – must have seemed alarming to the councillors and officials involved. Moreover, many councils went beyond the minimum role of building management and assumed the additional responsibility of employing direct labour teams up to several hundred strong. This is examined separately in the following section.

It will be helpful first to look briefly at the various stages in the process of building a council housing scheme. The first task was the appointment of an architect, either as an official of the local authority or on a commercial contract. The architect was responsible to the Council, either as employee or consultant, not only for designing a housing scheme but also for supervising its execution. Design broadly followed Ministry of Health patterns and was sometimes only a small element in the architect's duties. His more onerous work on site could only begin after several other stages of the process had been completed by the Council. These involved obtaining the Ministry of Health's approval in principle to the number and (particularly under the 1919 Act) the design of the proposed houses; drawing up bills of quantity and invitations to tender; selecting a suitable contractor; obtaining the Ministry's approval of the tender price and with it the sanction to raise a loan; and finally the sealing of a contract with the chosen builder. Once the contractor had started work on site, the architect would make frequent inspections, examine claims against the Council for payment on account, eventually approve the finished work and deal with the contractor's final claim.

This ideal sequence was often disrupted or brought to a halt for various reasons. The most irksome delays occurred in County Durham during the Addison scheme. This was a time when local government was relatively inexperienced and central government interference in matters of detail was at its greatest. It was also the time when labour and materials were in shortest supply, for the house-building industry had withered away during the war years and recovered only very slowly in the dislocated conditions which followed. Some idea of the labour position can be obtained from census material for County Durham, which reveals that the number of men working in skilled building trades was significantly lower in 1921 than in 1911, and in most cases had been falling since 1901. There were, for example, 17 per cent fewer bricklayers in the county in 1921 than in 1911, 22 per cent fewer plasterers and 28 per cent fewer slaters and tilers. In many trades a full recovery to the 1911 manpower levels was not achieved even by 1931. The position was aggravated by the general policy of the unions in resisting the dilution of building trades by unskilled army-surplus labour. In County Durham the already high cost of building labour was increased by union demands for additional allowances (mainly for 'walking time' spent reaching a site) and the strong bargaining position of the skilled men occasionally spilled over into a strike.[82] There is less information available on the scarcity of building materials in the county, but the indications are that difficulties were at least as great in Durham as they were in the country as a whole.

A further problem in County Durham just after the First World War was the tendency of builders in the larger towns to operate in confederations in order to avoid competitive tendering. The most powerful of these were based in Newcastle, Sunderland and West Hartlepool. By refusing to tender except on a collective basis within their own areas, these cartels attempted to push building costs even higher than the already inflated level. The Sunderland federation, for example, submitted a tender to the Rural District Council of about £1,300 per house, at the same time as a builder outside the group was quoting about £950 per house.[83] Similarly, the Newcastle federation, which had originally quoted the Gateshead Council a figure of £1,300 per house, was prompted by fear of outside competition to drop its own price to £950 only a fortnight later.[84] Fortunately, although the action of the federated builders slowed down the process of letting a contract, it did not usually result in the payment of excessive prices. The Ministry of Health's housing commissioners would not sanction acceptance of unreasonable group tenders[85] and it was usually possible, after a time, for the Council to find a willing non-federated builder in the locality[86] or even from outside the county.[87] Ultimately, the action of the federated builders rebounded on them with an unforeseen vengeance: not only did they lose work to outside contractors, but they also helped to promote the first direct labour schemes. As the Housing Committee of Stockton reported after a visit to the West Hartlepool direct labour scheme, the Council there had taken the initiative because of 'the excessive prices at first put in by the Builders, and the apparent ease with which the same [were] reduced, at various meetings with the Housing Commissioner, to a sum per house considerably lower than the original price.'[88]

One interesting result of the shortage of labour and materials during the Addison Act period was the encouragement which it gave to the use of new methods of house building. By far the most important break with traditional methods in County Durham was the use of the Dorman Long construction system. This had been developed by Dorman Long & Co. in a housing estate built near Redcar for its own workers (unimaginatively christened 'Dormanstown'). The company then began to make a commercial venture of the system, selling kits of steel girders to local authorities, who could have them bolted together on site and fitted out with walls and floors fashioned from concrete slabs.[89] Most of the more energetic councils in County Durham sent parties on guided tours of Dormanstown and most councillors were impressed with what they saw.[90] Consequently, with encouragement from the housing commissioner, several councils erected 'Dorlonco' houses. Though no cheaper than more conventional dwellings built in this period, they could be completed in a much shorter time, the Ministry of Health estimate being nine weeks.[91]

Unfortunately, the Dorlonco experiment was not a success. As some councillors had observed on their visit to Dormanstown, the houses were liable to cracking and dampness.[92] The Ministry's inspector conceded that there was 'a certain amount of "sweating" . . . which might be mistaken for dampness by unenlightened members of a visiting delegation.'[93] In fact the problem was far more serious than mere perspiration and ten to fifteen years later most of the Dorlonco houses built in Durham needed extensive repairs. As the surveyor to Chester-le-Street UDC reported in 1936, the cracking of the concrete slabs not only caused dampness but also exposed the steel frame to rust. The only lasting solution was to encase each house in a shell of traditional brick, at a cost of £120 a time.[94] Such drastic action had already become necessary to Dorlonco houses in Felling, Brandon and Auckland rural district.

It was probably because of these early failures, and of the falling cost of traditional building methods, that no further attempt was made between the wars by councils in County Durham to experiment with new construction ideas. Although some large English towns built some low-rise blocks of flats in the 1930s, it was quite rare even for the borough councils in County Durham to depart from the new 'Tudor Walters' tradition of two-storey houses. Nevertheless, there was one peculiarity of construction sometimes necessary in the coalfield. This was the special strengthening of foundations to minimize the effect of mining subsidence, and either involved reinforcement of brick foundations with concrete or the use of a ferro-concrete 'raft' on which a house could safely be perched.[95]

It was sometimes possible for a council to avoid the difficulties inherent in construction projects simply by buying and converting existing property. Only very rarely did this involve taking over inhabited buildings, for the theory behind national housing policies of the 1920s demanded additions to the total housing stock. There were cases, however, of war-surplus buildings being converted for use by council tenants. One example is that of a block of disused barracks bought by Barnard Castle in 1930 and converted to provide 25 dwellings.[96] Darlington and Ryton, on the other hand, purchased some less substantial ex-army huts which could be moved and reassembled to provide temporary accommodation.[97] The most important case, however, is that of the takeover of more than 600 two- and three-bedroom dwellings contained in huts at Birtley. These had been run up during the First World War to house a colony of Belgian refugees who had been put to work in the Birtley munitions factory. After the war, when the refugees had been repatriated, the huts were largely taken over by squatters. Management of the buildings was apparently assumed in 1924 by Chester-le-Street RDC,[98] which eventually purchased the site from the government in 1932 in order to demolish and rebuild.[99]

Another way of avoiding the problems inherent in a major construction scheme was to persuade another body to do the building. No council in County Durham was able to convince the Ministry of Health in 1919 that the housing needs of the district could be met solely by the efforts of private enterprise. Nevertheless, one council – Hebburn – managed to pass responsibility for construction of its 1919 Act estates to another public body – the Office of Works.[100] This was a rare instance of central government assistance in project management. It was over-shadowed in the late 1930s by the intervention of the North-Eastern Housing Association, which (as we saw earlier) was set up by the national government to relieve local authorities of the financial burden of building and running their own housing schemes.

After the period of building under the Addison Act, when a number of contracts were let to firms based outside the county, the great bulk of work went to local builders – usually within the Council's own district. This was mainly a reflection of the steadying market, for in stable conditions most firms were reluctant to tender for contracts advertised in an inconveniently distant district; and the inconvenience was likely, in any case, to dictate a tender price unacceptable to the Council. Building contracts did not, however, necessarily go to the lowest bidder. Although the Ministry of Health would not allow councils to accept, for example, the tender of a local builder in favour of a lower bid from an outsider,[101] local authorities still had to ensure that a contractor would be able to do the job properly. Not all successful tenderers were suitable contractors: for example, Easington RDC had to cancel two contracts because the building firms failed to produce securities[102] and Gateshead had the misfortune to engage a builder from Stanley whose creditors intervened after six months' work to prevent the contract being completed.[103]

There were cases, perhaps like the one just quoted, where builders submitted dangerously low tenders in order to clinch a contract. On the other hand, it was possible for someone with inside knowledge of current tender levels to play the system to his own advantage. One such person was the chairman of the Durham City Housing Committee, whose finely-judged tendering earned his building firm at least one contract with Durham Rural District Council.[104] Several other councils had members with business interests in building firms but in most cases their knowledge of the trade was put to positive use in housing committees. Only in Gateshead, it seems, did a private builder and landlord try to use his position on the Council to prevent a housing programme getting off the ground.[105]

In the same way as the distribution of building contracts settled down after the period of the Addison scheme, so did their size and form. Whereas 1919 Act contracts might cover from four houses[106] to a thousand,[107] the standard number in most medium-sized districts settled down later to about fifty houses per contract. This was partly due to the Ministry of Health's policy in 1921 of taking advantage of falling prices by only sanctioning smaller contracts – a policy to which the Ministry clung for several more years in a general attempt to control local authority programmes more closely. In fact, many councils found that there were practical advantages in using smaller contracts – their only fear was that changes in government policy might preclude later instalments of housing. Similarly, the conditions of contracts also hardened into a form which generally suited most parties. After some attempts during the Addison period to ride out the vagaries of the market with forms of prime-cost contracts (in which the Council and the contractor would share any savings or any extra costs on an agreed price) the standard form soon became that of a simple fixed-price agreement.

There is enough information in local authority records up to about 1926 to show that contract prices in County Durham were generally higher than in the rest of England and Wales. This is particularly noticeable in the early stages of the Addison scheme. It is difficult to speculate on whether or not the scarcity of labour and materials was any more acute in Durham than in other regions at this time, but one factor may have been the involvement of contractors from outside the county: their prices may have included a 'long-distance' element which would have been absent if tenders had been submitted by local, non-federated builders. The less complete evidence which is available for the late 1920s and the 1930s suggests that the prices in County Durham grew closer to the national averages but still remained slightly above them. A possible, though again speculative, explanation for this may be the pattern of urban settlement in the Durham coalfield. The scattering of small mining villages, which were in fact urban in character and had a high demand for council housing, was in contrast with the concentrated larger settlements usual in most other regions, where the larger building firms were more conveniently centred. Thus in many parts of County Durham it is possible that building firms attracted greater overheads than elsewhere in getting skilled men, building materials and plant on to site. Unfortunately, there is not enough evidence to test this possibility with a satisfactory comparison between the Durham coalfield and the towns of South Tyneside.

d. Direct labour

The direct employment of building labour by district councils was in one sense an extension of the philosophy behind council housing itself. Just as state intervention in the housing market had broken the hold of private developers and landlords, the aim of using direct labour was to cut private profit out of the construction process. The main argument for the use of direct labour was that, assuming a saving of the profit element charged by a private builder on contract, houses would be built more cheaply and thus either council tenants would pay lower rents or taxpayers and ratepayers would pay less in subsidies. But sometimes councils had the further aim of ensuring that local labour would be employed on housing schemes. Some councils in County Durham actually developed a systematic policy of using direct labour to reduce local unemployment and to increase the welfare benefit entitlements of the unemployed. Sometimes, as we shall see below, this function of direct labour was inconsistent with the original concern to keep construction costs to the minimum: the element of contractor's profit was replaced progressively by the cost of an additional, though not unjustifiable, social policy.

As mentioned in the previous section, the first impetus to the use of direct labour in County Durham was given by the attempt of certain local builders in 1919 and 1920 to operate cartels. The Ministry of Health had at first been rather sceptical about direct labour, informing its regional housing commissioners that 'it is not at present intended that a Commissioner should suggest recourse to this method'.[108] The Ministry was forced to modify its attitude when it emerged that councils obliged to negotiate with a federation of builders could rarely obtain a tender acceptable to the housing commissioner. The first Council compelled to take the initiative in seeking approval for a direct labour scheme was West Hartlepool, which decided to approach the Ministry in March 1920.[109] In the next few months several other districts followed suit. Seaham Harbour, for example, decided to build 50 houses by direct labour 'after considering tenders received and conferring with the local Builders' Federation [and] having failed to get a price fixed which the Housing Commissioner could approve'.[110]

After several early successes, direct labour was established in some districts as an important element in the housing programme for the rest of the inter-war period. In other districts it made no appearance at all. None of the genuinely rural districts ever used direct labour on their (necessarily limited) housing schemes. But of the larger towns only Stockton appears to have rejected the method out of hand.[111] Most of the main urban centres and nearly all the coalfield districts used direct labour, although in widely varying degrees.[112] Details of the number of houses built by this method and the number of men employed are available for only a few districts, but at least an impression can be formed of the scale of activity over the whole county. In the Easington district, where direct labour was much favoured, 547 of the council houses standing in 1927 (or 47 per cent of the total built since 1919) had been erected by this method. The proportion of the direct labour contribution in the district had risen steadily over the period: it accounted for 16 per cent of the houses built under the 1919 Act, 39 per cent under the 1923 Act and 70 per cent under the 1924 Act.[113] In Chester-le-Street Urban District, where direct labour had got off to a slower start, 211 houses in 1932 (or 32 per cent of the total) had been built by this method,[114] but in Felling the number by that time was 453 (a proportion of 56 per cent).[115] Some idea of the numbers employed is obtained from the fact that in 1926 Jarrow had 67 men working on direct labour schemes (or 80 per cent of the total workforce engaged on council house building)[116] and in 1927 Gateshead was employing 400 (and no private contractors).[117]

There was rarely any doubt in the 1920s that the use of direct labour achieved considerable savings over private contracts. The savings were greatest during the time of the Addison programme, a period of unstable building costs when contractors were obviously inclined to include a wide safety margin in their tenders. In West Hartlepool houses completed by direct labour in 1921 were more than 25 per cent cheaper than the contract price, but for schemes completed in 1922 the saving had narrowed to 13 per cent on 'parlour' houses and 6 per cent on 'non-parlour' houses.[118] By 1926 the Washington Housing Committee found that the average saving on recent schemes was about 7 per cent.[119] The general evidence is that savings in the mid-1920s were on average between 5 and 10 per cent of current contract prices. One recorded case in the 1920s of direct labour costs exceeding the lowest tender price for the job concerns the Carr Hill estate in Gateshead. Following a complaint by the National Federation of Building Trades Employers, the Ministry of Health found that the final direct labour costs for one batch of houses were 'about £1,500 more than the lowest tender received.' In fact this represented only an over-spending of about 3 per cent and the Council had, in any case, been 'doubtful about the contractor's capacity to carry out the work.'[120] The only other recorded case of over-spending in the 1920s concerns Blaydon UDC, which exceeded its own direct labour estimates during the Addison scheme by an average of £176 per house.[121] This was viewed by the Ministry with more concern, but it is now impossible to ascertain by how much (if at all) the final direct labour costs exceeded the lowest private tender figures.

Unfortunately, as with details of local building costs generally, there is very little information on direct labour prices in the 1930s. This is largely because building both by contract and by direct labour had by then become so much more of a routine

matter that a decreasing amount of detail was included in records of council and committee meetings. Because cases of over-spending were not routine they received dispropor-
tionate attention, in council records as well as in the press. Cases of over-spending on
direct-labour schemes were certainly more common in the 1930s, but it cannot be
proved one way or the other whether the system still produced savings overall. The general position is probably well represented by the example of Chester-le-Street UDC.
This was a council which the Ministry of Health viewed with some suspicion of financial
and administrative incompetence.[122] But, as the Council's figures for 232 houses
showed in 1935, there had been a saving of 11 per cent on the original direct labour
estimates, which themselves had necessarily been less than the lowest tender prices.[123]

On the other hand, a number of cases of over-spending could be cited, but probably
the most serious involved Felling UDC. By 1939 the Council realized that it had
exceeded its direct labour estimates by £33,782 over a total of 1,129 houses –
equivalent to an over-spending of about 9 per cent.[124] The result of this rather belated
realization was a further increase in what was already the highest local rate levied for
housing purposes in the whole county. This example, and no doubt several others, may
have arisen from administrative inefficiency (that is, from bad estimating) rather than
from inefficiency on the part of the direct labour team itself. But a problem common to
all councils using direct labour was the great revival in building activity from the early
1930s. Tender prices became much keener and, since councils could obtain Ministry of
Health approval for direct labour only by submitting an estimate lower than the best
private tender for an individual scheme, this put more pressure on direct labour managers to submit unrealistic estimates. Another problem which the building boom
created for direct labour organizations was the difficulty of retaining the most skilled
and productive workmen. Given a staff management policy traditionally less flexible
than in the private sector, local authorities could not compete with the offers of over-
time, bonuses and other concessions made by private contractors with plenty of business. Thus it was that Easington RDC, for example, found itself in 1936 with an acute
shortage of bricklayers and was forced to transfer responsibility for 100 new houses
from its direct labour department to a private contractor.[125]

A more serious problem in Easington, however, was a fall in the productivity of its
direct labour team on those houses which it *was* able to build. As the Ministry of
Health observed, the labour hours spent on building one of the Council's two-
bedroom houses had risen from 413 in 1933 to 796 in 1935–6.[126] The Council could not
dispute that this was due to 'the employment of men who had been out of work for a
long time.' There had been a deliberate policy of picking the requisite number of
unskilled men from the labour exchange lists of unemployed, engaging them for
a period of 18 weeks (the minimum period needed to establish entitlement to state unemployment benefits) and then replacing them with a new batch of local unemployed
from the exchange. Having received a deputation of councillors from Easington,

. . . the Ministry expressed the view that it was impossible to combine the relief of
unemployment with housing schemes. In one or two other places where this had
been tried the Ministry had been obliged to stop the practice owing to the increased
cost of houses, e.g. Blaydon. At Felling the cost had risen to such an extent that the
Council could not compete with the contractor's prices.[127]

Another example which the Ministry might have cited was that of Jarrow, where the
Borough Engineer was directed in 1933 to 'employ labourers who have not been on the

job before.'[128] It was undoubtedly true that this policy did not promote efficiency in building, but it was understandable that some councils should strive to kill the two birds of bad housing and unemployment with one of the few stones to hand.

It is reasonable to conclude that the direct labour system worked well for most of the councils which used it in the inter-war period. It usually produced savings from which tenants or local ratepayers as a whole derived benefit.[129] Even when, in the 1930s, some councils distorted the financial picture by using direct labour to reduce the distress caused by high unemployment, the system can still be said to have worked to the advantage of the local community. There were some, like the 'moderate' or rate-payers' group on the Gateshead Council, who objected to direct labour on principle, to avoid 'the usual tangle of affairs when the cobbler leaves his last and the miner wants to oust the builder from his legitimate calling.'[130] The moderates' official view of the direct labour team, propagated in their free news-paper, is captured in the cartoon reproduced in fig. 8: the directly employed brick-layer dozes contentedly as the cobwebs gather around his trowel. It is not surprising, therefore, that the moderates, having gained control of the Gateshead Council in 1926, would only allow direct labour on schemes which had already started; by September 1927 about 400 men were to be laid off and the building plant put up for sale.[131] It is quite likely that this policy reflected the long-standing interest of private builders on the Gateshead Council, but it is interesting that there is no record – in any district of County Durham – of official complaints from builders themselves that direct labour was forcing them out of business.

e. Planning and design

The quality of inter-war council housing schemes represented an enormous advance on the standards of earlier working-class housing. This improvement was particularly marked in the north-east of England, for the existing standards in this region were considerably lower than in the rest of the country. Some idea of the improvement can be obtained by considering simply the average number of rooms in a dwelling at the beginning of this period. In County Durham this figure was 3.89 at the 1921 Census (5.14 in England and Wales as a whole) while the Addison houses then being erected were mainly of five and six rooms. As well as being far superior to the existing working-class housing in the private sector, inter-war council schemes were an improvement on the estates built by local authorities before the First World War. Some of the pre-war council houses were designed very well, but they generally followed the traditional terrace style and were smaller (usually only four rooms) and more densely packed (between 20 and 25 to the acre)[132] than the inter-war variety. Standard inter-war council houses were of five rooms and stood about ten to an acre.

This great improvement in quality was largely the result of a report in 1918 by a government committee chaired by Sir John Tudor Walters.[133] The details of the report have been adequately described elsewhere[134] and it is sufficient here to note that its approach drew heavily on the example of model towns and the garden city movement before the First World War. The planning ideals of such progressive housing architects as Raymond Unwin – himself a member of the Tudor Walters committee – clearly emerged in the report, with its emphasis on light and spacious house designs, low-density development and healthy out-of-town sites. The report was forward-looking in nearly every respect. Its recommendations covered, for example, the co-ordination of public transport with estate growth, the manufacture of standardized and inter-changeable building components, and the use of waste energy from power stations to run district heating schemes. The standards of house design recommended by the report (and subsequently incorporated in the Ministry of Health's manual for local authorities)[135] stand up favourably to comparison with the recommended standards of the 1960s[136] and were actually better, in terms of living space per person, than standards 40 or 50 years later.[137]

The Tudor Walters recommendations were adopted as part of the feverish 'homes for heroes' movement at the end of the war. The government was willing to accept these high standards in the same way that it was prepared to render local authorities generous financial assistance. It was unfortunate, however, that one effect of applying these standards was to accentuate the high cost of building under the Addison programme – and, like the subsidy itself, the full Tudor Walters ideal fell a casualty to the Government's waning enthusiasm for housing its heroes. The recommended standards for the rest of the inter-war period, which were imposed on local authorities by the conditions attached to the particular Exchequer subsidy, were pared down considerably from the original Tudor Walters recommendations.[138] In essence, however, they were only a scaling down of the 1918 designs, not a fundamental revision.

One of the major influences exerted by the Tudor Walters report was on the use

Figure 8.   'GATESHEAD SOCIALISTS will RE-START "DIRECT LABOUR" if YOU let them': cartoon reproduced from the *Gateshead and District Municipal News*, August 1935.

made of land after the First World War. Apart from slum redevelopment schemes in some of the larger towns, most inter-war council houses were built on the edge of existing settlements, or away from them entirely. An obvious reason for this was the lack of building space within the limits of existing settlements, but there were also financial and environmental factors. Peripheral sites, usually on agricultural land, were advocated because land was cheaper, and because conditions were more pleasant and physical restrictions on planning fewer, than in the case of central sites. In the mining districts of County Durham, where existing settlements were small and scattered, this policy had little impact: the limited schemes required could be grafted on to these villages and the settlement remain fairly compact. Even in the smaller towns there was no remote 'council suburb'. In Chester-le-Street, for example, where earlier residential development had taken place along a strip of land between the main street and the railway line, the local authority built its inter-war estates along the same axis on the other side of the railway: the most distant council house was only half a mile from the town centre.[139] In the case of the large conurbations, however, council estates tended to be more remote. In Sunderland, for example, the main inter-war schemes were about two miles from the town centre,[140] while Gateshead and South Shields both had detached estates, at Wrekenton and Cleadon Park respectively. It was in these more distant estates that the low level of amenities common to much twentieth-century residential development – the lack of schools, shops and pubs – was of most significance: in 1951 Gateshead admitted that 'comparatively new housing estates are grossly uncatered for.'[141] The isolation of families even on these estates was not as great, however, as in the case of the largest English cities.[142]

The Tudor Walters report also influenced the use of land within council estates themselves. Instead of following the grid-iron patterns of wide streets engendered by the old building bye-laws, local authority architects were shown (by the Ministry of Health's manual) how to lay out an estate more imaginatively, exploiting the physical configuration of the site. The houses themselves were generally laid out in blocks of two or four, although blocks of six or eight were sometimes used. The arrangement of blocks was also held to be important, in order to maintain visual interest and to make the best use of land for gardens, allotments or open spaces.[143]

The most common type of council house erected in County Durham between the wars was of the A3 variety – consisting of three bedrooms, living room, kitchen-scullery, bathroom and water-closet. Houses of the B3 type (which had a parlour as well) and sometimes of the B4 type (which also had a fourth bedroom) were fairly common in schemes under the Addison Act and might comprise more than half of the total on a particular estate.[144] Under later housing schemes, however, the parlour was very rarely included and the A3 type came to the fore, followed by the A2 (which was similar, but had only two bedrooms). Although the latter type of house was not favoured by the Ministry of Health,[145] it was widely used in County Durham because of its relative cheapness for both the Council and the tenant.[146] Another house type more common in Durham than in most of the country was the A1 – a single-bedroom, one-storey dwelling for 'aged persons'. The problem of housing the elderly was particularly marked in the mining areas of the county, given the interaction of the colliery 'free house' system and, from the last quarter of the nineteenth century, the general rise in life expectancy. The bungalows which local authorities in the county built for the elderly owed some of their design to Tudor Walters principles, but they also drew on the example of the aged miners' homes which had been provided through trade union initiative since about the turn of the century. The least common dwelling type used by councils in County Durham between the wars was the low-rise flat. This only made an appearance in a few town-centre slum redevelopment schemes in the later 1930s.

The facilities within council houses generally improved over the inter-war period. The installation of electricity, for example, became more common and the gas cooker gradually took over from the solid-fuel kitchen range. And though a post-Addison house was not likely to have a parlour, it usually sported a separate bathroom. There was no rule about fixed baths under the Addison Act, although 'when there is an adequate water supply and the structure of the house makes it practicable, the Ministry consider that baths should be provided.'[147] Tenants were finally denied the pleasures of the zinc tub by Neville Chamberlain, whose Act of 1923 laid down the enduring condition that houses must contain a fixed bath to qualify for subsidy. Toilets were served, except on the more remote rural sites, by the water-carriage system and were generally inside the house. Even in the 1930s, however, some local authorities were building houses with outside toilets: commenting on proposals by Lanchester RDC in 1934 for 17 new houses to be served in this way, the Ministry of Health's adviser wrote: 'I don't much like the detached w.c.s in new housing but it is a pretty well established local method.'[148] In fact, not everyone was happy with an indoor toilet, especially if it was upstairs. The local Trades and Labour Council complained to the Ministry about council houses in Stockton being erected with this feature: 'a workman returning from his work in his dirty clothes and boots who desires to use the w.c. should have it downstairs.' They begged the Ministry to ensure in future 'that the convenience of workmen will be considered.'[149]

While the internal facilities of council houses tended to improve over the period, the dimensions and overall living space gradually shrank. In the 1920s the County Unionist Association declaimed to the local electorate about the extravagance of 'palatial dwellings' erected under the Addison scheme[150] and the Ministry of Health was sometimes concerned that a few councils, like Easington, were building houses of up to 20 per cent greater superficial area than the national recommendations. Although Easington was criticized by the area housing commissioner for this policy, the Council stoutly refused to compromise its own high standards.[151] The point which the local authorities and the Ministry appreciated – but the Unionist Association did not – was that the Exchequer, rather than the local ratepayer, actually footed the bill under the Addison scheme for any standards above the average. The Gateshead ratepayers' organization was cheered, however, by the smaller houses erected under the Chamberlain and Wheatley Acts and did 'not agree with all this twaddle talked at Conferences at Newcastle and elsewhere by Gateshead Aldermen and others.' After describing one of the new council houses, which had been criticized by the local Labour Party for their smallness, the ratepayers' publication concluded, 'not much like a kennel or slum house, is it? . . . the tenants are delighted.'[152]

In the 1930s, however, the further economies of design required by the Ministry of Health and dictated by the pressures of local government finance led to some rather more serious criticisms of new council houses. In 1936 the Medical Officer of Health for Houghton-le-Spring complained vehemently to the Council about

. . . the inadequacy of the size of the bedrooms. In the smaller houses they are nothing more or less than boxes and will not take ordinary sized furniture . . . There is better accommodation in some ships at sea than these rooms provide.

I would advise as a minimum that bedrooms should be of regular shape and of such a size as will take ordinary furniture and leaving enough room to move about without having to jump over the bed to get from one side of the room to another.[153]

A similar complaint was made to the Ministry by the Conservative MP for Wallsend about Chester-le-Street RDC's estate at Birtley, where 'some perfectly appalling new council houses have been erected . . . they are highly unsuitable and it is impossible to get a double bed into the bedroom without putting the head of it into a cupboard.'[154] The MP imputed a sinister motive to the Labour-controlled local authority: 'knowing that district very well I do not put it beyond the council, either themselves or through some other method, to arrange for this unsatisfactory type of house to be built in order to demonstrate against the National Government.'[155] In fact, the problems were caused by a combination of economic pressure and bad design: the Council had amended its plans for subsequent estates.[156]

The standard of architecture in council house building between the wars varied considerably between districts in the county and between individual schemes. Anyone making a survey of inter-war estates will find that many Addison Act houses were designed to a high standard of domestic architecture, drawing heavily, of course, from the Tudor Walters models, but often showing good individual treatment of style and proportion. The financial constraints upon architects under later schemes, however, are only too apparent. There are exceptions, but in comparison with Addison Act houses many other inter-war council dwellings appear box-like, with uninteresting proportions and unrelieved features: even in 1934 the correspondent of *The Times* stressed the need in County Durham for 'more taste and less unnecessary ugliness.'[157] Nevertheless, local authorities maintained a great degree of pride in their achievements throughout the period. Ceremonies were frequently conducted for the ritual of 'sod-cutting'[158] and at the opening of the 1,000th or 2,000th house, or at any other suitable stage.[159]

This sense of pride can sometimes be detected in the naming of streets on council estates, which occasionally lapsed into a catalogue of flowers, trees and rural beauty-spots, but often commemorated the councillors themselves; and in a few districts there was tribute paid to the political thinkers most respected by the councillors – Marx, Engels, Lenin and Keir Hardie formed one quartet in Stanley.[160] The MP for Hartlepool was even moved to send the Council a begging letter, asking for a new street or square to be named after him 'in view of his long association with the Borough.'[161] It is not surprising, perhaps, that some civic figures enjoyed being celebrated in this way, for council housing schemes were a particularly tangible and enduring expression of local government achievement, large enough to transform the landscape of a district. Nor is it surprising that councils, in the same way as any other builders, could stand back and view their work with a certain professional pride. It was no doubt in just such a frame of mind that the Felling Council particularly called the attention of the Royal Commission on Local Government on Tyneside to its 'beautiful Housing Schemes which have been very artistically laid out with gardens, open spaces and grass plots and are much admired.'[162]

4 The Council as landlord

By 1939 about 300,000 people in County Durham, or about 20 per cent of the population, were officially resident in council houses. Bearing in mind the unusually high incidence of sub-letting in the county (discussed in section *b* below) the actual number of occupants may have been considerably higher. Between the wars most councils had to cope with responsibilities even less familiar than those encountered in the role of builder. The role of landlord involved the Council in selecting tenants, overseeing their behaviour and collecting their rent. Apart from the sheer scale of these responsibilities, the Council often had to face a dilemma that did not exist for the private landlord. The problem was expressed quite well in the Ministry of Health's *Annual Report* for 1929–30, in which it was recognized that local authorities could not

> . . . be governed by the same considerations as other property owners. The latter naturally select the most eligible, i.e., the most respectable and prosperous, tenants available and may even take into account the absence of children who may knock the house about. Local authorities on the other hand have to provide for those tenants, amongst others, who are least eligible in the eyes of the private owner.

Taking the argument a little further, should the Council of a district where there was severe housing shortage actively prevent sub-letting of its property? Or in trying to recover arrears of rent, should the Council take legal proceedings against tenants who were out of work or on strike, or against widows? Whatever his personal predisposition, a private landlord was not expected to be philanthropic; the Council, on the other hand, had not entered the housing market for commercial purposes and was expected to follow considerations apart from the purely economic. The consequent difficulty of reconciling estate management with social policy is a theme which underlies the rest of this section.

a. Tenants

The first task of the Council as landlord was to select its tenants. This was by no means easy, for the number of applicants was always many times greater than the number of vacant houses. In Darlington, for example, there were 1,368 applicants in June 1922, but even by the end of 1924 the Council had not built more than 300 houses.[163] In Chester-le-Street there were over a thousand names on the waiting list by 1935, but the Council's rate of building was only about 70 houses per year.[164] With such a high degree of competition for tenancies it was clearly essential for the Council to apply systematic procedures and priorities in selection.

It was necessary first to establish who would be responsible for setting the priorities and for applying them. Most councils delegated responsibility to a housing committee or its equivalent, but some delegated further to a sub-committee of local men for each parish, others to a housing manager. In most cases, however, the decision to award a tenancy rested with councillors, who consequently found their goodwill to be much in demand. The proffering of bribes, though rarely mentioned in council records,[165] was probably quite common – one councillor from the Durham Rural District complained to the press that he had habitually to run for his bus to avoid the solicitations of desperate applicants.[166]

The influence of councillors in the selection process sometimes produced questionable decisions: for example, one of the parish sub-committees in the Easington district awarded a council house to its own chairman.[167] Whatever the merits of individual cases, this kind of decision could not fail to arouse suspicion. As one applicant of four years' standing commented to a journalist in Gateshead, 'the fact that three members of the Committee occupy Council houses does not inspire confidence.'[168] Gateshead was, in fact, the only place where allegations of organized corruption were made. In October 1925 the local moderate party claimed that one Labour alderman and three councillors were living in council houses;[169] six years later they claimed that this had grown to eight councillors 'and over 40 "Labour" delegates, ward officials and leading workers of the Gateshead Labour party and I.L.P.'[170] Propaganda evidence must be treated cautiously and it should be noted that for most of the period in question the Gateshead Council was in fact under Moderate control, but the substance of these allegations was apparently never challenged in print. On the other hand, in the whole of the county there is not a single case where the District Auditor found that a tenancy had been granted improperly.

The priorities for dealing with applications for houses were usually laid down formally by the Council. During the period of the Addison scheme the highest priority was generally given to the applications of ex-servicemen and their families. This policy was encouraged by the government[171] and the underlying idea of 'homes for heroes' was administered almost literally by many councils in County Durham, with preference usually given above all to men who had served in the forces overseas. An equal consideration was that applicants should be residents of the particular district, either at the time of application or (in a few districts) before the outbreak of war. This residential qualification was not required by law, but the administration of the 1919 Act was conceived in terms of local authority areas and councils were thus inclined to tackle the housing problem on a rather parochial basis.

A fairly typical composite of these considerations was the statement of priorities laid down by the Hebburn Council, where top of the list came 'men from Hebburn who have served in H.M. Forces, preference given to men engaged overseas, and to those who gave up their houses when joining the Forces, or whose houses were given up subsequently, and to the widows of ex-servicemen in Hebburn.'[172] Jarrow went so far as to entertain no other applications than those made by local ex-servicemen,[173] but most councils tried to apply the notion of housing need as well as that of military service. Gateshead, for example, while giving priority to ex-servicemen over 'civilians', recognized within these categories the superior claim of applicants with large families.[174] Similarly, while Felling gave top priority to applicants who had served in the forces overseas, it would consider no claim where the family numbered fewer than six.[175] It was unusual in these early stages, however, for a council to make the relief of overcrowding its sole criterion in allocating council houses: this appears only to have happened in Ryton and in the rural districts of Easington and Sedgefield.[176]

The preference allotted to ex-servicemen by most councils in the early post-war years gave way by the mid-1920s to criteria directly related to housing need. Priority came gradually to be given to families whose existing accommodation was judged inadequate. The most systematic demonstration of this principle was in Darlington, where applicants were graded on a 'points' table: a family scored 30 points, for example, if its members were living more than three to a room, and a further ten points for each member above that level.[177] Some councils, like Washington, also gave priority to applicants on medical grounds – particularly where there were cases of tuberculosis in a family.[178] A married couple invariably had a stronger claim than a single person and this evidently was an inducement to marriage: in order to deter nuptial opportunists the Washington Council required applicants to furnish proof of at least five years' wedlock.[179]

In the 1930s councils were faced with a new obligation arising from the clearance of slums and overcrowded areas. As the building of council houses for 'general needs' declined, it was mainly the families displaced by clearance schemes which went to the top of the waiting list. A fairly typical list in the 1930s was based on priorities such as those observed by the Darlington Council: first came families displaced by the Council, with preference going to the larger families, then tuberculosis sufferers living in unsuitable accommodation, then childless couples displaced by the Council, followed by single persons displaced by the Council.[180] There was, however, an important proviso to this order of precedence, in that a tenancy would be given only to those families which satisfied the Medical Officer of Health that they were 'desirable' and the Borough Treasurer that they were able to pay the rent and rates.[181] Or as the Council of Sunderland Rural District decided, 'preference shall be given to the applicants whose previous rent record is satisfactory and who are known to be clean and tidy.'[182]

The concern to select tenants who were able and willing to pay the rent was evident in some councils much earlier than in others. Felling made it a factor in its selection procedures as early as 1921[183] and Hetton made it a condition in 1924 that applicants had to present a current rent book as evidence of their previous record.[184] But this concern became much more widespread in the 1930s, partly because the accumulation of rent arrears (particularly during the 1926 coal dispute) was a reason given to many councils by the Ministry of Health for refusal to sanction the building of additional houses, and partly because councillors came to appreciate that arrears had to be balanced by unpopular increases in local rates. The inspection of applicants' previous rent books consequently became standard practice in many districts.

An interesting indication of the factors considered by local authorities in selecting tenants is given in the 'Instructions to Enquiry Officers' which the West Hartlepool Council issued in 1932 to officials responsible for investigating applications.[185] Some of the instructions were designed to establish the financial standing of the applicant. Enquiry officers had to 'inspect the rent book and enquire at Rates Office as to rates outstanding' and to ask 'whether applicant is employed or unemployed at date of visit, and, if employed, where – amount of income.' Other procedures were used to assess the general 'suitability' of an applicant. As well as having to call on the applicant's landlord and referees, the enquiry officer was instructed to interview the applicant at home and to report on the 'condition of rooms – whether clean and tidy or otherwise' and 'whether furniture sufficient or only partly sufficient for a Corporation house.'

The difficulty which councils experienced in catering for the poorest applicants was relieved considerably by the 'sanitary' Housing Acts of the 1930s. Their emphasis on the rehousing of slum-dwellers, at a time when building costs were lower and Exchequer subsidies higher than in the late 1920s, meant that families with the greatest housing need could be given help in a more direct way. But though rent levels grew more accessible to the lower-income groups and more applicants could thus satisfy housing officials of their ability to pay, there usually remained the requirement for a family to establish its 'suitability' in broader terms. This generally came to mean satisfying the local Medical Officer of Health that the family's furniture and effects would not constitute a health hazard when moved to a new estate. Many families failed to do this at the first attempt: in Sunderland, for example, 103 out of the 179 new tenants in 1934 needed to have their furniture and bedding disinfested before they were accepted.[186] Some local authorities had to equip themselves with fumigation chambers for this purpose, while others relied on the issue of disinfectant and kerosene soap-sprayers: 'it is wonderful how effective the simple methods are, backed up by hot water and supervision,' the Medical Officer for South Shields enthused zeugmatically.[187] A few councils took a more positive approach to the problem and followed the example of Gateshead, where 1930 Act houses were made available with essential items of new furniture which tenants could buy from the council at 3s. per week over three years.[188]

Unfortunately, there is very little statistical evidence to show the effect that different selection policies exercised on the social composition of housing estates. Details exist for a few estates: for example, in the parish of Tunstall in the Sunderland rural district 90 per cent of the council houses in 1931 were occupied by miners and their families, and in the Wearside parish of Castletown the proportion was about 50 per cent.[189] Or in two streets in Hetton (which were examined by the Council in detail in 1928) one can see that out of a total of 31 tenants there were 24 miners (including a 'deputy' and a disabled pitman living on compensation), four unemployed, a blacksmith, a rent collector and a billiard-hall attendant.[190] Although detailed information is lacking, the indications are that the proportion of working-class tenants was relatively high in County Durham; in London, by contrast, tenancies in the 1930s were held predominantly by 'small clerks and tradesmen, artisans and the better-off semi-skilled workers.'[191]

An interesting feature suggested by the available evidence is that councils often made social distinctions between applicants when vacancies arose for the larger, 'parlour' houses. In the Easington district, for example, a batch of six new parlour houses was allocated to five schoolmasters and a senior pitman.[192] A later example from the same district shows that vacant parlour houses were awarded to a schoolmaster, a butcher and a cinema manager, while the non-parlour houses went largely to miners.[193] The justification for this was probably financial, for the rent of a parlour house was usually about 25 per cent higher than that of a non-parlour house. The Darlington Housing Committee found it particularly difficult to find 'suitable' tenants for its parlour houses and had to place special advertisements when vacancies arose: the Borough Accountant personally decided whether or not an applicant's resources were adequate.[194] The danger of this approach was that, if carried too far, help was given to people who could already afford adequate housing in the private sector. West Hartlepool was the only council which went to the lengths of fixing official limits on income: the waiting list was restricted in 1933 to applicants whose annual income did not exceed £300.[195]

Once tenants had been selected and installed, the attitude adopted by councils towards them could vary considerably. Some councils, like Stockton, felt it necessary to make detailed regulations forbidding, for example, the keeping of pigs or the disposal of household waste down water closets.[196] Others had a more enlightened approach, issuing tenants with handbooks of advice rather than with instructions. A particularly good example is the book given by South Shields to its tenants in the 1930s, which even contained a section on preparing cheap, high-protein meals.[197] A few councils actively encouraged discussions with tenants' associations.[198] The points which they most often raised with councils were connected with rent levels, but there were cases where a council might be lobbied, for example, to adapt its older houses for electricity.

Of all the difficulties which councils were caused by the conduct of tenants, the greatest arose from the sub-letting of property and the non-payment of rent. These questions are examined separately later on. By comparison the other problems were slight, but there were two broad classes of objectionable behaviour with which councils had to deal – the anti-social (causing offence to other tenants) and the destructive (causing damage or undue wear to the property). As an example of the former, there is the bizarre case of two neighbouring tenants in Washington who were, after mutual complaints, instructed by the Council to refrain respectively from holding unruly spiritualist meetings and from keeping a disorderly goat.[199] Equally anti-social was the tenant at Wingate who, for some arcane reason, kept a shed full of dead rabbits.[200] Damage to council property was generally just a matter of broken window panes, although one Washington tenant did manage to destroy his front door in a brawl.[201] Concern for property led most councils to forbid tenants to carry out a trade on the premises; this was taken so far in one district as to prevent a doctor from seeing patients in his council house.[202] By far the most outrageous recorded misuse of council property was perpetrated by a Consett man who, in addition to sub-letting parts of his house, removed the bathroom window, replaced it with wire mesh and converted the room into an aviary.[203]

Apart from a few serious cases, however, the general behaviour of tenants caused few problems and, needless to say, 'the old bogey about the baths being used for the storage of their coals has about as much truth in it as the battalions of Russian soldiers coming through Newcastle Station during the War with snow on their boots.'[204] Indeed, the arch-Conservative publication which bore this comment had been moved to swallow its earlier regurgitation of the familiar argument that 'you cannot convert a brutish and soulless being into a gentleman by putting him in a garden city.'[205] In 1936, under the headline 'slum tenants rise to it', the paper was pleased to note that families from condemned areas, no doubt overcoming their innate brutishness, 'have developed a house-proud and garden-proud attitude' when rehoused on a council estate.[206]

b. Sub-letting and overcrowding

One of the most difficult problems which faced the Council as landlord was what to do about tenants who sub-let their houses. It is necessary, before going further, to make clear the distinction between 'lodgers', who within certain limits councils were prepared to tolerate, and 'sub-tenants', to whom they usually took exception. In the present context, a lodger was a single person whose rent paid for a furnished room and often for meals taken with the family of the council tenant; a sub-tenant paid for accommodation which was more self-contained and usually unfurnished, and in which he lived with wife and children.

'Lodging' was traditionally very common in mining districts, because of the high level of labour migration in the industry. The usual rule applied by councils in County Durham to tenants wishing to take in a lodger was that the written approval of the Council should first be sought; the addition of a lodger to the household should not create overcrowded conditions; and the lodger should have a furnished bedroom.[207] Under such conditions the practice was to the advantage of all parties: the Council had the satisfaction of seeing its accommodation occupied to an optimum level, while the tenant and the lodger in theory enjoyed an arrangement of mutual benefit. The Council rarely interfered in such arrangements – although there was an intriguing case in which the Washington Housing Committee required a tenant to remove a couple of lodgers whom it discreetly described as 'lady theatricals'.[208] In most cases, however, local authorities were prepared to look on the arrangements benevolently and the Ministry of Health was broadly in favour.[209]

On the other hand, most councils took a stronger line on the question of sub-letting. Their objections were threefold. In the first place, the presence of an extra family in a council house very often led to overcrowding – an aspect of the problem which is examined later in this section. Secondly, the separation of unfurnished bedrooms to serve as bed-sits not only created undesirable living conditions, but also led to undue damage and deterioration of the Council's property. During a Ministry of Health inquiry into housing defects in Hetton, much of the blame for dilapidations was attributed to the widespread practice of sub-letting.[210] A particular problem was the use of bedroom fireplaces for cooking and continuous heating – purposes for which they had not been designed and constructed. This often resulted in the smouldering of surrounding floorboards and joists.[211] The third objection was that sub-tenants, once installed with their own family and furniture, were very difficult to shift. This caused grave problems when, for whatever reason, the official tenant moved away; for unless the Council took legal action to remove the sub-tenant, it could not allocate the house to anyone on the official waiting list. The Easington Council had encountered this problem at an early stage, in its 1890 Act houses at Murton, and had apparently taken a hard line with the squatters;[212] but other councils chose a line of less resistance and recognized these families as the new tenants in preference to more deserving cases on the waiting list.[213]

It would be quite wrong, however, to imagine that sub-tenants were themselves the cause of the problem. The root of the evil was the severe shortage of working-class housing that prevailed in most of the county. Few families would choose to live in a room or two within someone else's home if a structurally separate dwelling were available nearby. The question of money does not affect the argument: sub-tenants, as we shall see below, paid as much in rent for bed-sit accommodation as they would have had to pay for a larger, self-contained dwelling in the same district. The problem arose because there was a dearth of separate dwellings and because many existing tenants, some with generous motives but most with an eye to the cash, were prepared to open their doors to families who would otherwise have 'doubled-up' somewhere else or moved right away from the district.

As this implies, sub-letting was not a practice confined to council estates. An impression of its general extent can be obtained from a study of the working-class housing in the South Shields rural district made by its sanitary inspector in 1924.[214] This was predominantly a mining district, situated between the Tyneside and Wear-side conurbations, and overcrowding there (about 25 per cent at the 1921 census) was slightly lower than the county average. The inspector's report to the Council took in just under 2,700 houses (about three-quarters of the total housing stock of the district), of which council housing represented about 6 per cent. The report showed that just over 10 per cent of the houses inspected had one or two rooms sub-let. It also showed that sub-tenants paid over 30 per cent more in rent than tenants who occupied the same space in a separate dwelling. On average, the cost of renting two rooms as a sub-tenant (about 7s. 6d. per week) was the same as the rent for a separate dwelling of four rooms. This trend was more marked in the parish of Boldon Colliery: there the rent for one and two sub-let rooms (6s. 6d. and 7s. 6d. per week) was respectively the same as the rent of separate dwellings of three and five rooms.[215]

There are no figures to show how the incidence of sub-letting in council houses compared with the level in the remainder of the housing stock. It is clear, however, that the inducements to sub-letting were stronger for the council tenant than for the private tenant. Council houses were generally larger than existing working-class dwellings and their rents were higher than those prevailing in the private sector for the same number of rooms. Thus it was much easier to absorb a sub-tenant in a council house than, for example, in a colliery house, and the financial constraints to do so were greater. A possible result of financial pressure on tenants was that sub-letting may have increased during and after the coal dispute of 1926. Unfortunately, only one local authority – Easington RDC – conducted surveys at the relevant times, but its figures show that the incidence of sub-letting rose from 16 per cent of council houses in February 1926 to 26 per cent in February 1930.[216]

The most detailed source of information which still survives on the sub-letting of council houses is the report of a survey conducted by Hetton UDC in January 1931.[217] The main purpose of the report was to illustrate a drop in the level of sub-letting (from 30 per cent of houses to 18 per cent) following a campaign of legal threats against offending council tenants, but the details provided of individual households enable other interesting conclusions to be drawn. For example, the rents paid by sub-tenants ranged from 2s. 6d. to 8s. per week;[218] the mean 'sub-rent' of 5s. 2½d. per week was roughly half that of the rents payable to the Council, which ranged from 10s. 1d. to 11s. 5d. per week (including rates). An intriguing feature is that a very high proportion (over 90 per cent) of the tenants sub-letting were themselves in arrears with their rent to the Council; the average arrears per sub-let house were also about 7 per cent higher than the average for other council houses in the district. This is open to two interpretations: either the tenants who sub-let were desperately short of money or they had an entirely casual attitude to their obligations to the Council. Neither alternative can be proved to be the general case, though it should be noted that about one in seven tenants who sub-let was in turn owed arrears of rent by his sub-tenant. In households where this was the case, an average of just over 30 per cent of the arrears owed by the official tenant to the Council was in turn owed to him by the sub-tenant.

It is also possible to derive from the survey of sub-letting in the Hetton district some idea of the overcrowding which the practice caused. The average family of 'sub-landlords' in Hetton was of roughly the same size (about five persons) as the average family of all council tenants in the district; the average family of sub-tenants contained about 3½ persons. In about two-thirds of the houses which were sub-let there lived eight or more persons, and in about a third there were ten or more persons. Taking the common overcrowding yardstick of 'more than two persons to a room', this reveals that about half of the people living in sub-let houses were living in overcrowded conditions. This compares with an overcrowding figure of 16 per cent for the whole of the Hetton district at the census of 1931.[219]

In general, however, there was significantly less overcrowding in council houses in County Durham than in other forms of working-class accommodation. The major survey of working-class housing conducted throughout England and Wales in 1936 showed that only 7.7 per cent of families in council houses in County Durham were overcrowded, compared with 12.4 per cent in other working-class dwellings.[220] Only in Darlington and Sunderland was overcrowding proportionately more common in council housing than in the private sector; while at the other extreme there were towns like Jarrow and South Shields where overcrowding was five times more common in the private than in the council sector.

Nevertheless, most of the coalfield local authorities maintained a persistent campaign against tenants who sub-let their houses. For legal and practical reasons the Council's efforts could only be levelled at the official tenant and not directly at the sub-tenant. The methods used to deal with the problem ranged in the early stages of a case from calling a tenant to the council offices for an interview to sending him a solicitor's letter of warning. Eventually, the Council might issue the offending tenant with a notice to quit and, as a last resort, obtain a possession order from the courts. Few councils were prepared to pursue a case through to the stage of eviction and many, indeed, were satisfied by a partial response to an intermittent campaign of threats. The Hetton Council, for example, issued 110 tenants on one estate (half the total number) with letters threatening eviction, but was content to drop all action a month later when it emerged that 36 of these tenants had responded by ejecting their sub-tenants.[221]

Although sub-tenants were the cause of one problem – the overcrowding and misuse of council property – they were, as we have seen above, the victims of a much wider problem, the serious overall shortage of separate dwellings. Councils which took a wider view of their housing responsibilities tended, therefore, to be somewhat ambivalent in their attitude towards sub-tenants. The Easington Council, for example, was moved at one stage to give nearly 400 tenants six months' notice to remove themselves or their sub-tenants, but then let the campaign peter out when a local miners' lodge politely enquired what provision the Council was making for the families which would be displaced.[222] At least two councils, Brandon and Willington, actively encouraged sub-letting for several years as the most beneficial way of putting their housing stock to the service of the community. The depression which blighted Brandon between the wars meant that council tenants could not afford the rents prescribed by the Ministry of Health. As early as 1922 the Council realized that the introduction of 'half-tenancies' – the doubling-up of families, each with its own council rent book – was a sensible answer to the problem.[223] During the coal dispute the Council actually pressured tenants into doubling-up if they could not find the rent for a house on their own[224] and by 1930 about a quarter of its housing stock was being shared.[225] Although the Ministry tolerated this policy in the short term as the only way to stop the accumulation of rent arrears, it was also concerned about the overcrowding which resulted. By the 1930s it had persuaded Brandon – and Willington, which had followed the example of its neighbour – to phase out the existing half-tenancies and to allow no new ones.[226] Whether they intended it or not, these two councils had effectively demonstrated to central government a key dilemma for housing authorities in depressed areas.

c. Rent

From the tenant's point of view, the most important element in his relationship with the Council as landlord was the level of rent charged for the accommodation. But rent levels were also of fundamental concern to central and local government, because of the obvious connection between current income and the need to meet running costs and repayments of capital debt: lower rents meant higher subsidies from public funds. Against the financial implications of rent policy both central and local government had to weigh the espoused social aim of providing good houses for a weekly sum that working-class tenants could afford. A local authority had to balance its concern to improve housing conditions in the area with another to keep local rates within reasonable bounds. Similarly, the Ministry of Health, while promoting the social policy of improving housing conditions, kept a sternly critical eye on the implications for Exchequer subsidies and – as part of its wider responsibilities as watchdog over local government – on the overall level and the acceptable deployment of local rates. On balance, local authorities in County Durham were more favourably disposed towards the tenant than were the agents of central government.

The tension between the two tiers of government was most apparent in the case of housing schemes under the 1919 Act. Because the liability of local authorities was normally fixed at the product of a penny rate and the Exchequer had to make good the remaining loss, councils had nothing to lose in pressing for lower rents. On the other hand, the high capital cost of Addison Act schemes increased the pressure on the Ministry of Health to keep the level of Exchequer liability under control: each local authority proposal to reduce rents threatened to aggravate the financial embarrassment which the programme was generating in central government. In fact, the original intention of the Ministry's policy was a staged *increase* in council house rents up to 1927, until the full economic cost was being recovered.[227] In Stockton this would have meant an increase in the rent of a standard A3 house from 10s. to £1 6s. 6d. per week (excluding rates) over a period of seven years: the troubled housing committee was doubtful whether tenants would be able to pay even the amount suggested for the first year.[228] It must quickly have become apparent to the Ministry that, if Addison Act houses were to be occupied at all, this policy could never be implemented; so that in 1921 it was actually on the insistence of the Ministry that Darlington's own plan to increase rents by annual stages of 1s. per week up to 1927 was dropped.[229] Therefore, while rents in the private housing sector gradually became 'decontrolled' as tenants moved on, it was soon accepted that, with the heavy costs of building under the 1919 Act, economic rents in the local authority sector could never be envisaged.

Far from rising towards the economic level, rents charged for Addison Act houses were to fall considerably in the 1920s and 1930s. This trend was due largely to pressure from the local authorities, reacting in turn to representations from their tenants. It owed little to the Ministry of Health, which resisted for as long as possible any reduction from the minimum rents (10s. per week for an A3 house, exclusive of rates, and 12s. 6d. for a B3) which it laid down in 1920 for council houses in urban areas and mining villages.[230] Only Sunderland cheered the Ministry by charging significantly more than the minimum (about 35 per cent overall).[231] Nearly all the other local authorities in County Durham were at some stage concerned to negotiate rents well below the 1920 minimum. Most cases were resolved by negotiation or by reference to a rent tribunal, and it was rare for a council to take unilateral action. But when this did happen, the Ministry acted firmly to impose financial liability on the local authority by refusing to subsidize the additional losses arising from the disputed rent reduction: this sanction was used against the Hetton Council in 1923 for charging rents below the level recommended by a tribunal.[232]

The case for lower rents under the Addison scheme was made by local authorities in County Durham on the basis of what working-class families themselves might expect to pay and what they would reasonably be expected to part with. It is clear that Addison Act houses were considerably more expensive to rent than older houses in the private sector. As part of the 'Survey of Housing Needs' which councils were required to make under the 1919 Act, information was sought on the rents prevailing in each district for accommodation of equivalent size (A3, B3, etc.) to the proposed council houses. This information survives for a useful cross-section of local authority areas – South Shields, Hebburn, Ryton, Consett, Benfieldside and Houghton rural district.[233] It shows that the average rent for an A3-size house in the private sector was about 7s. 1d. per week inclusive of rates, and for a B3-size house about 9s. 2d. per week. This means that the Ministry of Health's minimum rents of 10s. and 12s. 6d. per week for A3 and B3 council houses would, after the addition of rates, have represented at least double the prevailing level in these districts. Even the reduced rents which were eventually adopted in these areas were at least 50 per cent higher than levels prevailing in the private sector. Of course, Addison Act houses were far superior in quality to any existing working-class accommodation. As well as being anything from ten to a hundred years newer than other dwellings, these council houses probably had larger rooms and certainly were laid out in greater space and designed to a much higher standard.

The argument for lower rents in the 1920s was more compelling when related to working-class wage levels. In 1912, the average rent of a four-room house in the South Tyneside towns of Gateshead, Jarrow and South Shields had been about 5s. 9d. per week, including rates. This represented between 15 and 25 per cent of the gross weekly income of the average worker.[234] In the 1920s, however, the evidence adduced by some of the mining districts in County Durham showed that even those council house rents which had been fixed below the Ministry of Health's original minimum made demands on an uncomfortably high proportion of tenants' income. In the Easington rural district, for example, the main class of applicant was said to be the colliery surface worker, who was not entitled to a colliery house and whose gross weekly earnings averaged £3 4s. 6d.[235] This meant that the inclusive rents which the Council was obliged, after nearly a year's negotiation with the Ministry, finally to charge such tenants represented about 23 per cent of their gross earnings for an A3 house and about 27 per cent for a B3 house.[236] This was in a relatively flourishing mining area, but in the Auckland rural district, where the pits were rapidly becoming unviable, a worker was lucky to receive £1 10s. per week. This meant that the rent which the Council had to charge for an A3 house, including rates, took 45 to 50 per cent of the miner's income. The unlucky tenants in this district were the ones who had no work at all: in October 1922 the Council reported that 9 out of 21 pits in West Auckland had closed over the previous 18 months. The overall result was that 'whenever a house happened to be empty other than those provided by the Council, the Council's tenants left and went to the other house because the rents are so much less.'[237]

None of the negotiations between councils and the Ministry of Health before 1923 produced significantly lower rents than those which had been set in the early stages of the programme. In January 1923, however, the Ministry and the dissatisfied local authorities persuaded the Annfield Plain council 'to accept an arrangement for a test case . . . on behalf of local authorities in the County of Durham.'[238] The matter was duly referred to a rent tribunal, which operated under powers granted by legislation secondary to the 1919 Act. Details of the reduction in rents recommended by the tribunal in this test case are not available, but it can be seen that a year later the average rents in a selection of mining districts were (at 7s. per week for an A3 house and 8s. for a B3, exclusive of rates) 30 to 35 per cent lower than the rents originally advocated by the Ministry of Health.[239] A further indication of the trend is available for the industrial towns of south Tyneside, thanks to summaries prepared by officials of the Jarrow and Gateshead Councils. These summaries show that the average rents of A3 and B3 council houses in the conurbation stretching from Whickham to South Shields were respectively 10s. 4d. and 12s. 4d. per week (exclusive of rates) when first negotiated with the Ministry of Health in the middle of 1921.[240] By the middle of 1922 there had been a slight fall in rent levels of about 5 per cent (down to an average of 9s. 11d. and 11s. 6d. per week),[241] but by April 1924 – after stronger appeals to the Ministry and the Annfield Plain test case – there had been a dramatic reduction of a further 20 per cent (to an average of 7s. 8d. and 9s. 8d. per week).[242]

This was a notable victory for the local authorities, particularly as the cost of the extra subsidies was being thrown on central government. Unfortunately, the economic conditions that had originally prompted the campaign for lower rents did not improve sufficiently to eradicate the difficulty of letting the houses at a sum within the reach of working-class tenants. Councils like that of Hetton continued to press for reductions, claiming that 'wages have generally decreased'[243] – although economic conditions there were much better than in the south-west coalfield and council house rents (at 9s. 6d. and 11s. 6d. per week, including rates) were among the lowest in the county. Even so, in 1925 the rent of an A3 house claimed 15 to 20 per cent of the average weekly income of employed tenants in Hetton and the rent of a B3 house some 20 to 25 per cent.[244] In the second half of the 1920s, however, the Ministry of Health dug in its heels to resist further reductions in the rents of Addison Act houses. A request from the Brandon Council was given a particular dusty reception: in response to descriptions of the effect of severe economic depression and of the protracted coal dispute on tenants' incomes the Ministry made the astonishing statement in February 1927 that 'there would not appear to have been any material change in the position of the working classes for whom the houses were erected since the time when the present rents were fixed [in January 1924].'[245] As we have seen in the previous section, this led the Council to sanction the 'doubling-up' of families. In the following section it will be shown how economic depression interacted with unrealistic rent levels to produce rent arrears and further problems.[246]

Under the Chamberlain and Wheatley schemes it was much easier for the Council to determine its own rent policy. As the liability of central government was limited to an annual flat-rate sum per house, any further reduction from an economic rent had to be subsidized by the ratepayers. But though the Ministry of Health was unable to prevent councils charging rents which it considered undesirably low, there were other constraints acting on local authorities. A good example is the case of Sunderland RDC, which in May 1928 decided on a 25 per cent reduction in the rents of its Chamberlain and Wheatley Act houses.[247] This clearly enraged many local ratepayers and resulted in an official complaint to the Ministry of Health by one of the parish councils. The Ministry responded by telling the district council that its reductions 'had been drawn up without any proper consideration.'[248] Next to join in was the District Auditor, who 'declared that the council had no power to subsidise the wages of a particular few at the expense of the remainder of the mining community and other ratepayers.'[249] The auditor returned to the fray in the following year and gave the opinion that 'those Members of the Council who are responsible . . . render themselves liable [to a] surcharge.'[250] The councillors were eventually saved from having to dig into their own pockets by the intervention of another party – the rent tribunal. The arbitration of this body resulted in the original rents being restored and the Council spared.[251]

More important than constraints such as these was the sheer cost of building. Given on the one hand the relatively modest flat-rate Exchequer contributions in the later 1920s and the level of working-class incomes on the other, only a substantial fall in building costs would have enabled councils to achieve their aim of charging lower rents without intolerable demands being made upon local ratepayers. A further problem was the simple fact that council tenants themselves had to pay rates (in the 'inclusive' rents charged by local authorities). This usually represented about 50 to 55 per cent on top of the purely 'rent' element. Being new and relatively spacious, council houses attracted higher rating assessments than other working-class accommodation in a particular area; and the effect was compounded by very high rate poundages levied in the county. The combination of these factors finally moved the South Shields Rural District Council to complain in 1930 that council houses at Boldon Colliery were standing empty,

> . . . because the people cannot pay out of their wages the rent (including rates) which the Council is compelled to charge. At the present time, if further houses were erected at Boldon Colliery, owing to the condition of the Mining Industry and high rates levied in the area they are not likely to be occupied. When the rates are reduced and the rents of the Council Houses reduced accordingly to a figure which the Working Classes in this area can reasonably pay, further houses could be built, and overcrowding abated.[252]

The problem is further exemplified by a study made of estates in Stockton by the Medical Officer of Health.[253] By analysing the health records of families which had been moved in 1927 from a slum clearance area (Housewife Lane) out to a large new council estate (Mount Pleasant) he showed that there was a significant increase in the death rate (from 22.9 to 32.5 per thousand) in the five years following the move over the previous five years spent in the slums.[254] This had nothing to do with housing and environmental standards, which were vastly superior on the new estate; nor was it the result of any epidemic or upsurge in the common infectious diseases. The phenomenon was put down to dietary deficiencies which had been aggravated by an increased proportion of family income being taken by rent (the mean rent in the slums had been 4s. 8d. per week, including rates; on the new estate it was 9s.).[255] In families where the husband was employed the proportion of family income taken by the council house rent was 20.5 per cent. This rose to 31.3 per cent in families where there was no wage-earner. In the latter circumstances, where the rent level was obviously critical, an average of only 2s. 11d. per week was available to feed each member of the family; back in the slums the figure had been 3s. 10d. per week.[256] The same conclusions above poverty and health had already been reached by the medical officer for West Hartlepool:

> it has not been found possible to build [council] houses for letting at an economic rent to meet the great bulk of distressed people who are living on unemployment benefit or transitional benefit. It is hopeless to demand rent of even [6s.] out of an income . . . of [£1 3s. to £1 5s.] and expect at the same time to retain their health and character.[257]

It was only after the Greenwood Act of 1930 that it became possible for councils to build houses at rents which most low-income families could afford. The combination of more generous Exchequer subsidies with lower builing costs and interest rates in the 1930s meant that slum replacement housing could be let at low rents without undue strain on the local rates. The effect of these more favourable circumstances is illustrated by information collected in 1936 by Seaham Harbour UDC from every other urban district council in the county.[258] This shows that in the mining districts the average rent of an A3 house built under the Addison and Chamberlain Acts was then 6s. 9d. per week, excluding rates; for a Wheatley Act house it was 6s. 6d.; but for an

A3 house built under the Greenwood Act it was only 4s. 6d. Similarly, on Tyneside in 1936 an Addison or Chamberlain house averaged 7s. 4d. per week and a Wheatley House 7s.; but the average weekly rent for a Greenwood house was only 5s. 3d.[259]

This represented substantial progress, although tenants of the older council houses did not receive any immediate benefit. The Housing Act of 1935 did, however, cut through some of the knots of accounting practice which had previously tied most councils to separate accounts for each housing scheme and, as we have just seen, to different rents for similar accommodation. Many councils moved to an arrangement whereby housing accounts were consolidated and rent income pooled. Thus it became possible for a district like Consett to fix a graduated scale of rents, ranging from 5s. 3d. for an A2 house to 6s. 11d. for an A6 house, based purely on the size of accommodation provided.[260] On the other hand, at least two councils introduced income-related scales of rent, though only for tenants who had been forced to leave their previous (slum) accommodation. As early as 1933 the Gateshead Council agreed to a sliding scale which provided that, for example, a couple with six or more children would pay an inclusive rent for an A4 house of 6s. per week if their income was no more than £1 6s., but 14s. 6d. per week if their income exceeded £2 10s.[261] And in Felling, 60 per cent of rehoused tenants started off on the new estates with a rebate of between 1s. 6d. and 3s. 6d. per week.[262]

In the 1930s, therefore, there were greater opportunities for councils to charge rents which were low enough for even some of the poorest working-class families to afford, and to make more flexible arrangements for families in special need. Conversely, there was less reason for councils being 'forced in a large number of cases to let houses to a class of tenants who could reasonably have found their own accommodation.'[263] A measure of the progress made is that in 1936 the average 'exclusive' rent of a council house in County Durham was 6s. per week[264] – which, even in a region of high rate bills, gave an inclusive weekly sum below the 10s. which had become accepted in the 1930s as the reasonable limit for working-class families.[265] The fact that by 1939 many families might hope to obtain decent new housing, at a rent which left them with sufficient income for other necessities, was an important breakthrough in the standard of living.

d. Arrears

The greatest single obstacle to good relations between the Council and its tenants was the problem of rent arrears. The cost of an individual tenant's arrears had to be borne by the rest of the ratepaying community;[266] moreover, the sum total of arrears in a particular district could influence the Ministry of Health to refuse to sanction the building of additional council houses. But though it was clearly in the interests of both the Council and the local community for regular recovery of rent to be established, there were major difficulties in actually achieving this. Most significant of these was the industrial depression which plagued the county for much of the inter-war period: as we shall see below, councils found it difficult to recover rents from families whose income had been hit by falling wages, unemployment or industrial disputes. Sometimes the problem was aggravated by the fixing of rents which, as we have seen in the previous section, were not in reasonable keeping with working-class incomes. There is also the possibility, examined below, that some councils did less than they might in pursuing the arrears owed to them.

The general course of rent arrears in the county is well illustrated by the examples of South Shields, Seaham Harbour and Chester-le-Street Rural District – the three local authorities for which most precise information exists. In fig. 9 this information is expressed in terms of the average amount outstanding at a particular time for each year of a council house's life. This shows very clearly the pattern of indebtedness and recovery being influenced by economic conditions. Most striking is the case of Chester-le-Street Rural District, where a fairly low level of arrears (about 2 per cent of the total rent due each year) climbed steeply during the 1926 coal dispute, at the end of which the Council had received only about 30 to 40 per cent of the rent due for the financial year. From the beginning of 1927 the level of arrears fell quite steadily, so that by the late 1930s most of the debt from 1926 had been recovered. Similar trends may be seen in the case of Seaham Harbour and South Shields, although the lower proportion of miners resident in the latter meant that the coal dispute had less impact on the overall level of arrears. It is interesting to note that the recovery in South Shields was fairly quick and that by the end of the period over 98 per cent of the rent due to the Council had been collected. In Seaham Harbour, however, there was a second peak of arrears in 1930 before the recovery really began.

The basic pattern of arrears is apparent in all districts on the coalfield for which evidence survives. The salient feature in all cases is the coal dispute, which in the Sunderland rural district, for example, gave rise to a tenfold increase in rent arrears between March 1926 and February 1927.[267] An analysis of the arrears accumulated in different parts of the district by 1931 shows that in the parish of Ford, where there were only two miners in council houses, the arrears stood at an average of £3 12s. 3d. per house; but in the predominantly mining parishes of Ryhope, Tunstall and Hylton the figures were £11 11s. 3d., £11 14s. 10d. and £12 11s. 2d. respectively.[268] The same overall pattern can be seen in the mining area of Hetton, where the total amount owed to the Council rose from £144 in November 1925 (a mere 14s. 5d. per house) to £3,087 in January 1927 (£9 10s. per house).[269] A further factor in the general course of arrears, reflected possibly in the figures for Seaham Harbour, may have been the wider economic depression from 1929 to 1931. This appears to have been the case in Darlington, where the Council, having ascertained from the town's five largest employers that the average wages paid had fallen by 24 per cent between 1929 and the beginning of 1932, discovered by interviewing tenants who had recently fallen in arrears that their average weekly income had dropped by 26 per cent (from £3 2s. 8d. to £2 6s. 2d.) over the same period.[270]

Before looking at the various methods by which councils attempted to recover arrears from their tenants, it will be useful to consider the means by which rent payments normally changed hands. The standard procedure was door-to-door collection on a weekly basis. This meant that much depended on the rent collector who regularly came into personal contact with tenants over a round of between 300 and 500 houses. He was generally a salaried employee of the Council, earning £4 to £5 per week (substantially more than most council tenants). Some of the more rural districts, where the number of houses did not warrant a full-time collector, farmed the job out on commission – usually 4 to 5 per cent of total receipts. In more urban areas, with a greater concentration of council houses, it was more economical to employ salaried staff: the average cost to the Council was about 3 to 4½ per cent of the rent recovered.[271] Some councils may have regarded the commission method as an incentive to sharpen the rent collector's approach. It may have been for this reason that Chester-le-Street UDC took the unusual step of hiring a firm of estate agents to handle all collection on a commission of 3 per cent. This arrangement, which lasted throughout the 1930s, was undoubtedly a financial success for the Council.[272]

Because most rent collectors handled over £5,000 per year each, it was usual for councils to insist on some kind of insurance against the risk of embezzlement. Either the Council made arrangements of its own or, as was quite common, the collector had to deposit with the Council a 'bond' issued by his own insurers. This was no mere formality – there are several cases on record of a collector having gone astray. The Easington Council, after experiencing problems with the Wheatley Hill collector, who was made to disgorge £25 on pain of being reported to his insurers,[273] eventually had to take proceedings against the Shotton collector who had pocketed £96 and represented it as tenants' arrears.[274] In another case, one of Chester-le-Street RDC's rent collectors was acquitted of theft by a court of magistrates, but his insurers had to pay the Council £207 which had been lost due to 'bad accounting'.[275] Other cases did not reach court: an action against one of Sunderland RDC's collectors was dropped when, after 'negotiations with relatives', the outstanding sum of £384 was to be repaid in full.[276] Despite the responsibilities and temptations, the job evidently still had its attractions, for the applications to replace this collector numbered 282 by the following month.[277]

Nevertheless, the occasional difficulty with a knavish rent collector was fairly small in comparison with the widespread problem of tenants' arrears. The prevalence of debt (in some districts nearly half of the council tenants might be behind with their rent at any time) and the severity of individual cases (sometimes involving more than a year's unpaid rent) forced local authorities to develop an armoury of devices for recovering money. The basic methods are still in operation today. Most common was

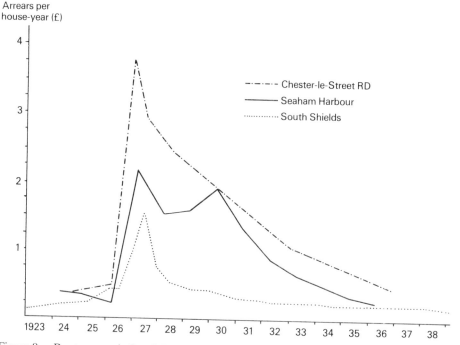

Figure 9. Rent arrears in South Shields, Seaham Harbour and Chester-le-Street RD, 1923–38.

a written 'notice to quit', usually allowed to lapse if payment was made by the effective date. The next stage in the process was obtaining a court order for repayment of the debt by instalments. If a tenant failed to keep up with these payments, the Council could obtain a distress warrant and, with help of bailiffs, seize furniture and effects to off-set the debt. The final step, which rarely befell council tenants in County Durham, was eviction. In fact, it was more common for tenants in arrears to move out of council houses in the early stages of debt recovery; indeed, the ease with which council tenants could slip into arrears was probably the most important factor in determining the rate of removals. At different stages of the period it can be seen that for every ten council houses in a district there might be anywhere from two to six former tenants who had moved out and were still being pursued for rent arrears.[278]

A method adopted by some councils, particularly in pursuit of money owed by previous tenants, was to hire a firm of professional debt collectors. The leading exponents of this business were the Northern Guild of Commerce and Trade Protection Society, whose recorded dealings were with the councils of Blaydon, Felling, Stanley, Washington and Auckland.[279] These debt collectors had some success, but their services cost about 15 per cent of the arrears actually recovered.[280] Another agent, hired by the Hetton Council, operated on a commission of 20 per cent.[281] There was thus some justification for the unusual experiment in Chester-le-Street, during which tenants and ex-tenants with arrears of more than £5 were allowed a discount of 5 per cent if they settled the sum in full.[282]

There were other methods, apart from straightforward debt collection, by which councils could reduce their overdue accounts. The most effective was an agreement with a tenant's employer to deduct a certain amount from his wages and pay it direct to the Council. There appears to have been only one recorded case where this happened – involving a colliery in the Stanley area[283] – and no case at all where the now familiar arrangement of direct deductions from state benefits was used. A more common arrangement was the contribution of strikers' rent allowance from the Durham Miners' Association (DMA).[284] After the 1926 dispute miners in the Easington district were allowed £3 each towards rent arrears[285] and in a strike at Ryhope which had started in 1932 each man was allowed 2s. per week.[286] Not all lodges were prepared to hand over the allowance direct to the Council but, when pressed, they might agree to disclose a statement of individual allowances, so that the Council could pursue tenants who had failed to hand over the full amount.[287] The DMA's contribution would have had a considerable effect in reducing strikers' arrears in mining districts: in the Sunderland rural district, for example, its payment of £1,570 served to clear 42 per cent of the arrears that had accumulated in the district during the 1926 coal dispute.[288] The final solution for dealing with arrears was the accounting expedient of writing them off. Inevitably there were debts which could never be recovered – for example, if a tenant disappeared from the area, or if he died penniless. Quite a large proportion of arrears was, therefore, lost for good: in Chester-le-Street, for example, out of a total of £7,423 outstanding at September 1930, £2,545 (or 34 per cent) had been written off by September 1940.[289]

Of course, some councils were better than others in preventing arrears from piling up and in clawing back the debts which did arise. Jarrow, for example, managed to recover 99.8 per cent of the rent due up to the end of 1927[290] and Durham City had no arrears at all by the middle of 1932.[291] In Blaydon, on the other hand, rent arrears stood for some time at an alarming £15,000.[292] The County Medical Officer of Health was moved to include in his report for 1925 a statement that 'in some districts in the county, housing schemes . . . have not involved any serious losses [whereas] in others the arrears of rent have reached very considerable sums, but whether this loss of money is a result of laxity or inefficient management is not for me to say.'[293] The official whose job it was to make such judgments was the District Auditor. In his report on the affairs of the Brandon Council, for example, he asserted that 'the Council is a Labour Council and I think has failed to take all possible and reasonable steps to collect rents from the tenants of the Council houses.'[294] The same auditor made similar claims about Hetton UDC in 1936, which prompted one councillor to remark that the matter had become 'a political vendetta'.[295]

The value of the auditor's claims can be assessed by a closer examination of the situation in the Brandon district. The main problem here was the poverty of the tenants: the majority were dependent on the mining industry and suffered badly because of local pit closures in the 1920s as well as in the 1926 dispute. Nevertheless, the Council had carried through its first eviction as early as 1923 and resolved to issue notice to all tenants more than £1 10s. in arrears.[296] Other sanctions included cutting off the electricity supply and seeking court orders for repayment[297] – although, as the Council's Clerk observed, the latter step usually meant a year before even the court costs were recovered.[298] The pressure of debt and of council sanctions forced many families out into cheaper accommodation, sometimes to another district: many council houses at New Brancepeth stood empty (following pit closures) and lost the district over 5 per cent of its total rental capacity.[299] From a total stock of 337 Addison Act houses, over 200 tenants had moved out by 1929 and were still being pursued for rent arrears.[300] As we have seen above, the Council was forced to condone sub-letting on a large scale, in order to bring rents more within the reach of tenants.[301] In 1930 the Council decided on a policy of giving every new tenant notice to quit on the first occasion a weekly payment was missed[302] and in 1931 it hired debt-collecting agents to recover arrears from former tenants.[303] The only policy for which the councillors could be criticized was their refusal to give tenancies to applicants from outside the district who were better able to pay the rent, on the grounds that 'they preferred to keep the houses for their own people who were of the working class, for whom the houses were intended.'[304] It was this approach, together with the Council's repeated requests for lower rents, that led the Ministry to remark that 'assisted scheme houses were not "poor law houses"'.[305]

It can be seen, then, that the Brandon Council did about as much as could reasonably be expected to prevent the accumulation of arrears. But the debts still mounted and stood in the way of any new housing schemes in the district for over ten years. There were undoubtedly cases – in several districts – where bad management crept in: the occasional instances of individual tenants owing over £50 (or, in Blaydon, sometimes over £100)[306] indicate poor control. It is also likely that councils were much more lenient than private landlords in their attitude towards tenants in arrears of rent. Evidence is not available to allow direct comparison with the private sector, but clearly the small landlord, whose operating margins (particularly if the rent was 'controlled') were very narrow, would be less favourably disposed to defaulting tenants than would a large institutional landlord like the District Council, which could easily bear a shortfall in receipts. The Council had also to apply other considerations than the purely commercial in its dealings with tenants. Thus while the Council's attitude to tenants laid off from work was generally sympathetic, institutions like the coal companies were more hard-hearted: for example, a miner's free colliery house would often become subject to a market rent while he was involved in a strike or lock-out, or when he was made redundant.[307] No doubt some tenants were inclined to take advantage of the Council's more lenient attitude; so that in opening a new estate at Chilton Moor the chairman of Houghton-le-Spring UDC appealed to the tenants, 'because you have a Labour Council that does not mean you have not to pay rent.'[308]

On the whole, councils did a reasonable job in dealing with a very difficult problem. There was little action they could take against tenants affected by the coal dispute, when in many districts the vast majority of the population was affected. It was difficult too, in areas of general economic depression, to find working-class tenants whose budgets would always be adequate to cover all of their liabilities. In the Sunderland Rural District, for example, even after the coal dispute (when 87 per cent of tenants had fallen in arrears)[309] the proportion of tenants in debt to the Council was still high in the 1930s – a fairly constant 40 per cent.[310] Even districts like Stockton, where the level of arrears was generally low, had problems on the poorer estates: in the slum rehousing estate of Mount Pleasant, mentioned in the previous section, arrears were three times higher than in the rest of the borough.[311] It is likely, therefore, that even in the more favourable conditions of the 1930s, when rents were lower and incomes more stable, the rent for a council house could still be beyond the comfortable reach of some of the poorest working-class families.

5 Conclusion

It might help first to point out some of the limitations in the general content of this paper, and to some extent of the thesis from which it is drawn. There is the obvious regional horizon, which means that however interesting the lessons that emerge – and County Durham is a particularly interesting region for the study of housing – they will stand up better when set alongside examples from other parts of the country. Equally obvious is the fact that no one region, nor any one local authority, operated in a vacuum outside the changeable atmosphere of central government policy. It was central government which directed a programme of subsidized public sector house building after the First World War and which changed its priorities in line with national politics. Local government put these policies into practice, with more or less enthusiasm for some aspects rather than others. The point of this study has been to look at how a certain group of local authorities carried out their responsibilities and how this affected their relationship with central government.

The other limitations are sectoral. The rise of the council house sector between the wars took place alongside a major structural change in the private sector – the decline of the private rented market and the growth of owner-occupation. A detailed analysis of this change, based on regional examples, would be valuable in helping to understand how the housing market came to be transformed from the turn of the century, when the vast majority of people rented their accommodation from a private landlord, to the present, with its sharp social division between owner-occupiers and public sector tenants. On a more down-to-earth level, readers will have noticed that this study has left out one area of housing activity into which many local authorities did put a lot of effort – the clearance of slums, which gathered momentum after the 1930 Act. This is a deliberate omission. Slum clearance has a longer and less controversial history, grounded in the public health movement of the mid-nineteenth century, than state-assisted house building by public authorities. There is plenty of work that could be done on slum clearance, but the rewards of study are probably more limited.

What this study has tried to show is that the policy of active intervention by the state was of vital importance in dealing with the particular housing problems of a very hard-pressed region. Indeed, the significant improvement in the housing conditions of County Durham between the wars sounds one cheering note in what is otherwise a dirge of decline and depression in that region. Market forces were responsible for pushing the county into economic decline after the First World War: equally, and especially in those circumstances of depression, they were not the mechanism for making good the serious deficiencies in the quality and the quantity of the housing stock. At the very least, the local implementation of national housing policy in County Durham demonstrated the principle that improvement and recovery in an economically declining region requires that the state should step in to make up for the failures of private enterprise.

NOTES

The status of a council in the local government hierarchy is referred to frequently in abbreviated form. These abbreviations, which were in common use before the 1974 reorganization, are as follows: CB County Borough; MB Municipal Borough; UDC Urban District Council; RDC Rural District Council.

Most references to the districts of Brandon and Byshottles, Houghton-le-Spring and Hetton-le-Hole have been shortened to Brandon, Houghton and Hetton.

1 Ministry of Health, *Housing Act, 1935. Report on the Overcrowding Survey in England and Wales, 1936*.
2 E.H. Hunt, *Regional Wage Variations in Britain, 1850–1914* (1973), 44–7.
3 For details of rents and wages in some of the major towns of the North-east in 1905 see Board of Trade, *Report of an Enquiry into Working Class Rents, Housing, Retail Prices and Standard Rate of Wages in the United Kingdom, 1908*, PP 1908 (Cd 3864), cvii. For an analysis of rents on the Durham coalfield in 1903 see R. Ryder, *Council House Building in County Durham, 1900–1939: the Local Implementation of National Policy* (M.Phil. thesis, University of Durham, 1979), 98–107.
4 See Ryder, *op. cit.*, 79–85.
5 *Report of the Royal Commission on the Coal Industry, 1925*. PP 1926 (Cmd 2600), xiv. About 49,000 of the houses were in County Durham.
6 Returns made by individual collieries in 1903, in DCRO: NCB 1/CO/86/511.
7 Land Enquiry Committee, *The Land: the Report of the Land Enquiry Committee* (2 vols, 1913–14), II, 199.
8 Further to n. 3 above, see A.L. Bowley and A.R. Burnett-Hurst, *Livelihood and Poverty* (1915), 140–5, for an account of rents in the mining town of Stanley.
9 A.G. Kenwood, 'Residential building activity in north eastern England, 1853–1913', *Manchester School of Economic and Social Studies*, xxxi (1963), 115–28.
10 Calculated from colliery returns in DCRO: NCB 1/CO/86/778.
11 Sunderland CB Council Minutes, 8 July 1903, SLS.
12 See Ryder, *op. cit.*, 124–32, for an analysis of the motivation behind council house-building schemes in this period.

13 Local Government Board, *Annual Reports* (1902–3 to 1913–14).
14 The most comprehensive sources for statistics on the number of houses built are the annual reports of the medical officer of health for the county and for the county boroughs. These can be supplemented by information in individual council and housing committee records. Nonetheless, there are some gaps: in particular, the figures for 1939 are not very reliable.
15 In this table the districts as constituted in 1939 have been arranged in seven groups. This has been done principally for the convenience of being able to examine wider regions of the county – each of a fairly homogeneous nature. There is also the question of the major boundary changes of 1935–7, which make it difficult to calculate certain statistics other than for wider groups of districts. Housing association dwellings have been included, as far as possible, in the figures for private house building.
16 The exhaustive overcrowding survey of 1936 was conducted on a basis entirely different from the census 'more than two persons to a room' standard.
17 D.C. Galleymore, *The Effects of Economic and Social Development on Local Government in an Urban District of North East England* (*Blaydon*) (MA thesis, University of Durham, 1970), 29.
18 E. Wilkinson, *The Town that was Murdered: The Life-Story of Jarrow* (1939), 247.
19 *Northern Echo*, 1 October 1935.
20 *North Mail*, 31 January 1934.
21 *Gateshead and District Municipal News*, June 1936.
22 These local authorities were the boroughs of Jarrow, Sunderland, West Hartlepool and Stockton; the urban districts of Consett, Leadgate, Stanley and Washington; and the rural districts of Easington and Sedgefield.
23 Stockton paid £15 extra per house (Housing Committee Minutes, 16 October 1923, CCRO); Leadgate £10 (Council Minutes, 13 November 1923, DDC); and Easington £37 (Housing Committee Minutes, 20 September 1923, DCRO: RD/Ea).
24 West Hartlepool CB Housing Committee Minutes, 5 February 1924, HBC.
25 Easington RDC Housing Committee Minutes, 26 July 1923, DCRO: RD/Ea.
26 *Ibid*; 26 April 1927.
27 Circular letter to local authorities, dated 23 December 1935, quoted in Whickham UDC, Housing Committee Report, 14 January 1936, GLS.
28 Details are in a report from the NEHA dated 12 July 1938 in PRO: HLG 52/826; and also in the *Sunderland Echo*, 29 March 1939.
29 NEHA report, dated 12 July 1938, in PRO: HLG 52/826.
30 North Eastern Housing Association, *The North Eastern Housing Association Ltd: 25 Years of Housing, 1935–1960* (1960), 24.
31 *Ibid.*, 11–13.
32 West Hartlepool CB Housing Committee Minutes, 23 March 1939, HBC.
33 South Shields CB Housing Committee Minutes, 14 January 1930, STLS.
34 Letter from Council to Ministry, dated 10 November 1927, in PRO: HLG 48/792.
35 The other elements in running costs were 'repair and maintenance' and 'management expenses', but little information is available about the scope for economy exercised in these areas. The maintenance budget was initially fixed at 15 per cent of the gross income from rents and the management budget at 5 per cent. (Ministry of Health, *Housing Accounts: Assisted Schemes of Local Authorities* (1921), xx.)
36 Easington RDC Housing Committee Minutes, 17 October 1922, DCRO: RD/Ea.
37 Stanley UD Council Minutes, 17 August 1920, DCRO: UD/Sta.
38 South Shields CB Finance Committee Minutes, 2 May 1922, STLS.
39 Easington RDC Housing Committee Minutes, 22 March and 20 April 1926, DCRO: RD/Ea. Shaw tempered his concern for housing reform with good business sense: Easington secured the loan by offering him $\frac{1}{4}$ per cent more in interest than the London County Council.
40 Stanhope UD Council Minutes, 21 February 1927, DCRO: RD/We.

41 Jarrow MB Housing Committee Minutes, 14 September 1922, T&WCRO: JRU.

42 Sedgefield RD Council Minutes, 16 September 1926, DCRO: RD/Se.

43 Annfield Plain UD Council Minutes, 17 August 1920, DCRO: UD/Sta. The coal company no doubt also saw this as a good public relations gesture.

44 Easington RDC Housing Committee Minutes, 13 October 1925, DCRO: RD/Ea.

45 See, for example, Washington UDC Housing Committee Minutes, 31 August 1926, T&WCRO: WGU, and Sedgefield RD Council Minutes, 5 August 1927, DCRO: RD/Se.

46 Hetton UDC Housing Committee Minutes, 22 November 1926, T&WCRO: HTU.

47 Minute dated 3 January 1928 by J. C. (later Sir John) Wrigley, then a principal at the Ministry of Health, in PRO: HLG 49/152.

48 Ministry of Health, *Annual Statements of Rates and Rateable Values in England and Wales*, 1913–44. The chief offenders were the urban districts of Chester-le-Street (on six occasions), Houghton, Brandon, Washington (four occasions each), Blaydon, Seaham Harbour, Spennymoor and Bishop Auckland (three occasions each). The lean years were mainly from 1926 to 1929.

49 See correspondence in PRO: HLG 48/54.

50 See Ministry of Health, *Annual Report*, 1927–28. The reason for this action was not so much the incompetence of the board as its alleged over-generosity to miners involved in the coal dispute.

51 Brandon UDC built 337 houses under the 1919 Act (Council Minutes, 4 February 1935, DCRO: UD/BB) and the product of a penny rate was £146 (*ibid.*, 3 September 1928).

52 In 1936, 15.8 per cent of families in Felling were living in overcrowded conditions, compared with 3.2 per cent in Darlington (Ministry of Health, *Housing Act, 1935. Report on the Overcrowding Survey in England and Wales*, 1936).

53 Preston Borough Council, *Rates Levied in Various Towns* (Preston, 1940).

54 In 1933 a Ministry of Labour report revealed that over 30 per cent of the insured population of Felling were unemployed: P.P. 1933–34 (Cmd 4728), XIII, 117.

55 Ministry of Health, *Statement of Rates and Rateable Values in England and Wales* (1938–39).

56 Ministry of Health, *Statement of Rates* (1920–40) and Preston Borough Council, *op. cit.* (1920–40).

57 This is on the basis that about 60,000 council houses were built in County Durham between the wars at an average density of ten houses to the acre. In addition, when the Second World War brought building to a halt, local authorities held a certain amount of undeveloped land – perhaps a further 10 per cent on the developed area.

58 This is on the basis of an average cost to local authorities of between £200 and £250 per acre purchased.

59 Jarrow Borough Engineer's report, July 1919, T&WCRO: JRU.

60 Tanfield UDC Housing Committee Minutes, 24 September 1919, DCRO: UD/Sta.

61 Letter dated 16 November 1921 in PRO: HLG 48/238.

62 Darlington CB, Report of Housing Committee, 9 May 1921, DCRO: CB/Da.

63 See, for example, conveyance details in the Statement made by Felling UDC in 1935 to the Royal Commission on Local Government on Tyneside, GLS.

64 Brandon UD Council Minutes, 11 August 1919, DCRO: UD/BB.

65 Darlington CB, Report of Housing Committee, 24 March 1920, *DCRO*: CB/Da.

66 Gateshead CB Housing Committee Minutes, 11 August 1919, 9 February 1925 and 13 April 1928, GLS.

67 Consett UD Council Minutes, 25 February 1919, DDC; Lanchester RD Council Minutes, 10 April 1919, DCRO: RD/La; Leadgate UD Council Minutes, 22 May 1919, DDC.

68 Letter dated 5 February 1919 in PRO: HLG 47/248.

69 Easington RDC Housing Committee Minutes, 19 December 1918, DCRO: RD/Ea.

70 *Ibid.*, 6 April 1920.

71 Darlington CB, Report of Housing Committee, 13 June 1919, DCRO: CB/Da.
72 *Ibid.*, 9 May 1921.
73 Sunderland RD Council Minutes, 20 March 1919, T&WCRO: SDR and *Sunderland Echo*, 21 March 1919.
74 Auckland RDC Housing Committee Minutes, 1 December 1919, DCRO: RD/Au.
75 Easington RDC Housing Committee Minutes, 19 December 1918 and 6 April 1920, DCRO: RD/Ea.
76 *Ibid.*, 1 June 1920.
77 Stanley UD Council Minutes, 8 June 1920 and 14 September 1926, DCRO: UD/Sta.
78 Stockton MB, Minutes of General Purposes Committee, 3 June and 22 July 1938, CCRO.
79 Darlington CB, Report of Housing Committee, 27 June 1922 and 13 September 1927, DCRO: CB/Da.
80 Brandon UD Council Minutes, 1 March 1920 and 4 August 1925, DCRO: UD/BB.
81 Jarrow Borough Engineer's report, July 1919 and February 1923, T&WCRO: JRU.
82 See, for example, South Shields CB Housing Committee Minutes, 30 November 1920, STLS.
83 Sunderland RD Council Minutes, 10 August 1920, T&WCRO: SDR.
84 Gateshead CB Housing Committee Minutes, 28 May 1920 and 11 June 1920, GLS.
85 See, for example, South Shields CB Housing Committee Minutes, 11 May 1920, STLS.
86 In the example of Sunderland RDC quoted above, the contract went to a small builder operating in the rural district instead of to the larger federated firms based in the borough itself. (Sunderland RD Council Minutes, *loc. cit.*)
87 Easington RDC managed to break its deadlock with the Sunderland and West Hartlepool federations by negotiating separately with a builder from Leeds (see Housing Committee Minutes for March 1920, DCRO: RD/Ea).
88 Stockton MB Housing Committee Minutes, 12 November 1920, CCRO. The same considerations had prompted the use of direct labour by Easington RDC (see Housing Committee Minutes, 6 April 1920, DCRO: RD/Ea).
89 Ministry of Health, *Housing*, 22 December 1919, 164.
90 Only the delegation from Stockton considered that the steel and concrete houses 'hardly appeared suitable' (Stockton MB Housing Committee Minutes, 21 November 1919, CCRO).
91 Minute dated 8 May 1920 in PRO: HLG 49/11. It was possible in the difficult conditions of 1920 for construction by traditional methods to take over a year.
92 *Ibid.*
93 Minute dated 14 May 1920 in PRO: HLG 49/11.
94 Chester-le-Street UDC Housing Committee Minutes, 1 October 1936, CDC.
95 See, for example, Easington RDC Housing Committee Minutes, 24 July 1919, DCRO: RD/Ea.
96 Barnard Castle UD Council Minutes, 8 April 1930, DCRO: UD/BC.
97 Darlington CB, Report of Housing Committee, 24 March 1920, DCRO: CB/Da, and the statement made by Ryton UDC to the Royal Commission on Local Government on Tyneside, July 1935, GLS.
98 Chester-le-Street RDC, Architect's report, 1 May 1924, CDC.
99 *Newcastle Journal*, 22 July 1932.
100 Hebburn UDC Housing Committee Minutes, 7 October 1920, T&WCRO: HBU.
101 See Hetton UDC Housing Committee Minutes, 18 May 1932, T&WCRO: HTU.
102 Easington RDC Housing Committee Minutes, 7 December 1920, DCRO: RD/Ea.
103 Gateshead CB Housing Committee Minutes, 24 January 1929, GLS.
104 *Durham County Advertiser*, 9 September 1932.
105 *North Mail*, 17 April 1919 and 3 July 1919.
106 Barnard Castle RD Council Minutes, 15 December 1920, DCRO: RD/BC.

107 South Shields CB Housing Committee Minutes, 10 August 1920, STLS.
108 Ministry of Health Memorandum to Housing Commissioners, No. 34, 21 August 1919, PRO: HLG 31/1.
109 West Hartlepool CB Housing Committee Minutes, 31 March 1920, HBC.
110 Seaham Harbour UDC, Report of Housing Committee, 8 June 1920, DCRO: UD/Sea.
111 Stockton MB Council Minutes, 7 October 1924, CCRO.
112 The following Councils are known definitely to have used direct labour at some point in the inter-war period: the boroughs of Gateshead, Jarrow, Sunderland, Stockton and West Hartlepool; the urban districts of Whickham, Felling, Hebburn, Blaydon, Benfieldside, Tanfield, Annfield Plain, Stanley, Chester-le-Street, Washington, Houghton, Seaham Harbour, Willington and Spennymoor; and the rural districts of Lanchester, Chester-le-Street, Houghton, Durham, Easington and Sedgefield.
113 Easington RDC Housing Committee Minutes, 11 October 1927, DCRO: RD/Ea.
114 Letter dated 7 November 1932 from the clerk of the Council, in PRO: HLG 49/152.
115 Felling UD Council Minutes, 3 August 1932, GLS.
116 Jarrow Borough Engineer's report for May 1926, T&WCRO: JRU.
117 Gateshead CB Housing Committee Minutes, 20 May 1927, GLS.
118 West Hartlepool UDC Housing Committee Minutes, 26 February 1924, HBC.
119 Washington UDC Housing Committee Minutes, 6 April 1926, T&WCRO: WGU.
120 Ministry of Health minute dated August 1926, in PRO: HLG 49/200.
121 Note of meeting, dated 21 May 1924, in PRO: HLG 48/49.
122 See, for example, minutes dated 6 April and 21 December 1927, in PRO: HLG 49/152.
123 Chester-le-Street UDC Housing Committee Minutes, 7 February 1935, CDC.
124 Felling UD Council Minutes, 4 April 1939, GLS.
125 Easington RDC Housing Committee Minutes, 24 August 1936, DCRO: RD/Ea.
126 Report of deputation to Ministry, in Easington RDC Housing Committee Minutes, 6 February 1936, DCRO: RD/Ea.
127 *Ibid.*
128 Borough Engineer's report for September 1933, T&WCRO: JRU.
129 In the case of savings under the Addison scheme it was, of course, the taxpayer who gained most.
130 *Gateshead and District Municipal News*, April 1930.
131 Gateshead CB Housing Committee Minutes, 30 September 1927, GLS.
132 Average of schemes in County Durham approved by the Local Government Board in 1913–14. (Local Government Board, *Annual Report*, 1913–14.)
133 *Report of the Departmental Committee on Questions of Building Construction in Connection with the Provision of Dwellings for the Working Classes in England, Wales and Scotland.* PP 1918 (Cd 9191), vii, 391.
134 For recent examples, see C. Powell, 'Fifty years of progress: the influence of the Tudor Walters report on British public authority housing' in *Built Environment* (1974), 532–5, and J. Burnett, *A Social History of Housing, 1815–1970* (1978).
135 *Manual on the Preparation of State-Aided Housing Schemes* (1920).
136 Powell, *op. cit.*, 533–4.
137 Ministry of Technology, *Houses and People: A Review of User Studies at the Building Research Station* (1966) 48–9.
138 *Ibid.*
139 See maps of urban growth in G.A. Nadur, *Some Aspects of the Urban Geography of Chester-le-Street and Houghton-le-Spring and Other Small Urban Settlements in North Durham* (Ph.D. thesis, University of Durham, 1967).
140 See B. T. Robson, *Urban Analysis: A Study of City Structure with Special Reference to Sunderland* (1969), 97, and D. A. Burgess, *Some Aspects of the Geography of the Ports of Sunderland, Seaham and the Hartlepools* (M.A. thesis, University of Durham, 1961), 59.

141 County Borough of Gateshead, *Gateshead Development Plan, 1951* (Gateshead, 1951), 59.
142 See R. Durant, *Watling: A Survey of Social Life on a New Housing Estate* (1939) for a study in the alienation of families on a London estate.
143 Even in 1938 the Ministry of Health might remind a council of the need for varied grouping and layout of house types in a particular scheme. (Letter from Ministry to Stanley UDC, dated 13 July 1938, in PRO: HLG 49/1120.)
144 For example, in Stockton's Addison Act estates 57 per cent of the houses were B3 and the remainder A3. (Stockton MB Housing Committee Minutes, 14 January 1927, CCRO.)
145 See, for example, Stockton MB Housing Committee Minutes, 10 December 1920, CCRO, and Easington RDC Housing Committee Minutes, 17 November 1932, DCRO: RD/Ea.
146 For example, in four estates built in the urban district of Felling between 1929 and 1933, 69 per cent of the houses were A2 and the remainder A3. (Felling UDC, Register of Houses 1929–33, GLS.)
147 Ministry of Health, *Housing*, 19 July 1919, 2.
148 Minute dated 3 October 1934, in PRO: HLG 49/1120.
149 Letter dated 19 December 1925, in PRO: HLG 48/227.
150 Durham County Unionist Association, circular No. 2, November 1923, DCRO: D/MCF 27.
151 Easington RDC Housing Committee Minutes, 9 December 1920, DCHO: RD/Ea.
152 *Gateshead and District Municipal News*, August 1929.
153 Copy of report by Medical Officer of Health to Houghton UDC, dated 16 May 1936, in PRO: HLG 48/792.
154 Letter to Ministry from Irene Ward, MP, dated 12 June 1935, in PRO: HLG 49/532.
155 *Ibid.*
156 Undated comments by Ministry staff, *ibid.*
157 *The Times*, 22 March 1934.
158 See, for example, Leadgate UD Council Minutes, 12 April 1921, DDC.
159 For example, Jarrow MB Housing Committee minutes, 16 June 1936, T&WCRO: JRU, and Felling UD Council Minutes, 8 June 1938, GLS.
160 Stanley UDC Housing Committee Minutes, 28 March 1933, DCRO: UD/Sta.
161 Hartlepool MB Housing Committee Minutes, 11 February 1932, HBC.
162 Statement made by Felling UDC to the Royal Commission on Local Government on Tyneside, dated November 1935, GLS.
163 Darlington CB, Report of Housing Committee, 27 June 1922; Report of Streets Committee, 20 January 1925. DCRO: CB/Da.
164 Chester-le-Street UDC Housing Committee Minutes, 19 May 1935, CDC.
165 One example may be found in the Easington RDC Housing Committee Minutes, 7 September 1933, DCRO: RD/Ea.
166 *Durham County Advertiser*, 5 July 1935. The district rent collector, even though he had no part in selecting tenants, was also solicited for support: he occasionally received the odd ten-shilling note through the post. (*Ibid.*, 6 September 1935.)
167 Easington RDC Housing Committee Minutes, 31 August 1921, DCRO: RD/Ea.
168 *Evening World*, 5 December 1931.
169 Local election poster, GLS: accession no. 66497.
170 *Gateshead & District Municipal News*, October 1931.
171 Commons written answer, *Parliamentary Debates*, 5th series, vol. 121, col. 943, 19 November 1919; and *Housing*, 8 December 1919, 164.
172 Hebburn UDC Housing Committee Minutes, 2 May 1921, T&WCRO: HBU.
173 Jarrow MB Housing Committee Minutes, 10 November 1921, T&WCRO: JRU.
174 Gateshead CB Housing Committee Minutes, 28 December 1920, GLS.

175 Felling UD Council Minutes, 3 November 1920, GLS.
176 Ryton UD Council Minutes, 30 June 1920, GLS; Easington RDC Housing Committee Minutes, 16 September 1920, DCRO: RD/Ea; Sedgefield RD Council Minutes, 26 August 1921, DCRO: RD/Se.
177 Darlington CB Housing Committee Minutes, 15 June 1926, DCRO: CB/Da.
178 Washington UDC Housing Committee Minutes, 2 September 1925, T&WCRO: WGU.
179 Ibid.
180 Darlington CB Housing Committee Minutes, 11 December 1936, DCRO: CB/Da.
181 Ibid.
182 Sunderland RD Council Minutes, 15 October 1935, T&WCRO: SDR.
183 Felling UD Council Minutes, 2 November 1921, GLS.
184 Hetton UDC Housing Committee Minutes, 11 February 1924, T&WCRO: HTU.
185 West Hartlepool CB Housing Committee Papers, 17 November 1932, HBC.
186 Annual Report of the Medical Officer of Health for Sunderland, 1934, SLS.
187 Annual Report of the Medical Officer of Health for South Shields, 1934, STLS.
188 Gateshead CB Housing Committee Minutes, 4 October and 22 November 1934, GLS, and Gateshead Herald, November 1937 issue.
189 Sunderland RD Council Minutes, 28 July 1931, T&WCRO: SDR.
190 Hetton UD Council Minutes, 14 February 1928, T&WCRO: HTU.
191 Burnett, op. cit., 233. His conclusion is based on surveys of six major LCC estates in the 1930s, details of which may be found in Durant, op. cit., 124.
192 Easington RDC Housing Committee Minutes, 14 February 1922, DCRO: RD/Ea.
193 Ibid., 26 January 1927.
194 Darlington CB Housing Committee Minutes, 17 January 1928, DCRO: CB/Da. Crook UDC was also forced to advertise for families to fill its parlour houses (Housing Committee Minutes, 22 November 1927, DCRO: UD/CW) and South Shields was forced to split some of its B4 houses into three-room flats (Housing Committee Minutes, 20 November 1928, STLS).
195 West Hartlepool CB Housing Committee Minutes, 23 March 1933, HBC.
196 Stockton MB Housing Committee Minutes, 10 September 1920, CCRO.
197 A copy is retained in STLS.
198 For example, Gateshead CB Housing Committee Minutes, 21 June 1923, GLS.
199 Washington UDC Housing Committee Minutes, 13 September 1927, T&WCRC: WGU.
200 Easington RDC Housing Committee Minutes, 6 March 1923, DCRO: RD/Ea.
201 Washington UDC Housing Committee Minutes, 1 November 1926, T&WCRO: WGU.
202 Chester-le-Street RDC Housing Committee Minutes, 7 August 1924, CDC.
203 Consett UDC Housing Committee Minutes, 31 March 1932, DDC.
204 Gateshead & District Municipal News, March 1936.
205 Ibid., December 1928.
206 Ibid., March 1936.
207 See, for example, Stanley UD Council Minutes, 21 February 1922, DCRO: UD/Sta.
208 Washington UDC Housing Committee Minutes, 12 July 1926, T&WCRO: WGU.
209 Ministry of Health, Housing, 19 July 1919, 2.
210 Hetton UDC Housing Committee Minutes, 18 October 1938, T&WCRO: HTU.
211 Easington RDC Housing Committee Minutes, 28 November 1922, DCRO: RD/Ea.
212 Ibid., 25 May 1922.
213 See, for example, several instances in the Hetton UDC Housing Committee Minutes for 1927, T&WCRO: HTU.
214 Copy of report dated 8 December 1924 in PRO: HLG 48/367.
215 Ibid.
216 Easington RDC Housing Committee Minutes, 23 February 1926 and 25 February 1930, DCRO: RD/Ea.

217 Hetton UDC Housing Committee Minutes, 23 January 1931, T&WCRO: HTU.
218 This compares quite favourably with the Leadgate area, where rents paid by sub-tenants were said to range from 4s. to 10s. per week. (Leadgate UD Council Minutes, 14 April 1925, DDC.)
219 Hetton UDC Housing Committee Minutes, 23 January 1931, T&WCRO: HTU.
220 Ministry of Health, *Housing Act, 1935. Report on the Overcrowding Survey in England and Wales, 1936.* The criteria used in this survey to determine overcrowding were far more refined than the earlier 'two-to-a-room' standard and the results were expressed in terms of families, rather than persons, overcrowded.
221 Hetton UDC Housing Committee Minutes, 22 December 1930 and 26 January 1931, T&WCRO: HTU.
222 Easington RDC Housing Committee Minutes, 20 May 1930, DCRO: RD/Ea.
223 Brandon UD Council Minutes, 6 November 1922, DCRO: UD/BB.
224 *Ibid.*, 6 September 1926.
225 Ministry of Health note of a meeting with a deputation of Brandon councillors in November 1930, in PRO: HLG 48/54.
226 Brandon UD Council Minutes, 5 November 1934, DCRO: UD/BB, and Willington UD Council Minutes, 9 July 1935, DCRO: UD/CW.
227 Ministry of Health, *Annual Report*, 1919–20. As with the theory behind rent control in the private sector, the Government's belief was that 'normal' market arrangements could gradually be resumed as economic conditions stabilized after the war.
228 Stockton MB Housing Committee Minutes, 28 June 1920, CCRO.
229 Darlington CB, Report of Housing Committee, 9 May 1921, DCRO: CB/Da.
230 Ministry of Health memorandum dated 9 August 1920, in PRO: 48/13.
231 Rents of 17s. per week for B3 houses in Sunderland were fixed in 1920 and were kept up for several years. (Sunderland CB Council Minutes, 13 October 1920, SLS.)
232 Hetton UDC Housing Committee Minutes, 23 May 1923, T&WCRO: HTU.
233 Copies of Ministry of Health from D89, in PRO: HLG 48/118 (Hebburn); 48/70 (Consett); 48/69 (Benfieldside); 48/123 (Houghton RD); and in South Shields CB Housing Committee Minutes, 20 October 1919, STLS, and Ryton UD Council Minutes, 8 October 1919, GLS.
234 Board of Trade, *Report of an Enquiry into Working-Class Rents and Retail Prices, together with the Rates of Wages in Certain Occupations in Industrial Towns in the United Kingdom*, P.P. 1913 (Cd 6955), LXVI, 393.
235 Easington RDC Housing Committee Minutes, 28 September 1920, DCRO: RD/Ea.
236 *Ibid.*, 26 July 1921.
237 Auckland RDC Housing Committee Minutes, 23 October 1922, DCRO: RD/Au.
238 Annfield Plain UD Council Minutes, 16 January 1923, DCRO: UD/Sta.
239 Summary of council house rents as at April 1924 in various districts, in Gateshead CB Housing Committee Minutes, 1 May 1924, GLS. The mining districts in question were Stanley, Tanfield, Chester-le-Street, South Shields RD, Brandon, Crook, Willington and Shildon.
240 Summary of rents in Jarrow Borough Engineer's report for July 1921, T&WCRO: JRU.
241 Summary of rents in Gateshead CB Housing Committee Minutes, 20 July 1922, GLS.
242 Summary of rents, *ibid.*, 1 May 1924.
243 Hetton UDC Housing Committee Minutes, 18 February 1924, T&WCRO: HTU.
244 *Ibid.*, 23 February 1925.
245 Brandon UD Council Minutes, 28 February 1927, DCRO: UD/BB.
246 It is worth noting that the Ministry did eventually agree to a $12\frac{1}{2}$ per cent reduction in rents – but only in 1931, when most of the damage had been done (*ibid.*, 4 May 1931).
247 Sunderland RD Council Minutes, 8 May 1928, T&WCRO: SDR.
248 *Ibid.*, 5 June 1928.
249 *Sunderland Echo*, 6 November 1929.
250 Sunderland RD Council Minutes, 21 October 1930, T&WCRO: SDR.

251 *Ibid.*, 13 January 1931.
252 Report of South Shields RDC to Durham County Council, 1930, DCRO: CC/H/90.
253 G.C.M. M'Gonigle and J. Kirby, *Poverty and Public Health* (1936).
254 *Ibid.*, 108–13.
255 *Ibid.*, 117–18.
256 *Ibid.*, 120.
257 Annual Report of the Medical Officer of Health for West Hartlepool, 1931, WHR.
258 Seaham Harbour UD Council Minutes, 27 October 1936, DCRO: UD/Sea.
259 *Ibid.*
260 Consett UDC Housing Sub-committee Minutes, 17 December 1940, DDC.
261 Gateshead CB Housing Committee Minutes, 5 January 1933, GLS.
262 Felling UDC, Register of 1930 Act Houses (2 vols), GLS.
263 Gateshead CB, Report of Letting Sub-Committee, 12 September 1929, GLS.
264 Calculated from Ministry of Health, *Rents of Houses and Flats owned by Local Authorities* (*England and Wales*), 1937. The average in the rural districts of Durham was 5s. 4½d. per week, in the urban districts and municipal boroughs 5s. 11d., and in the county boroughs 6s. 6½d. – all exclusive of rates. These rents were 10 to 12 per cent lower than for the rest of England and Wales.
265 This figure was enshrined in the report by Political and Economic Planning, *Housing England* (1934) and was confirmed by the experience of the Unemployment Assistance Board: B.B. Gilbert, *British Social Policy, 1914–1939* (1970), 201.
266 Exceptionally, under the Addison Act, the cost would be sustained by the Exchequer, but the Ministry of Health had to be satisfied by the District Auditor that all reasonable efforts had been made to recover the debt.
267 Sunderland RD Council Minutes, 16 October 1934, T&WCRO: SDR. The total amount owed to the Council had risen from £432 to £4,199.
268 *Ibid.*, 28 July 1931.
269 Hetton UDC Housing Committee Minutes, 23 November 1925 and 24 January 1927, T&WCRO: HTU.
270 Darlington CB Housing Committee Minutes, 19 April 1932, DCRO: CB/Da.
271 These estimates have been calculated from county-wide summaries given in Sunderland RD Council minutes for 15 September 1931 and 11 December 1934, T&WCRO: SDR.
272 Chester-le-Street UDC Housing Committee Minutes, 14 November 1940, CDC.
273 Easington RDC Housing Committee Minutes, 26 June 1923, DCRO: RD/Ea.
274 *Ibid.*, 19 December 1929, 9 January and 21 January 1930.
275 *Northern Echo*, 13 June 1936.
276 Sunderland RD Council Minutes, 22 July 1924, T&WCRO: SDR.
277 *Ibid.*, 19 August 1924.
278 See, for example, Stanley UD Council Minutes, 24 July 1928, DCRO: UD/Sta; Brandon UD Council Minutes, 4 February 1929, DCRO: UD/BB; and Sunderland RD Council Minutes, 31 December 1939, T&WCRO: SDR.
279 Auckland RDC Housing Committee Minutes, 28 November 1933 (including reference to Blaydon UDC) DCRO: RD/Au; Felling UD Council Minutes, 5 July 1933, GLS; Stanley UD Council Minutes, 24 July 1928, DCRO: UD/Sta; and Washington UDC Housing Committee Minutes, 29 May 1934, T&WCRO: WGU.
280 Auckland RDC Housing Committee Minutes, 28 November 1933, DCRO: RD/Au.
281 Hetton UDC Housing Committee Minutes, 6 November 1933, T&WCRO: HTU.
282 Chester-le-Street UDC Housing Committee Minutes, 19 July 1932, CDC.
283 Stanley UD Council Minutes, 12 July 1927, DCRO: UD/Sta.
284 The first recorded instance of such an arrangement in County Durham was a payment made to Sunderland RDC by the Silksworth miners' lodge in 1912. (Sunderland RD Council Minutes, 18 May 1912, T&WCRO: SDR.)
285 Easington RDC Housing Committee Minutes, 14 June 1927, DCRO: RD/Ea.
286 Sunderland RD Council Minutes, 31 January 1933, T&WCRO: SDR.

287 See, for example, Brandon UD Council Minutes, 7 November 1927, DCRO: UD/BB.
288 Sunderland RD Council Minutes, 16 October 1934, T&WCRO: SDR.
289 A further 49 per cent had been recovered direct from tenants and ex-tenants; the remaining 17 per cent was still being fought over (Chester-le-Street UDC Housing Committee Minutes, 16 October 1941, CDC).
290 Jarrow MB Housing Committee Minutes, 19 January 1928, T&WCRO: JRU.
291 *Sunderland Echo*, 2 June 1932.
292 *North Mail*, 17 July 1929, and *Northern Echo*, 15 July 1932.
293 Annual Report of the Medical Officer of Health to Durham County Council for 1925, DCRO.
294 District Auditor's report, dated January 1928, in PRO: HLG 48/54.
295 *Northern Echo*, 26 May 1936.
296 Brandon UD Council Minutes, 5 February 1923, DCRO: UD/BB.
297 *Ibid.*, 4 June 1923.
298 Note of meeting with council deputation, dated November 1930, in PRO: HLG 48/54.
299 Report by Clerk of Council to Ministry of Health, dated April 1930, *ibid*.
300 Brandon UD Council Minutes, 4 February 1929, DCRO: UD/BB.
301 See notes 223–6 above.
302 Brandon UD Council Minutes, 2 June 1930, DCRO: UD/BB.
303 *Ibid.*, 1 June 1931.
304 Note of meeting with deputation, dated October 1934, in PRO: HLG 48/54.
305 Note of meeting with deputation, dated November 1930, *ibid*.
306 *Northern Echo*, 6 October 1932.
307 See, for example, the Holmside and South Moor Collieries Ltd 'house rents book', 1928–31 (DCRO: NCB 3/69). This shows that rents of between 4s. 6d. and 5s. 10d. per week were charged for a total of 127 houses in the Stanley and Annfield Plain area.
308 *Northern Echo*, 10 September 1936.
309 Sunderland RD Council Minutes, 10 February 1931, T&WCRO: SDR.
310 *Ibid.*, 15 October 1935 and 31 December 1939.
311 Stockton MB General Purposes Committee Minutes, 11 November 1938 and 5 May 1939, CCRO.

Council housing in Leeds, 1919–39: social policy and urban change

ROBERT FINNIGAN

Council housing in Leeds, 1919–39: social policy and urban change

ROBERT FINNIGAN

1 Introduction

The growth of council housing is undoubtedly one of the major themes in recent urban history, for it is through this phenomenon that the development of the Welfare State has left its clearest impression on the modern British city. This paper aims to elucidate this theme by examining the housing policies pursued by Leeds City Council during the inter-war years. It is based on the contents of an M.Phil. thesis, entitled 'Housing Policy in Leeds, 1919–39', presented to the University of Bradford in 1981 as the result of postgraduate research carried out under the supervision of Professor Derek Fraser.[1]

The paper is concerned primarily with two aspects of housing policy in inter-war Leeds: the evolution of council housing as a social service and the impact of this process on the city's environment. Throughout, these issues are discussed within the context of national housing policy, to which any local study of this subject must refer. At this point, however, additional influences on the development of council housing in the locality need to be introduced to the framework.[2] The initial requirement is an analysis of the housing situation in Leeds during the early part of this century, because it is clear that differences in local housing conditions create a pattern of housing problems which makes some central government initiatives more relevant than others to individual housing authorities. Secondly, some knowledge is required of the local political system, given its role as the link between national policies and local problems, and the ability of local politics to affect the implementation of housing policies. Thirdly, the structure and performance of the local economy after 1919 form a general background against which political change and the evolution of housing policy should be set. Therefore, the following introduction focuses on Leeds' housing problems before the local authority emerged as a major house-builder and landlord, and on the city's economic and political history during the inter-war years.

In 1914 Leeds was the fifth largest city in England with some 450,000 inhabitants. Since the first census of 1801 the city's population had increased eightfold, for Victorian Leeds became one of the country's main industrial and commercial centres.[3] During the nineteenth and early twentieth centuries house building in Leeds was dominated by the construction of 'back-to-backs', until these became a distinctive feature of life in Leeds.[4] By 1914 there were more than 78,000 back-to-backs in Leeds, representing 71 per cent of the city's total housing stock.[5] To many contemporary housing reformers the back-to-back was, by definition, an unfit dwelling but in Leeds' case, certainly, it needs to be said that this was 'a general type of housing which embraced important variations in the standard and density of groups of dwellings.'[6] In effect there were three broad categories of back-to-back housing in Leeds at this time.[7] First, there were 14,000 so-called 'modern' back-to-backs which had been built since the 1890s. These had between three and five rooms (including a scullery) and were provided with a fixed bath and private w.c., neither of which were included in earlier versions of the back-to-back. Externally the modern variety were easily distinguishable by their small front gardens or forecourts. The second group comprised 29,000 houses of 'intermediate' vintage, dating from the 1870s and 1880s. These were built in the wake of an 1866 bye-law which limited the development of back-to-backs to blocks of no more than eight houses, each one opening directly on to the street; along the length of the street the blocks of houses were separated from one another by yards containing the toilets. In the third, and largest category, were some 35,000 dwellings, built in long, unbroken rows or enclosed courts, of which 14,000 had only two rooms. Whereas the modern back-to-backs were built at about 40 dwellings per acre, and the intermediates at between 50 and 60, in some districts the oldest type reached densities of 70 to 80 per acre; they dated from the pre-bye-law era when the rate of population growth in Leeds had been most rapid.

Living conditions in a Leeds back-to-back before the First World War therefore varied considerably, depending on the age of the dwelling, the amenities it offered and its location within the city – all these factors being inter-related. Few people at that time considered either the intermediate or modern types to be bad housing, for they provided a reasonable standard of accommodation, in terms of living space and sanitation, and were to be found mainly in those districts developed in the later nineteenth century when the pace of urbanization slowed. However, attitudes towards the remaining 35,000 back-to-backs were more ambivalent. On the one hand it was felt that Leeds' working class benefited from the prevalence of the back-to-back because it was a separate, single-family dwelling. As a director of the Leeds Permanent Building Society told the Building Societies' Association annual meeting in 1909, 'We prefer in Leeds that a working man should have his house to himself, that he should not take in lodgers, and that he should not live in flats. We prefer he should have his little house to himself.'[8] But it could not be denied that unhealthy and altogether undesirable environmental conditions existed in the working-class areas of central Leeds where the 'ancient type' of back-to-back was the standard form of housing. Indeed, between 1905 and 1914 the City Council actively pursued a policy to deal with what its Medical Officer of Health considered to be the worst examples of this problem. In this period more than 1,600 slums were demolished in what amounted to a process of 'nuisance removal', for as yet the main political parties remained convinced that house building was one enterprise in which the municipality should not become involved.[9] Under both Conservative and Liberal control the Council would sanction neither subsidized housing for the poor nor the building of houses to let at an economic rent for fear of undermining the position of the private landlord. Before 1914, therefore, council housing in Leeds comprised a mere three dozen dwellings,[10] built on the few occasions when the Local Government Board insisted that the Council replace properties included in its slum clearance schemes, or those demolished to make way for street improvements or redevelopment. When these three categories are added together the total number of houses demolished in Leeds between 1895 and 1914 exceeds 2,300.[11]

Leeds' pre-war policy of clearing insanitary housing while making every effort to avoid municipal involvement in house building was condemned by Labour as 'a gigantic conspiracy of the powers that be acting on behalf of the Property Owners' Association.'[12] Allegedly, the property interest on the Council sought to create a shortage of working-class housing and thus enable landlords to charge higher rents. Clearly, not every landlord approved of slum clearance and the liquidation of his investment, but equally Leeds did experience the beginnings of a housing shortage and higher working-class rents in the years immediately before the First World War. Since the 1890s Labour had argued in favour of municipal house building, as well as slum clearance, 'in order that the people displaced by the removal of unfit dwellings may not be driven to create more crowded districts.'[13] In the absence of a rehousing policy greater overcrowding was, indeed, the corollary to slum clearance in Edwardian Leeds. Between 1901 and 1911 the city's population increased by 4,077 or 3.9 per cent, compared to 16,582 or 16.7 per cent in the previous inter-censal period.[14] Despite the sharp decline in population growth after the turn of the century house building remained buoyant; at 15,654 the increase in the number of houses between 1901 and 1911 was only 531 less than that registered between 1891 and 1901.[15] However, the 1911 census also showed that 48,057 people in Leeds were living in overcrowded conditions (i.e. at a density of more than two persons per room), representing 11.2 per cent of the city's total population, whereas ten years before the corresponding figures had been 43,239 and 10.1 per cent.[16] Further evidence of increasing demands on the city's housing stock is to be found in the emergence of rent as a political issue. Historically, rent levels in Leeds were not high in comparison to other areas of the country. When the Board of Trade surveyed working-class rents in 73 English and Welsh towns in 1908 it listed 31 where they were higher than those charged in Leeds, but only 14 where the general level of prices was higher.[17] In 1908 the weekly rent of a back-to-back in Leeds ranged from 3s. for some of the oldest two-room types up to 6s. 6d. for examples of the modern variety.[18] By 1914, however, Labour were claiming that houses in Leeds were not only more overcrowded than in the recent past but also more expensive.[19] Following rent increases imposed during 1913 a further rise of 6d. per week in January 1914 occasioned the formation of a Tenants' Defence League to resist this latest attempt by the landlords to 'exploit' the city's working class.[20] From then until the outbreak of the war the League's activities centred on a campaign to persuade the City Council to ease the housing situation by adopting a programme of municipal house building, but this made little impression on a body still wedded to the view that the provision of working-class housing was a matter either for commercial investors or for those motivated by philanthropy.[21]

When the trend towards higher rents is considered alongside the housing situation and the condition of the slums it is clear that the major components of Leeds' post-war housing problem were already in being in 1914. The war and its aftermath served to exacerbate these difficulties and to transform political attitudes towards the housing question. During the last year of the war housing became as important a political issue locally as it was at the national level. In September 1918 a conference was held in Leeds to discuss the prospects for housing after the war at which Seabohm Rowntree told the audience he 'did not think the Prime Minister was putting it too strongly when he proclaimed housing to be the most urgent problem that awaited solution.'[22] All shades of local opinion, from the Chamber of Commerce to the Trades Council, shared this view of the housing problem's significance at the end of 1918.[23] Meanwhile nearly 80,000 Leeds men were waiting to leave the armed forces and return home to a 'Land Fit for Heroes'. To that end the City Council had already made preparations for a municipal housing scheme, mindful, too, of the imminent prospect of government housing legislation. The first part of the scheme comprised 2,000 houses and was approved by the Council in July 1918 by 68 votes to three. Before the vote was taken the Conservative leader of the Council, Alderman Charles Wilson, had stated that 'it was time to get out of the old rut. . . . they ought to go through with this scheme regardless of any cost.'[24] Wilson was no doubt thinking of the generous financial assistance the city would receive from the Exchequer, but nevertheless his remark, and the size of the majority in favour of municipal house building, contrast sharply with the ethos which had long prevailed in Leeds politics.

After the First World War council housing in Leeds developed as the city's political system passed through a period of transition. The municipal elections held in November 1919 were the first for six years, and as a result of franchise reform in the previous year there were now 184,580 voters in Leeds, more than twice the size of the electorate in 1914.[25] The election results confirmed the trends which had been apparent before the war, namely the dominance of council politics by the Conservatives and declining Liberal representation caused by a rise in Labour's support and the defection of traditional Liberal voters to the Conservatives.[26] Labour emerged in 1919 as the second largest party on the Council with 22 members, compared to 29 Conservatives and 17 Liberals.[27] This pattern was to be repeated annually until 1926, leaving the Conservatives as a minority administration supported by Liberal votes. In 1926 the process which transformed the party structure of the City Council was accelerated, due to Wilson's growing impatience with the need for co-operation with the Liberals. In June of that year he offered important committee posts to certain Liberal councillors as an inducement for them to join the Conservative Party. At a time of renewed divisions within the Liberal Party at national level five councillors accepted Wilson's offer.[28] While this move ultimately led to the eclipse of the Liberals in Leeds the short-term consequences were not altogether favourable for the Conservative administration. Angered by the defections the Liberal Party decided on a comprehensive electoral campaign and fielded candidates in 13 of Leeds' 17 municipal wards in November 1926. Although they lost a third of their 1925 vote the Liberals' action produced a large number of three-cornered contests which split the anti-Labour vote. Thus, Labour gained ten seats in 1926 and following the aldermanic elections became the largest group on the Council.[29]

The events of 1926 represent a watershed in the history of inter-war Leeds because thereafter local politics polarized into a two-party system once again, with the Liberals replaced by Labour as the Conservatives' main challengers for power. Between 1926 and 1939 there were two periods of Labour control, 1927–30 and 1933–5, but for the most part the city's municipal administration remained in Conservative hands. The fact that Leeds did not become a Labour stronghold during the inter-war years must to some extent be a reflection on the nature of the city's economic development in this period. Leeds was unlike many other established industrial centres in that it enjoyed a degree of relative prosperity between the wars. The level of unemployment, for instance, fluctuated in line with the general trend but was consistently below the national average. In 1932, when unemployment in the United Kingdom stood at 22.1 per cent of the the insured workforce, the rate in Leeds was 20.4 per cent, at a time when the rate was three or four times the national average in some localities.[30] Leeds undoubtedly benefited from the breadth of its manufacturing base and from the success of its clothing industry in particular; between 1921 and 1938 the number of workers in Leeds' clothing factories more than doubled from 25,000 to 51,000, and of these 70 per cent were female.[31] Moreover, Leeds prospered with its development as an important business and administrative centre. In 1931 the proportion of the city's total workforce employed in manufacturing was 55.7 per cent compared to 64.5 per cent twenty years before.[32] After 1918 Leeds acted as a 'provincial capital city' providing a range of services, in both the private and public sectors, for a large part of northern England.[33]

It is possible that the vitality of the Leeds economy at this time also assisted in bringing to a halt the outflow of population from the city. The extent of out-migration from Leeds between 1901 and 1921 is unclear because of the changes made to the city's administrative boundaries during this period. If Leeds is defined as the area governed by the City Council in 1931, then the city probably lost upwards of 19,000 people on the balance of migration between 1901 and 1921.[34] During the next two decades that trend was reversed. Taking the administrative boundaries used by the 1931 census, the population of Leeds increased by 33,878 between 1921 and 1939, from 463,122 to 497,000. Of this increase 20 per cent resulted from a net gain of 6,833 by migration.[35] The revival of in-migration provided some compensation for a declining rate of natural population increase in Leeds after 1918. While the local death rate changed little, from an annual average of 13.7 between 1920 and 1929, to 13.2 between 1930 and 1939, the birth rate fell sharply from 18.5 in the 1920s to 14.8 in the 1930s.[36]

From being an essentially Victorian city at the end of the First World War Leeds had evolved into a recognizably modern city by 1939. Between the wars the structure of the city's political and economic base underwent fundamental changes, along the lines outlined above. Moreover, this was a period which saw rapid environmental change despite the fact that Leeds' population was growing more slowly than at any time since the onset of industrialization. Central to this process was housing policy, and in particular the intervention of the local authority in the housing market. It is the growth of council housing between 1919 and 1939 and its implications for the development of the social and physical environment in Leeds which forms the subject matter in the remainder of this chapter.

2 Council housing and social policy

Hitherto the history of council housing between the wars has been written mainly from a national rather than a local viewpoint. This emphasis is understandable since the phenomenon itself represents the sum total of localized responses to policies which were determined centrally by government. Although local authorities were consulted at various times during the making of national housing policy, this process

always related to detailed matters rather than issues of principle, which all govern-
ments considered to be 'non-negotiable'.[37] Thus, any local case-study in the history
of council housing is concerned with the implementation of national policies at the
local level, and the effect of these policies on housing conditions in the locality.[38] In
this section, therefore, attention will focus on the changing role of the local authority
on the supply side of the housing market in Leeds, and on the pattern of housing
consumption created by the successive policies pursued between 1919 and 1939.

Table 3.   Council dwellings in Leeds, 1933 and 1939

Housing Act	Nov. 1933	Sept. 1939
Addison, 1919	3,329	3,329
Chamberlain, 1923	430	430
Wheatley, 1924	5,521	5,733
Greenwood, 1930	144	8,588
1938	—	1,845
Local Acts	604	643
	10,028	20,710

Table 4.   House building in Leeds, 1919–40

years ending 31 March	total completions	municipal total	municipal av./p.a.	private total	private av./p.a.
1920–26	6,114	3,786	541	2,328	333
1927–33	16,037	5,902	843	10,135	1,448
1934–40	32,200	11,692	1,670	20,508	2,930
	54,351	21,380		32,971	

In the twenty years up to September 1939 Leeds built more than 20,000 council
dwellings, and ranked as one of the 'big five' provincial housing authorities which
together accounted for 20 per cent of all council housing built in England and Wales
during the inter-war years.[39] The dwellings built in Leeds were the product of two
distinct periods of development separated by the political events of November 1933
when the election of a Labour Council led to a reorientation of housing policy towards
'welfare housing' and away from 'general needs', along the lines already laid down by
the National Government's slum clearance drive. Table 3 shows the composition of
the municipal housing stock, in both 1933 and 1939, in relation to the various subsidy
schemes of the inter-war years.[40] By 1939 council houses represented some 14 per
cent of Leeds' total housing stock, while a further 21 per cent was accounted for by
dwellings which had been built by private enterprise during the previous twenty
years. Over a slightly longer period, from April 1919 to March 1940, total house
building in Leeds amounted to more than 54,000 dwellings; the balance over time of
the contributions from both municipal and private enterprise is shown in table 4.[41]
Clearly, for the first seven years after the end of the First World War the City Council
was the major supplier of new housing in Leeds, in itself an unprecedented situation.

After 1926, however, private enterprise reverted to that role, partly as a result of the Chamberlain subsidy, introduced in 1923, which helped to finance the building of 5,269 houses in Leeds during the following six years.[42] Thus, whereas the Council built 61.9 per cent of all new dwellings between 1919 and 1926, the proportion fell to 36.8 per cent between 1926 and 1933, although in absolute terms the number of houses it provided rose by more than 2,000. Overall during the era of building for 'general needs' from 1919 to 1933 the Council accounted for 43.7 per cent of all house building in Leeds. Given that taxpayers and ratepayers contributed towards the cost of a further 24 per cent in the private sector, nearly seven out of every ten new houses built in the city at this time were subsidized to some extent by the public purse. After 1933 local authorities ceased to build for the purpose of increasing the housing stock, and their efforts were concentrated on a policy of 'welfare housing' through the slum clearance drive and, later, the Overcrowding Act of 1935: measures which were consolidated in the Housing Act of 1938. In Leeds this was effectively a period of housing renewal as far as municipal enterprise was concerned, for although nearly 11,700 council dwellings were completed between April 1934 and March 1940 at the same time the slum clearance programme resulted in the demolition of 11,132 houses.[43] As table 4 indicates, however, the private sector achieved a rate of building which more than compensated for the ending of council house building for 'general needs'. Between 1933 and 1940 private house builders alone provided 4,000 more dwellings than the combined total of municipal and private enterprise output during the previous seven years.

The changing role of local authorities in the housing market between 1919 and 1939 was essentially a function of developments in national housing policy, in so far as the various subsidy schemes of the period dictated the priorities in council housing. But although local authorities acted within a common framework of housing legislation and Ministry of Health policy, individually their conduct was also governed by factors such as political circumstances in the locality and the attitude of council officers.[44] In Leeds it is clear that such influences played an important part in determining the scale of council house building during the inter-war years. As we have seen, the Conservatives were the dominant party in Leeds politics at this time and their attitude towards council housing had a significant impact on its development. Initially they were caught up in the general post-war enthusiasm for public housing, once it became certain that the Exchequer would effectively foot the bill. In 1920 the Ministry of Health agreed that Leeds should build a total of 5,800 Addison houses,[45] but as table 3 indicates only 57 per cent of these were eventually completed. During the Addison era Leeds shared the problems of cost inflation, delays and shortages which beset house building in general, and which ultimately undermined the Addison scheme itself.[46] Locally this experience led to a re-emergence of traditional Conservative hostility towards municipal involvement in housing, on the grounds that this was a recipe for continued disruption of the market.

The ending of the Addison scheme in 1921 rekindled party conflict on the housing issue in Leeds. Between 1921 and 1923 the Conservative administration had no policy other than to 'wait and see' what would result from the government's review of the housing question. As ever, Labour argued that the answer to Leeds' housing problems lay in the hands of the City Council. This view was reinforced by warnings from the local building trade that there was little prospect of house building being undertaken as a strictly commercial venture.[47] The reality of the housing situation influenced the Conservatives to introduce two schemes in 1922 which were aimed at increasing the rate of house building in the city. The first allowed for the sale of municipally owned land to private builders at little more than 10 per cent of the original cost, while the second envisaged a programme of municipal house building to promote owner-occupation through 'rental purchase'.[48] While both these schemes were superseded by the Chamberlain Act of the following year they shared the same premise: henceforth the private sector should again be the major source of new housing. However, in contrast to the pre-war situation it was clear that private enterprise would be based on the growth of owner-occupation rather than building to let. Labour councillors saw this trend as confirmation of the need for council housing to be provided on a large scale, supplying working-class tenants with rented accommodation. Leeds Conservatives, however, were great believers in the social and political value of an increasing number of small-scale property owners. As the *Yorkshire Post* noted, this development would have a 'valuable stabilizing effect on public opinion' and was 'possibly the best and surest safeguard against the follies of Socialism.'[49] Specifically, the owner-occupier was seen as a natural Conservative voter.[50] Not surprisingly, therefore, Leeds built very few council dwellings under the Chamberlain scheme; instead the Conservatives preferred to capitalize the Exchequer and rate subsidies into a lump sum payment which reduced the selling price of new houses built by private enterprise.

By the mid-1920s the ruling party in Leeds had shown itself ill-disposed towards any policy which foresaw a major role for council house building, yet this was the very purpose of the 1924 Housing Act in the eyes of its promotor, John Wheatley. Between 1924 and 1933 local authority house building nationally was dominated by schemes financed under the Wheatley Act. In England and Wales during this period the county boroughs built on average 16.5 Wheatley dwellings per thousand of their 1931 populations; in Leeds the ratio was 11.9. By contrast, under the Addison Act Leeds completed 7.3 houses per thousand of the city's population in 1921 compared to an average of 4.0 for all county boroughs.[51] The high rate of Addison building came about more by accident than design, since the Ministry of Health determined the size of local schemes through detailed supervision of housing contracts. During the Wheatley era local authorities had much greater discretion in these matters, although in return for less central interference they ceased to enjoy open-ended subsidies from the Exchequer. In Leeds these factors, combined with a general antipathy towards council housing on the part of the Conservatives, produced the relatively low level of Wheatley house building. Indeed, it is worth noting that nearly four out of every ten Wheatley dwellings in Leeds resulted from contracts awarded during the two years from November 1928 when the Labour party had an overall majority on the City Council.[52]

A radical change in the character of council housing was promised by the passing of the Greenwood Act in July 1930. The second Labour government intended that house building for 'general needs' should be augmented by a programme of housing renewal based on slum clearance and rehousing by the local authorities. Along with the majority of housing authorities Leeds, which reverted to Conservative control in November 1930, did not find the prospect appealing. Consequently the local response to Greenwood's policy was decidedly cautious. In February 1931 it was announced that 2,000 houses would be demolished within five years, while a further 9,000 would be 'reconditioned'.[53] These proposals fell far short of being a real attempt to deal with the city's slum problem. In 1921 the Chamberlain Committee on Unhealthy Areas concluded that Leeds had some 33,000 back-to-back houses which were so unfit that it was 'difficult to suggest any method of dealing with them short of complete clearance.'[54] The committee's findings were based on evidence from the City Engineer and the Medical Officer of Health, Dr Jervis. Throughout the 1920s Dr Jervis constantly reminded the Council that in his opinion these 33,000 houses ought to be demolished at the first opportunity. His case rested on the damage to public health inflicted by bad housing, and in statistical terms can be illustrated by table 5.[55] The M.O.H. argued that although the cost of slum clearance and rehousing on the scale required would be high, it was doubtful whether it would be 'greater than is being borne at present in the shape of damaged lives, time lost through sickness, reduction of output, bodily disablement, to say nothing of the moral effects which are far reaching.'[56] It must be said, however, that Dr Jervis's view made little impression on the Council as a whole, concerned as it was with the economic costs of slum clearance to the ratepayers and property-owners.

Table 5.   *Mortality in selected slum areas, 1921–30: Average annual death rates per thousand for ten years, 1921–30*

area	death rate	infant mortality	tuberculosis	respiratory diseases
Meadow Lane	22.7	154	1.55	4.56
West St	22.1	169	2.99	4.95
York Rd	19.1	118	2.24	4.34
City	13.5	91	1.28	2.3

Following the appearance of the Chamberlain Report the City Council came under pressure from the Ministry of Health for action on the slum question. In response the Council adopted Dr Jervis's recommendation that 270 houses in the West Street area be demolished as he felt this to be the most insanitary area in the city.[57] (Moreover, its location near the main railway stations suggested that after clearance the site would not remain vacant for long, thus reducing the final cost of the scheme to the ratepayers.[58]) The scheme was approved by the Council in May 1923, but another four and a half years elapsed before the Ministry of Health's local inquiry was held — a delay explained by the Council's procrastination in formally presenting its proposals to the Ministry. The Conservative administration in Leeds deliberately dragged its feet in the interests of local property owners. In August 1927 the deputy Town Clerk noted in a letter to the Ministry of Health that 'consideration of this scheme has been postponed from time to time in anticipation of legislation dealing with the terms for the acquisition of property.'[59] Local landlords, represented by the Leeds and District Property Owners' and Ratepayers' Association, were vehemently opposed to the existing method of compensation, which they regarded as 'a system of iniquitous robbery and confiscation of the capital of private persons.'[60] The problem lay in the provisions of the 1919 Housing and Town Planning Act which allowed for owners of property condemned for slum clearance to be awarded compensation on the basis of site value rather than the full market value of the dwellings themselves. By 1927, however, it was clear that there was little chance of the existing legislation being amended and under renewed pressure from the M.O.H. and Labour councillors on the one hand, and from the Ministry of Health on the other, the Conservatives submitted the West Street scheme to the Ministry, and it was finally approved in June 1928.[61] However, slum clearance schemes in general were soon to be brought to a halt by legal judgments relating to disputed schemes in Derby and Liverpool, which in part prompted the drafting of new slum clearance legislation in 1929 to 1930.[62] Thus, in the ten years from 1923 to 1933 a mere 32 houses in the West Street area were actually demolished.[63]

Leeds' neglect of the slum problem was in no way unique; rather it was part of a wider pattern in the development of council housing during a period when priority was afforded to increasing the size of the total housing stock, and the elimination of substandard dwellings was mistakenly entrusted to the 'filtering up' process. Between 1919 and 1932 the 'big five' provincial housing authorities – Birmingham, Leeds, Liverpool, Manchester and Sheffield – built more than 100,000 council dwellings between them, yet they demolished fewer than 4,000 slums in the same period.[64] Even after the passing of the 1930 Housing Act the political problems associated with compensation together with the economic and social costs of rehousing discouraged local authorities from proceeding with housing renewal on a significant scale. They were ultimately galvanized into action by government initiative, when the slum clearance drive was launched early in 1933. In Leeds the Conservatives responded by increasing their five-year slum clearance target to 15,000 houses in total.[65] However, this decision resulted not only from pressure exerted by the Ministry of Health, but also from political pressures in the locality. During the previous two years the Labour party in Leeds had conducted a vigorous campaign against Conservative housing policy. Initially it was prompted by the minimal commitment to slum clearance adopted in the wake of the Greenwood Act, but later developed into a campaign for a fundamental reorientation in the city's housing policy. The leadership, and the inspiration, for the campaign was provided by Councillor Charles Jenkinson, an Anglican priest who represented a ward containing some of the worst slum properties in Leeds.[66] Supported by a few close colleagues, Jenkinson succeeded in rallying the Labour Party and then the electorate behind his plan for a massive extension of council housing in Leeds. Through his work in committee, and his speeches to the Council and public meetings (which gained extensive if not always favourable coverage in the local press) Jenkinson politicized the making of housing policy to a degree unprecedented in the post-war period. By 1933 clear inter-party differences on the issue had been exposed. For their part the Conservatives acknowledged that more than 30,000 houses ought to be demolished, but they persisted with the argument that to achieve this would take at least a generation. Thus caution remained the hallmark of the Conservative approach, whereas Jenkinson persuaded the Labour party to accept a fifteen-year programme for the clearance of more than 45,000 back-to-backs; this total would include all those houses previously condemned by the Chamberlain Report together with later examples of back-to-back housing whose condition the M.O.H. felt was almost as bad. On the basis of this bold and far-reaching commitment Labour fought the municipal elections of November 1933, when the party gained six seats and an overall majority on the City Council.[67]

In office Labour housing policy rested on somewhat different foundations from those outlined before the municipal elections. In January 1934 it was announced that after consultations with the Ministry of Health the Labour administration proposed to increase the rate of slum clearance to secure the demolition of more than 30,000 houses by the end of 1939. The object was to demolish, within six years, all those back-to-backs built before local bye-laws first laid down minimum standards for back-to-back development in Leeds.[68] A survey conducted by the M.O.H. early in 1934 identified 30,694 houses in this category, almost a quarter of the city's total housing stock.[69] On paper Leeds' slum clearance programme was the most extensive adopted by any provincial housing authority. As table 6 indicates it accounted for 11.2 per cent of all proposed demolitions in England and Wales, and for 9 per cent of the total population to be affected by slum clearance.[70] It was, therefore, a major element in the national policy of housing renewal.

Table 6.   Local authority slum clearance programmes, 1934

	as % of Eng. & Wales total		persons to be rehoused as % of 1931 population
	persons to be rehoused	houses to be demolished	
London	21.4	12.4	5
Leeds	9.0	11.2	23
Liverpool	4.8	4.5	7
Manchester	5.1	5.6	8
Sheffield	3.2	3.4	8
	43.5	37.1	

Kirby has argued that officials within the Ministry of Health never believed that any of the major housing authorities would complete their clearance schemes within six years, despite the propaganda which surrounded the slum clearance drive.[71] In practice such scepticism was fully justified by the local authorities' performance after 1933. In the case of Leeds, a total of 11,132 houses were demolished in the six years ending in March 1940, leaving 64 per cent of the slums designated in 1934 still standing.[72] Here as elsewhere the shortfall largely reflects the failure of the Ministry of Health to ensure that the local authorities maintained their commitment to slum clearance. As a result local circumstances exercised a major influence on policy-making in each area, as the Leeds case demonstrates. Although 13,406 houses in the city were 'represented' for demolition between 1934 and 1939, 58 per cent of these were 'represented' during the two years after November 1933 when Labour control-led the City Council. Thereafter, the Conservatives, while committed to the eventual removal of the 30,000 houses included in their opponents' programme, reverted to a policy of 3,000 demolitions per annum. This implied that 12,000 houses would be 'represented' between 1936 and 1939, but in the event only 5,646 houses were scheduled for clearance during this four-year period. Indeed, for two years after February 1936 not one house was 'represented' for demolition by the City Council.[73]

Leeds' slum clearance programme was retarded through a combination of political, logistical and economic factors. For the Conservatives the compensation issue remained a serious political problem, the more so as its resolution lay in the hands of the government rather than the local authority. Thus the Leeds Conserva-tive Association lobbied hard to gain concessions (i.e. higher rates of compensation) from the Ministry of Health, but although some changes were introduced in the Housing Act of 1935 these failed to satisfy the property owners and their allies in the local party.[74] Sympathy for the landlords' position influenced the Conservative Council of 1935–9 in so far as a slower rate of slum clearance was a basic element in its housing policy. To justify this change the Conservatives were able to point to the failure of municipal housing developments to keep pace with slum clearance. Two years into the rehousing programme the liquidation of a major contractor, bad weather and shortages of skilled labour had produced long delays in the completion of new houses. In the twelve months up to March 1936 a total of 672 dwellings were handed over to the City Council, in contrast to Labour's plan for at least 3,550 completions in that year.[75] With replacement houses unavailable slum clearance became a protracted business, with up to two years elapsing between the 'representation' of properties and their demolition. During this time houses which by definition were already in a poor condition deteriorated still further for want of maintenance and repair. The Conservatives, therefore, argued that by reverting to their original policy of 3,000 demolitions each year they would secure greater co-ordination between the clearance and rehousing schemes, reducing delays and dereliction in the slum areas.[76] But the revised programme was itself undermined by a sharp rise in building costs which occurred during 1936; by October of that year housing tenders showed that prices had increased by some 14 per cent in the previous 15 months. The Council, supported by the Ministry of Health, responded by imposing a moratorium on house building, pending a reduction in costs which would again allow dwellings to be let at rents which slum clearance tenants could afford.[77] Thus, whereas the Labour administration of 1933–5 awarded contracts for a total of 9,344 dwellings, during the following two years the Conservatives sanctioned only 2,466.[78] From October 1937, when the moratorium was lifted, until September 1939 contracts were let for a further 3,097 dwellings, but some of the schemes involved were later abandoned with the outbreak of war.

For many Conservatives the subsequent failure of Leeds' programme of housing renewal to proceed at the rapid pace envisaged in 1934 was not entirely unwelcome. Not only did it limit the impact of 'confiscation' on property owners but it also postponed the great expansion of council housing in Leeds which Labour had planned and which so alarmed their opponents. The Conservatives voiced their concern about the financial implications for the ratepayers of providing more than 30,000 council dwellings within seven years, and about the political consequences of the Council acting as landlord to a quarter of the city's population.[79] Nevertheless, as table 3 indicates, the years from 1933 to 1939 saw a significant increase in the size of Leeds' municipal housing stock, with more council dwellings completed in the six years after November 1933 than in the whole period from 1919 to 1933. Without doubt council housing in Leeds 'came of age' between 1933 and 1939 thanks to the impetus provided by Labour's housing policy at the start of the slum clearance era.

In examining the growth of council housing in Leeds between the wars we have so far concentrated on the factors which influenced the scale of local authority house building, with only brief references to the purpose of housing policy and its effect on the housing situation. Clearly, these too are issues which need to be discussed in order to assess the development of council housing in terms of social policy. In short, our attention must turn from the Council as house builder to the Council as landlord.

In Leeds as in other cities after 1918 the local authority became the major supplier of new housing to let, as private developers concentrated their efforts on providing houses designed for the owner-occupier. During the inter-war years it seems probable that almost nine out of every ten houses built by private enterprise in Leeds were purchased by owner-occupiers. Certainly, between October 1933 and March 1939 private builders in Leeds completed 16,003 new dwellings (with a rateable value up to £26 per annum) and of these only 1,774, or 11.1 per cent, were let.[80] The absence of comparable data does not permit an accurate measure of building to let between 1919 and 1933, but it is very unlikely that, as a proportion of the private sector's total output, it exceeded the level recorded after 1933. In the mid-1930s there must, if anything, have been a rise in the level of building to let in comparison to earlier years, given that the costs of construction and interest rates were lower and the local authorities were no longer building for 'general needs'.[81]

Houses bought by owner-occupiers were undeniably an economic commodity, supplied to meet housing demand rather than housing need: a fact demonstrated by the changing social background of house purchasers in Leeds during the inter-war years. In the 1920s members of social and economic classes I, II and III accounted for 97.5 per cent of all transactions, including rented properties converted to owner-occupation; this compares with 97.7 per cent between 1900 and 1909. Thus in the 1920s less than three out of every hundred purchases were made by people employed in semi-skilled or unskilled occupations. From 1930 to 1939, however, they accounted for 11.3 per cent of all purchases in an expanded housing market.[82] This group of workers included textile and clothing operatives, clerical, retail and transport staffs and many occupations in the service industries generally. As we noted earlier, it was the growth of employment in these very areas which ensured Leeds' relative prosperity during the inter-war period. Coinciding with a decline in the real cost of house purchase during the 1930s this trend formed the basis for the arrival of working-class owner-occupation in Leeds on a significant scale. Previously the demand for new housing at this level had been met by the local authority during the era of council housebuilding for 'general needs'. After 1933 the *raison d'être* of council housing in every locality was redefined, first by the advent of the slum clearance drive, and then by the Overcrowding Act of 1935, so that by the mid-1930s it was undeniably a welfare service. As local authorities withdrew from building houses for general rather than specific needs the scope of owner-occupation widened to involve the kind of household which represented the typical council tenant of the 1920s when council houses had been as much an economic commodity as anything produced by private enterprise.

Before 1933 council houses in Leeds constituted an economic commodity because rents were charged for them which were beyond the means of many working-class families in the city, despite subsidies from the Exchequer and the rates. Under both the Addison and Wheatley schemes subsidies provided insufficient compensation for the high cost of building council houses in relation to the rent-paying capacity of the low paid. In 1927 the M.O.H., Dr Jervis, complained that as a result 'the class of individual going into . . . the new houses [is] not the class that stands most in need of improved conditions.'[83] Dr Jervis contended that people lived in overcrowded or insanitary conditions simply because they could afford nothing better. In these cases there was effectively an economic barrier to better housing, in that the families concerned could on average pay no more than 6s. or 7s. a week for their accommodation. Thus they required cheap housing and what they were able to rent was bad housing, as those back-to-backs at the centre of Leeds' slum problem could be had for under 5s. per week including rates. New houses were never provided as cheaply as this by the City Council and therefore council housing made virtually no impression either on overcrowding or on the slums. As we have seen, slum clearance did not feature in municipal housing policy in the 1920s, and this is partially explained by the failure of the Council to devise any means of building houses within the rent-paying capacity of the average slum dweller. Although the scale of the slum problem in Leeds was in no way reduced during the 1920s, the 1931 census indicated that there had been some lessening of overcrowding during the previous decade. Compared with 1921 the number of overcrowded families (living at a density of more than two persons per room) had fallen from 7,370 to 5,640, and from 6.7 to 4.4 per cent of the total number of households in the city.[84] However, this improvement (which resulted from a decrease in average family size as much as in the growth of the housing stock) needs to be qualified in two ways. First, during the same period there was actually an increase in the number of shared dwellings from 1,335 to 1,850, and thus 1.5 per cent of all dwellings in 1931 housed more than one family compared to 1.2 per cent ten years before.[85] Secondly, the real level of overcrowding was masked by the Registrar General's insistence on counting living rooms as potential sleeping places when it was accepted locally that working-class families were averse to sleeping there except in times of severe illness. Given that more than 30,000 back-to-backs in Leeds had no more than two bedrooms, and of these some 14,000 had only one, overcrowding was far more extensive than the census data suggest.[86]

That council houses would be relatively expensive became apparent as soon as building began under the Addison Act. The rapid post-war increase in the cost of house building made high rents inevitable once the Ministry of Health had determined that local authorities should charge not less than two-thirds of the 'economic' rent for their dwellings in order to contain the Treasury's spending on the housing programme.[87] On completion, Leeds' Addison houses were let for 9s. per week in the case of the A3 type, while the B3 cost 11s.; when rates were added the gross rent amounted to 16s. 1d. and 19s. 6d. respectively.[88] Although there was no shortage of applicants for these houses, the local press reported in February 1922 that they were 'mostly better class artisans and members of the lower middle class.'[89] In later years Addison rents were reduced as interest rates fell and the City Council was confronted with organized pressure from the tenants themselves. But the power to make alterations lay with the Ministry of Health, as central control was the *quid pro quo* for the advantageous penny rate subsidy. Thus, on a politically sensitive issue the local authority was in the hands of the central department and could do little more than press the tenants' claims for lower rents in the hope of a favourable response. Under the Wheatley scheme, however, the administrative arrangements were very different, with fixed government subsidies and minimal central interference in the detail of local housing policy. Essentially, the onus was placed on the local authorities to determine rent levels, and few were inclined to finance cheap rents at the ratepayers' expense, especially as there was no problem in letting houses at relatively high rents. In Leeds, Wheatley houses were initially more expensive than their Addison counterparts with rents of up to 8s. 8d. for the A2, 9s. 9d. for the A3 and 12s. 2d. for the B3.[90]

The failure of the Wheatley Act to provide genuine 'working-class' housing – reported annually by the M.O.H. – prompted a political debate in Leeds as to how this might be achieved. The Labour Party saw direct labour as a means of reducing the cost of house building and therefore achieving lower rents. But this idea met with vehement opposition which persuaded the Labour administration of 1928–30 against a practical test of direct-labour house building. Instead they used direct labour estimates drawn up by the City Engineer to discourage high-cost tenders from private builders seeking housing contracts.[91] Also Labour pursued a policy of reducing the annual charges on new housing schemes by borrowing money over longer periods than had been the practice hitherto, and reducing those on existing properties by rescheduling the loan debt. This enabled an across-the-board reduction in Wheatley rents to be made in December 1929, after which A2s cost 7s. per week, A3s 8s. 6d. and B3s either 11s. or 12s. 6d.[92] Under Conservative control the Council followed the Ministry of Health's advice that municipal housing should be made less expensive by 'building down'. In 1927 Leeds began to build 'cottage flats' and eventually completed nearly 1,600 (including 568 approved by Labour between 1928 and 1930); in total they represented one in four of all Wheatley dwellings in the city.[93] After a general reduction of 6d. per week in Wheatley rents in December 1930 these flats cost 4s. 6d. for the two-bedroom type and 5s. 6d. for those with three bedrooms. Including rates the A2 flat cost 6s. 5d., a sum the M.O.H. considered to be 'reasonable and within the means of the majority of the working classes'.[94] However, the flats had been built mostly on suburban estates and tenants had to meet the additional cost of travelling to and from work and the amenities in the centre of the city. With this in mind the Conservative Council elected in November 1930 embarked on the development of estates close to the city centre, comprising A3 houses with a floor space of 724 sq. ft rather than the Wheatley 'norm' of 819 sq. ft. By 1933 these smaller houses in 'convenient' locations could be rented for 4s. 6d. per week, only 3d. more than the cost of a three-bedroom 'cottage flat'; as a result the building of the flats came to an end in the same year.[95] The effect of such innovations was essentially marginal, as the dwellings they produced accounted for no more than a fifth of the municipal housing stock in 1933, on the eve of the slum clearance drive. Moreover, they did little to alter the social bias in council housing in Leeds, for tenants were still described as 'artisans rather than members of the working class'.[96]

The launching of the slum clearance drive in 1933 was a landmark in the development of council housing, and one which pointed to its emergence as a social service. Jenkinson, the architect of Leeds' programme for housing renewal, believed that the slum problem was largely a symptom of a more deep-seated problem, that of poverty. He argued that people lived in conditions regarded as 'socially intolerable . . . mainly because their economic circumstances are such that better conditions have been beyond their reach.'[97] Implicit in this and similar statements made by Jenkinson was an attack on the way housing had previously been subsidized by the state. Instead of public funds being used to subsidize the rent of every council dwelling at the same rate (depending on the legislation under which they were built) Jenkinson wanted the money to be transferred to the tenants to allow rents to be fixed individually in relation to means; in this way it would be possible for new housing to be provided at a price within the means of those families living in the slums or in overcrowded accommodation. For him, therefore, differential rents held the key to the success of Labour's housing policy in securing a permanent improvement in working-class housing conditions. Local authorities had earlier been granted the power to introduce differential rents schemes by the Housing Act of 1930, and subsequent Ministerial speeches and circulars emphasized that 'the slum clearance scheme was intended . . . to be based on the general principle that subsidies should be varied according to the capacity of tenants to pay.'[98] Government policy was dictated by the search for economies in housing expenditure and by the realization that averaged subsidies had led to councils charging rents which were too high for the majority of working-class households. By 1938, therefore, more than 100 local authorities in England and Wales operated some kind of differential rents scheme, although these were usually limited to tenants rehoused under the slum clearance and overcrowding legislation.[99] Unlike Leeds, few authorities ever attempted to apply the principle of differential renting to their entire stock of council dwellings.

The essentials of Labour's differential rents scheme were outlined by Jenkinson in the following way:

> The rent of every council dwelling is fixed at the full municipal economic rent, that is, at a weekly sum which represents the actual cost of erection and maintenance. That rent every tenant is called upon to pay if he is adjudged capable of paying it. But if not so capable, then rent relief is granted to him according to his need, whenever such need arises, for so long as needs exist, but for no longer.[100]

To translate these principles into practice Labour created a complex and politically contentious administrative system, based on the introduction of a means test specifically designed for tenants living in council-owned properties included in the differential rents scheme. An individual tenant's entitlement to a rebate against the 'economic rent' was determined by the number of his dependents and their ages in relation to a scale of subsistence allowances based on a report by the British Medical Association's Committee on Nutrition. The sum of these allowances was deducted from total family income to show the amount available for paying rent. Rebates were granted on the basis that only part of this marginal income should be paid out in rent. The actual proportion in each case depended on the type of dwelling occupied and family size. For example, where the margin was 10s. and the dwelling was an A3 house the rent charged ranged from 5s. 6d. per week for a single person down to 2s. for a couple with five children.[101] In cases where total family income was actually lower than the subsistence allowance the tenant was not charged any rent at all. Whereas other differential rent schemes operated on the principle of all tenants paying some rent the Leeds scheme did not call on council tenants to pay rent until their family's income exceeded an official subsistence level. In this respect the Leeds policy was unique, a fact which fuelled the political controversy surrounding the provision of 'rent-free' houses.

In any scheme which sought to adjust rent in relation both to family size and to income some kind of means test was an administrative necessity, and the spread of differential renting in the mid-1930s produced a crop of means tests specifically designed for housing purposes.[102] In Leeds the Labour Party's intention that rent relief was to be granted on a week-to-week basis, varying according to changing domestic circumstances, obliged council tenants to furnish the Housing Department with a weekly record both of household income and of outgoings (such as travelling expenses, school meals and insurance premiums) for which allowances were made on the subsistence scales. The tenant's 'Grey Book', in which this information was recorded, had to be submitted for inspection whenever family circumstances changed and was automatically reviewed at six-monthly intervals by the Housing Department, which also verified statements about wages with the employers of tenants and their families.[103]

The imposition of a means test on council tenants who saw themselves not as claimants of public assistance but as individuals merely trying to avoid paying higher rents, created a political storm. To many in Leeds the Labour Party seemed intent on turning council housing into a Poor Law service, and the council estates into 'pauper settlements'. Jenkinson always insisted there was a vital distinction between the detested means test of the Public Assistance Committees and that employed in the differential rents scheme: 'one aimed at taking practically every penny out of the house. Ours aims at leaving in the house the maximum amount we believe is reasonable for life in the house.'[104] Despite the conviction which underlay this and similar utterances Labour's position was in truth untenable, given the party's history of opposition to means-testing in other social services. Within the Labour Party there were those who questioned the wisdom of this particular aspect of Jenkinson's policy. Electoral considerations aside, some feared that, as the Conservatives predicted, the means test would bring down the incomes of skilled and unskilled workers, of the employed and the unemployed to 'a common and reduced level.'[105] Jenkinson, however, saw it as a mechanism for raising the general standard of living among working-class families, especially for those who could never have afforded decent housing under previous subsidy policies.

Differential rents, more than any other issue, were responsible for the loss of popular support experienced by Labour in the two years after November 1933. (In November 1935 Labour lost control of the City Council and thereafter did not regain control until 1945.) Differential rents or, rather, certain features of the local scheme, alienated voters both on the council estates and elsewhere in the city. Not surprisingly many tenants bitterly resented the means test and it was reported that in some cases they chose to pay higher rents rather than submit to an investigation of their personal affairs.[106] For others the means test itself resulted in rent increases while their neighbours might well have been granted reductions or excused from paying any rent at all. Clearly, differential rents by their very nature affected individual tenants in various ways so that opinion on the estates was bound to be divided. Disaffected tenants, however, formed a vociferous lobby acting through the Tenants' Association to reverse Labour policy. They sought to do so initially by testing the Council's legal right to introduce differential rents. When this was reaffirmed by the Court of Appeal in October 1934[107] the Association was forced into an alliance with the Conservatives, who promised to abolish Jenkinson's scheme and the infamous 'Grey Books' when returned to office. For their part the Conservatives used the rent question to engage a much larger constituency than just council tenants. Supported by three of Leeds' four daily newspapers, they asked the public to consider both the financial and political implications of Labour's rent policy. It was argued that economic rents would quickly drive out 'good tenants', as these rents would be equal to the weekly cost of buying a new house from a private builder; given the aims of Labour's housing policy such tenants would inevitably be replaced by others who were asked to pay only a fraction of the economic rent – a process which promised to undermine the scheme financially.[108] The Conservatives also expressed alarm at the 'political' nature of a scheme which, by Labour estimates, would extend to more than 40,000 tenancies by 1941. The *Yorkshire Post* envisaged 'an increasing number of municipal tenants forming a solid block of votes, bringing pressure to bear at election times for a still further lowering of the rents and greater relief.'[109] Alderman Davies, the Conservative leader, warned ratepayers that the differential rents scheme provided evidence of 'a definite intention to put into force the first step in communal socialism in Leeds.'[110]

During 1934–5 opponents of Labour's differential rents scheme increasingly emphasized the 'political' arguments as the financial case against it was largely contradicted by the facts. Table 7 is based on returns prepared by the Leeds Housing Department in May 1934, one month after the scheme began, and in October 1935 on the eve of Labour's defeat in the municipal elections.[111] The marked increase in the number of tenancies covered by differential renting between these two dates is accounted for by new housing completions under the slum clearance rehousing programme and by the extension of the scheme to include more than 3,000 Addison houses. This followed the Housing Act of 1935 which allowed local authorities to consolidate the finances of all post-war housing schemes into a single Housing Revenue Account.[112] The inclusion of the Addison houses largely explains the increase in the proportion of tenants paying the full economic rent, since these were occupied by people in regular and relatively well-paid employment, with small families. Moreover, as Jenkinson had expected, the fact that industry and commerce in Leeds escaped the worst effects of the depression in the 1930s meant that there were enough tenants paying economic rents to keep the scheme solvent.[113] It would also appear that very few of these tenants – the 'good payers' as Conservatives called them – were driven to leaving the council estates by the coming of differential rents. However, in the autumn of 1935 the slum clearance programme was still at an early stage, and as yet only 11 per cent of all tenants received full rent relief. In this favourable climate the result was a healthy surplus in the subsidy pool which financed the rent scheme. In October 1935 the pool was valued at £1,789 per week, out of which £1,515 was paid in rent rebates; at this point, therefore, the differential rents scheme produced a surplus equivalent to £14,248 per annum.[114]

Table 7. Labour's differential rents scheme, 1934–5

	tenancies	no. paying economic rent	no. receiving rent relief	no. living rent free
May 1934	5,750	853(15%)	4.438(77%)	459(8%)
Oct. 1935	10,960	4,532(41%)	5,291(48%)	1,137(11%)

The Conservative administration elected in November 1935 was committed to the abolition of Labour's rent scheme, but before the election the party's spokesmen had been vague about the details of any alternative, beyond the principle of every tenant having some share of the housing subsidy. The details of the Conservatives' policy were announced in February 1936 and the revised scheme came into operation two months later.[115] The scheme was based on drawing a distinction between 'voluntary' and 'compulsory' tenants. The former comprised all those who had taken a council house out of choice, while the latter had done so under the slum clearance and overcrowding measures or on the recommendation of the M.O.H. Voluntary tenants paid a standard subsidized rent dependent on the type of dwelling they occupied, and these rents were on average 18 per cent lower than Labour's economic rents. The rents paid by compulsory tenants attracted a higher level of subsidy and were between 6d. and 2s. 3d. per week lower than those paid by voluntary tenants living in comparable houses. In addition compulsory tenants could claim further rent relief in relation to income and family size, but under the Conservatives' arrangements every tenant was obliged to pay a minimum of about 20 per cent of the standard rent. The new chairman of the Housing Committee, Alderman Blackah, repeated his party's belief that 'if a person was so poor that they were unable to pay any rent they were obviously cases for public assistance through the proper channels.'[116]

The new scheme affected tenants in three ways. First, those who had previously lived rent free now had to pay between 1s. and 2s. 1d. per week depending on the type of dwelling in which they lived. Secondly, about 5,300 tenants hitherto receiving partial relief against the economic rents had their rents revised and of these about 2,500 were asked to pay more. Thirdly, those who had paid the full economic rent had their rents reduced by anything from 6d. to 2s. 3d. per week.[117] Jenkinson argued that these reductions had been made possible only by calling on the poorest council tenants to pay higher rents, whereas Labour's scheme had been based on the notion that 'public money should not be given to those who do *not* need it [but] should be given to the fullest extent where it is needed' – a view implicit in a series of government circulars on rent policy issued during the previous five years.[118] He also predicted that before long the Conservative scheme would come to grief on two counts, one social and the other financial. In social terms Jenkinson maintained that the division of council tenants into the 'voluntary' and 'compulsory' categories was an arbitrary one with little relevance to reality in so far as experience showed that many of the 8,000 voluntary tenants could pay only minimal rents. His main criticisms, however, were directed against the financial implications of distributing housing subsidies in a 'wasteful' manner. In order to subsidize the rent of every tenant the Conservative scheme automatically used up to seven-eighths of the subsidy pool, leaving only one-eighth to finance the extra relief available to compulsory tenants.[119] In the spring of 1936, when the scheme began, there were some 3,800 compulsory tenants, almost a third of the total number of council tenants; but with the passage of time this number was bound to increase through slum clearance and the abatement of overcrowding, placing additional demands on only a small portion of the subsidy pool.

Within a year the weaknesses in the Conservative differential rents scheme became apparent. In February 1937 it was announced that by the end of the following month the scheme would have run up a deficit of nearly £28,000, having absorbed all monies in the subsidy pool and a surplus of £7,000 carried over from 1935–6 when the Labour policy was operative. To finance £15,000 of the deficit council rents were increased, while the balance was covered by a penny on the rates.[120] A loss had become inevitable when the Conservatives acknowledged that the distinction between compulsory and voluntary tenants was unrealistic. They had found that some of the latter had been rehoused by Labour from the housing waiting list and were unable to pay the higher rents subsequently imposed by the Conservative scheme. Thus, in March 1937, out of 7,341 voluntary tenants, 986 (13.4 per cent) were classified as 'voluntary tenants treated as if they were compulsory tenants', and received additional rent relief in the same way as compulsory tenants. When these were added to an increasing number of slum clearance tenants it was clear that insufficient money had been allocated for rent rebates; in March 1937 these were being granted to just over 4,600 tenants, or one in every three.[121] However, the measures taken at the end of the 1936–7 financial year were successful enough to enable the Conservatives to reduce the net rents of all tenants in receipt of rent rebates by 10 per cent in the following November.[122]

During the next two years no major changes were made to the rent scheme, despite persistent demands from the Tenants' Association (whose alliance with the Conservatives had long since broken down) for what it called a 'non-political and permanent' policy on council rents, to be based on standard subsidized rents against which all tenants would have the right to claim rebates.[123] By 1939 the electoral significance of the rent question remained high, as there were now in excess of 20,000 council tenants, almost double the number when differential rents were first introduced in 1934; hence it was the major 'unsettled question' in Leeds' housing policy on the eve of the Second World War.

Between 1934 and 1939 the often intense political controversy surrounding developments in rent policy in Leeds somewhat overshadowed the basic achievements which followed the advent of differential renting. In its Annual Report for 1939–40 the Housing Committee recorded that between November 1932 and March 1940 a total of 10,109 households were rehoused from slum clearance areas. Of these only one in twenty were found to have given up their tenancy during this period and returned to the private sector.[124] In this respect Labour's aim of keeping the former inhabitants of the city's slums in council housing was fulfilled. When the slum clearance programme was in its early stages much publicity had been afforded to a report from the M.O.H. in Stockton-on-Tees who suggested that many tenants rehoused by his local authority from slum clearance areas were facing a 'rent versus food' dilemma, which they tried to resolve by eating cheaper fare. The outcome was a lower resistance to disease, and more ill-health on new estates than ought to have been the case.[125] Thus in Leeds Dr Jervis was always a supporter of differential rents, since he saw 'no virtue in putting a family into a better house if as a result of the higher rent demanded, the nutrition of its members is going to suffer.'[126] What he and Jenkinson feared was that slum clearance tenants faced with higher rents and travelling expenses would gradually drift back to the centre of the city to find cheaper accommodation in the large Victorian properties in areas of declining status which had been sub-divided into 'tenements'.[127] In 1928 the M.O.H. had argued that the eradication of Leeds' slums was reliant on the provision of alternative housing which would cost slum clearance tenants no more than 7s. per week.[128] As we have seen, Leeds never really succeeded in bringing large numbers of new dwellings within the means of the lower paid, despite the policy of 'building down'. Thus until the early 1930s simple economics denied council housing to the majority of working-class households. In 1931 the net rents of Leeds' Addison houses ranged from 7s. 3d. to 12s. 3d. per week, with a mean of 9s. per week; those of the city's other council dwellings ranged from 5s. 11d. (for some A2 'cottage flats') to 13s. 7d. (for certain 'parlour houses') and here the average rent was 8s. 2d. per week.[129] Five years later, however, after the introduction of differential rents, the position was very different, as table 8 demonstrates.[130] By 1936, therefore, more than a third of all council tenants in Leeds paid no more than 5s. per week in rent, on a par with those who still lived in some of the city's worst back-to-backs. The coming of cheap council housing, through differential renting, enabled Leeds to avoid some of the social problems it had been feared might result from slum clearance rehousing. It is perhaps significant that the local press was devoid of reports about financial hardship among slum clearance tenants living on council estates after 1933.

The major objective of the rehousing policies pursued by both Labour and the Conservatives was to provide every family affected by slum clearance with an alternative dwelling of adequate size, and on this count too they were successful. In 1939 the Housing Committee carried out a survey of 9,791 council tenants rehoused under the Housing Acts of 1930 to 1938. Of this total 86 per cent were rehoused from slum clearance areas, 8 per cent were cases recommended by the M.O.H. (including overcrowded families), and 6 per cent were 'transfers', that is existing council tenants moving from one dwelling to another often because of overcrowding.[131] Table 9 shows the relationship between household size, income and dwelling size produced by the combination of 'welfare housing' legislation and differential rents in Leeds during the latter half of the 1930s.[132] These data confirm that after 1933 income was no longer the major factor which decided what type of accommodation a council

Table 8.   Council rents in Leeds, 1936

amount (net)	tenancies total no.	total %
Up to 3s.	2,208	19.2
3s.1d.– 4s.	903	7.8
4s.1d.– 5s.	1,047	9.1
5s.1d.– 6s.	1,861	16.2
6s.1d.– 7s.	1,108	9.6
7s.1d.– 8s.	2,690	23.4
8s.1d.– 9s.	295	2.6
9s.1d.–10s.	1,346	11.7
10s.1d.–11s.	34	0.4
	11,492	100.0

tenant occupied. For example, in 1939 income per head in the largest council properties (the B3 and B4 'parlour houses' and the A5 and A7 houses) was significantly lower than the mean value for all types of dwelling, which was 14s. 6d. per week. Thus, the success of differential rents policies can be seen in the way housing was allocated on the basis of 'need' rather than ability to pay. In itself this was an important development in the evolution of council housing as a social service both in the local context and from a wider perspective.

Table 9.   Rehousing in Leeds under the Housing Acts of 1930–8

	dwelling	av. no. persons per dwelling	av. weekly income (per head)
flats	A1	1.4	21s. 3d.
	A2	2.6	19s. 6d.
	A3	3.8	13s.11d.
	A4/A5	7.8	14s. 8d.
houses	A2	2.7	18s. 7d.
	A3	4.2	13s. 7d.
	A4	6.3	11s. 7d.
	A5/A7	8.6	9s. 3d.
	C3	6.2	9s.11d.
	B3/B4	6.4	11s. 9d.

Between 1933 and 1939 council housing ceased to be an economic commodity and thereby began to have an impact on the housing problems which had remained untouched by the policies pursued in the Addison and Wheatley eras. As a result, in Leeds more than 30,000 people were rehoused in dwellings which shared a common characteristic despite their design differences; when compared to the squalid legacy of *laissez-faire* urban development they represented a major advance in the quality of working-class house building.

3 Council housing and urban change

If its historical importance is to be fully appreciated the growth of council housing between the wars needs to be examined not only as an extension of social policy but also in terms of its effect on the urban environment. The most telling physical evidence of increasing state intervention in housing and the consequences for city development is to be found in the low-density council estates built after 1919. Through this kind of residential development on the urban fringe local authorities made a significant contribution to the general trend towards suburbanization in British cities during the inter-war years. In Leeds some 54,000 new dwellings were completed in this period and of these 40 per cent were built by the City Council in an enterprise which created more than twenty separate housing estates. But it is important to remember that as well as the rapid development of suburban residential areas the inter-war years also witnessed the beginnings of redevelopment in the urban core, following the reorientation of housing policy at national and local level between 1930 and 1933. By concentrating on slum clearance and therefore on housing renewal, local authorities also became *de facto* the agencies for a programme of urban renewal. Thus, a recurring theme in this as in other aspects of inter-war housing policy is the important chronological divide marked out by the slum clearance drive of 1933 which altered the nature of council housing and its impact on the urban landscape.

That the existence of council estates tells us much about the development of British society since the First World War is now widely recognized; witness the recently expressed belief of Asa Briggs that 'their importance to the social historian of the twentieth century is as great as the importance of the country house to the social historian of the eighteenth century.'[133] The significance of the inter-war council estate is essentially twofold and relates to the role of housing policy in raising the standard of working-class housing and in changing the social geography of the city. Initially, during 1918–19 such issues were of central importance to those responsible for making housing policy.[134] To achieve the quality of residential development desired by central government the local authorities were provided with a virtual blueprint for the development of housing schemes when the Local Government Board issued its *Housing Manual* in 1919 – a document based on the recommendations contained in the Tudor Walters Report of the previous year. Given the sense of urgency which attended the housing question after the Armistice, and the unfamiliarity of most local authorities (including Leeds) with large-scale municipal housing development, it is hardly surprising that the design of local Addison schemes in different areas bore a strong resemblance to the model devised at national level. Moreover, the penny rate subsidy itself meant that local authorities were not discouraged from building to a relatively high standard for fear of increasing the cost of Addison developments to their ratepayers. Therefore in terms of size and amenity council houses built at this time contrasted sharply with traditional forms of working-class housing.[135] This was particularly true in Leeds where low-density estates made up of 'cottages' set in gardens amidst semi-rural surroundings were introduced to a city in which seven out of every ten houses were back-to-backs, built at densities of up to 70 or 80 houses per acre in some districts. Little wonder, then, that in Leeds these early developments attracted extensive publicity, much to the annoyance of council tenants who had to contend with numerous weekend 'sightseers'.[136] The vision so long held by housing reformers and the town planning movement had become reality, or so it must have seemed.

In total Leeds completed 3,329 houses under the Addison Act between 1919 and

Figure 10. a. Examples of early Addison houses on the Hawksworth estate which were faced in local stone.

b. Addison houses at Middleton, exhibiting the 'plainness and economy' of which the City Council's Advisory Architect complained in 1922.

c. Addison houses built by the Airey company's 'Duo-Slab' prefabricated system.

d. Addison houses on the Cross Gates estate built by the 'Waller' method.

1924. They were designed by a full-time Advisory Architect, with the assistance of a panel of 21 local architects who worked on a part-time basis.[137] Before building work began the Advisory Architect and members of the Council visited a number of 'model' housing schemes such as New Earswick in York, Woodlands near Doncaster, Well Hall in Woolwich and the Ministry of Munitions' estates at Coventry and Gretna.[138] Subsequently, much of what the architect wanted to achieve was frustrated by the Ministry of Health in its search for cheaper forms of garden city development. In various ways the specifications of Leeds' Addison houses were amended to secure tender prices nearer the average of £800 per house desired by the Ministry.[139] For example, plans for half the houses to be faced in local stone were quickly abandoned and cheaper types of timber and roofing materials were used, while some internal walls were left unplastered and water pipes remained exposed. When faced with complaints about 'jerry building' the chairman of the Council's Housing Sub-committee 'agreed that the standard of the houses was not what [they] would have wished to start with'[140] (figs. 10a and 10b). Similarly, when tenants began to occupy them, the local press reported that many objected to paying high rents for houses with a 'generally . . . cheap and nasty interior appearance.'[141] In Leeds' case, however, the most significant result of the problems which beset council house building in 1919–20, both financial and logistical, was the adoption of non-traditional methods of construction on a large scale. Of all Leeds' Addison houses just over 50 per cent were built by prefabricated systems; 1,602 were built by the 'Duo-Slab' system developed locally by Wm Airey and Sons Ltd, and 88 were built by the 'Waller' system pioneered by the ill-fated Waller Housing Corporation[142] (figs. 10c and 10d). Encouraged by the Ministry of Health, the City Council saw these 'concrete houses' as a solution to the problems of cost inflation and delays, since they promised savings in the use of skilled labour and traditional materials, both of which were expensive and in short supply. The policy was pursued enthusiastically by the Conservatives but Labour councillors were generally hostile to it and instead advocated the use of direct labour building to reduce costs, together with a ban on 'luxury building' (of cinemas and the like) in order to divert resources into house building.[143]

In 1922 Leeds' Advisory Architect defended his own work against the general criticism that the ambitious plans of local authority architects had brought about the demise of the Addison scheme. He argued that his own designs had been 'exceedingly simple and economical' and much less elaborate than those shown in the *Housing Manual*; accordingly he noted how 'the criticism in Leeds has been that the houses are too economical and err on the side of plainness and economy.'[144] During the following decade 'plainness and economy' were to remain the watchwords which conditioned the design of more than 6,500 council dwellings in Leeds. When building under the Addison Act came to an end the City Council dispensed with the services of the Advisory Architect and from then until the formation of a separate Housing Department in 1934 all design work in connection with municipal housing was the responsibility of the City Engineer.[145] Most of this work related to developments financed by the Wheatley Act of 1924, which restored the potential for extensive local authority house building and accounted for more than 5,700 council dwellings built in Leeds between 1924 and 1933. In the Wheatley era fixed levels of government subsidy gave local authorities a greater interest in the cost of their housing schemes and therefore concerns about 'economy' affected local as well as national politicians. At both levels minimal attention was paid to questions of design as financial considerations became dominant. While the basic philosophy given expression in the

Housing Manual remained influential during the later 1920s most local authorities economized by increasing the density of development on housing sites and by keeping architectural and landscaping detail to a minimum. Above all, however, the houses they built were smaller than those provided under the Addison Act.[146] Thus a feature of the post-Addison period in Leeds is a sharp decline in the number of 'parlour houses' built by the City Council. Whereas 52 per cent of Leeds' Addison dwellings were of this type, providing both a living room and a 'parlour', the proportion fell to 11.6 per cent of total council house building between 1924 and 1933.[147] Except at Hollin Park, where the estate was made up entirely of such properties, the larger, better designed parlour houses were usually placed in strategic locations on the edge of an estate or overlooking a main road. As Jennings has shown, this was a common practice in the later 1920s, offering a 'visual apology' for the lowering of standards in municipal housebuilding[148] (figure 11a).

The demise of the parlour house began in 1923 when the Chamberlain Act excluded such dwellings from the subsidy scheme.[149] Although the power to build them was restored in the following year by the Wheatley Act financial considerations discouraged local authorities from building parlour houses in large numbers. With a fixed amount of government subsidy paid for every house local authorities acquired a vested interest in limiting the cost of their housing schemes, and in Leeds it was pointed out that 12 standard 'A' type houses could be built for the same amount as 9 'parlour' or 'B' type houses[150] (figure 11b). Towards the end of the 1920s growing concern about high rents and restricted access to council housing reinforced the trend away from the 'parlour house'. In 1929, for example, E.D. Simon published *How to Abolish the Slums* in which he wrote of the need for council houses to be 'as small and cheap as is possible, consistent with being a healthy house'; as a result he felt it was 'pretty clear that a parlour must be regarded as the beginning of luxury.'[151] This view became the dominant attitude of housing officials and local housing committees, but it was not accepted universally. The Leeds M.O.H., Dr Jervis, recorded his personal regret at the elimination of the parlour from council houses. In his opinion the second living room not only provided a place for study or a 'quiet hour', but one 'to which the mother can retire with the girls or the father with the boys in order to discuss matters which are of vital importance to their health.'[152] Today Dr Jervis's phraseology may appear rather quaint, but his basic point has proven to be a valid one in the long term, as the increasingly home-centred nature of family life since the 1940s has rendered the lack of a second living room or parlour an important defect in the typical inter-war council dwelling.[153]

The disappearance of the parlour from council house plans was only one consequence of a school of thought which saw 'building down' as the prerequisite for local authorities being able to accommodate the working class. This policy was urged on local authorities by the Ministry of Health in the late 1920s,[154] and in Leeds was implemented through a series of design changes between 1927 and 1933. In a major departure from previous practice the Council began, in 1927, to build flats. These were constructed in blocks of four, to a height of two storeys; each block had the outward appearance of a pair of semi-detached council houses, hence the term 'cottage flat' usually applied to these dwellings (figure 12a). Internally, living space in the two-bedroom flat amounted to 623 sq. ft, or 93 per cent of that in contemporary A2 houses; in the three-bedroom flat it was 85 per cent of that in the standard A3 house, which had an area of 819 sq. ft. Eventually 1,572 'cottage flats' were built and they accounted for nearly one in four of all council dwellings completed during the

Wheatley era.[155] But by 1933 the Council had already decided to build no more flats of this type as they had been found to provide unsuitable accommodation for 'the normal family.'[156] (The main problem, apparently, was the ease with which noise was transmitted from one flat to another and the ill-feeling between tenants this often caused.) Already, the emphasis in Leeds' 'building down' policy had moved away from the 'cottage flat' to the concept of providing small houses designed with lower income tenants in mind. In January 1932, the Ministry of Health issued a circular in which local authorities were recommended to concentrate their efforts on building A3 houses with a maximum floor area of 760 sq. ft. Four months later the Leeds Improvements Committee announced plans for A3 council houses with 724 sq. ft of floorspace, which compared with the previous norm of 819 sq. ft for such dwellings, and Addison A3s which provided 827 sq. ft of living space. In these new houses the bedrooms were of the usual size (150, 100 and 64 sq. ft) but the size of the kitchen was reduced from 93 to 60 sq. ft and the living room from 210 to 180 sq. ft to allow space for the bathroom on the ground floor.[157] By the middle of 1933 contracts were awarded for more than 550 of these houses, of which 64 per cent were financed by the Wheatley subsidy while the remainder counted as early completions under the 1930 Act. The rent of the Wheatley dwellings was 4s. 6d. per week (excluding rates), only 3d. more than that charged for the three-bedroom cottage flats.[158]

The Labour administration elected in November 1933 rejected from the outset any idea that 'building down' could solve the rehousing problem. While the previous Labour controlled council of 1928 to 1930 had built 'cottage flats' and an experimental development of a dozen A3 houses at 774 sq. ft,[159] Jenkinson was determined that every family 'regardless of its means' would be rehoused in the kind of dwelling it needed (in terms of bedroom accommodation) and that Labour's policy would provide 'precisely the same quality of dwelling for every tenant.'[160] As we have seen, the corollary to this aim was the introduction of the controversial differential rents scheme in April 1934. Another important change brought about by Labour at this time was the formation of a separate Housing Department, to incorporate functions hitherto divided between the City Engineer, the M.O.H. and the City Treasurer.[161] Henceforth this department was responsible not only for the development of new housing estates, but also for rent collection, tenancy administration and estate management. To lead the department a new post of Housing Director was created. Jenkinson's choice for this appointment was R.A.H. Livett, previously the deputy Housing Director in Manchester and an experienced local authority architect.[162] Some Labour councillors questioned the wisdom of selecting an architect to head what was developing into a social service, but the decision was indicative of the importance attached to planning and design issues by Jenkinson and his associates; they felt that Leeds had much to learn from the achievements of other housing authorities both in Britain and on the continent.[163] Moreover, the Labour party to some extent saw design as an 'ideological' instrument to legitimize council housing and demonstrate its superiority *vis à vis* the provision made by private enterprise.[164] Livett's appointment therefore added professional ambition to a renewed interest in design and a conscious attempt to improve the quality of council housing in Leeds. Generally, the trend at this time was in the opposite direction, as the reorientation of national housing policy in 1933 encouraged the building of smaller and simpler dwellings. It has been argued elsewhere that over time there was a close correlation between the quality of inter-war council housing and the income levels of the tenants for whom it was designed.[165] Thus in most areas during the mid-1930s 'building down'

Figure 11.   a. During the Wheatley era the larger, more elaborate type of council house was usually built on the edge of an estate. These 'parlour houses' on the Westfield estate overlook what was, in the 1920s, the main road between Leeds and Bradford.

b. The archetypal Wheatley dwelling: a three-bedroom, non-parlour (A3) house on the Dewsbury Road estate.

Figure 12.　a. Cottage flats on the Dewsbury Road estate. Beyond each front door a staircase leads to one of the two first floor flats; the two ground floor flats are entered through doors on either side of the building.

b. A block of four 'aged persons' flats' on the Sandford estate. Beyond the front door a staircase provides access to the two flats on the first floor; the two ground floor flats are entered separately through doors on either side of the building.

was 'an almost inevitable consequence of the drive to rehouse large numbers of former slum dwellers.' Unlike Livett, the majority of municipal architects exhibited 'an increasing tendency to regard the minimum as the maximum', when applying the Tudor Walters standards to the design of council houses.[166]

Council house building in Leeds between 1933 and 1935 was based on a plan which sought to match the provision of new dwellings to the demographic profile of the slum clearance areas and to create a housing stock capable of affording suitable accommodation at each stage in 'the life history of the average working-class family.' Labour's rehousing programme envisaged that total house building would comprise the following elements: aged persons' flats (30 per cent), A2 dwellings (10 per cent), A3s (50 per cent) and A4s (10 per cent).[167] However, this intention derived from financial as well as social considerations, given that the Greenwood subsidy was granted to local authorities in relation to the number of persons rehoused by them, rather than the number of dwellings they built. To provide alternative accommodation economically new housing had to be designed to maximize the density of occupation, short of overcrowding, so as to minimize the cost incurred by the local authority and keep rents low. The crucial factor was bedroom accommodation, since the under-use of this effectively resulted in a loss of subsidy from the Exchequer. Labour's formula was later revised by the Conservatives and after 1935 housing schemes were designed with fewer one-bedroom 'aged persons' flats' and A3 dwellings but with a greater proportion of two-, four- and five-bedroom properties.[168] By this time the extension of differential rents to all council housing in Leeds allowed slum clearance tenants to be rehoused in existing dwellings built under the Addison and Wheatley Acts when the three-bedroom house was by far the dominant type. (Of the city's Addison houses 98.8 per cent had three bedrooms and the remaining 1.2 per cent had four; between 1924 and 1933 when 6,502 dwellings were built, mainly under the Wheatley Act, 72.6 per cent had three bedrooms and 27.4 per cent had two.[169]) Therefore in the late 1930s new building began to make good the relative shortage of other kinds of housing in the council sector. During the six years 1934–9 a total of 10,883 council houses were completed, including some which resulted from contracts awarded before November 1933 when Labour came to power. Of these only 37 per cent had three bedrooms, while 26 per cent were 'aged persons' flats', 22 per cent were A2 dwellings, 9 per cent A4s and 6 per cent A5s.[170]

Apart from the final elimination of the 'parlour house' the main innovation of the post-1933 period, in comparison to the Addison and Wheatley eras, was the building of the 'aged persons' flats' (figure 12b). These were essentially three-room flats comprising a living room (167 sq. ft), kitchen (64 sq. ft) and a bedroom (104 sq. ft), together with a combined bathroom and w.c.[171] Clearly, the quality of accommodation provided by the 'aged persons' flats' cannot be compared to any dwelling previously built by the City Council, but the other two main types of housing, the A2 and A3 houses, had long been the mainstay of municipal house building in Leeds. After 1933 living space in the A2 house was little different from previous versions: the floor areas of the living room and second bedroom were identical, while the kitchen and first bedroom were only 4 sq. ft and 5 sq. ft bigger at 82 sq. ft and 156 sq. ft respectively. The same is true of the A3 house. Labour abandoned the policy of building A3s at 724 sq. ft and imposed a minimum size of 760 sq. ft, which allowed for a kitchen of 114 sq. ft, as opposed to 60 sq. ft in the smaller versions, and for the bathroom to be sited on the first floor.[172] However, the real comparison should be made with the standard Wheatley A3 at 819 sq. ft and this shows that while the third

Figure 13. a. Semi-detached houses at Gipton, Leeds' first slum clearance estate, designed by the Housing Director, R. A. H. Livett.

b. Variations on a theme. An alternative design employed by Livett to relieve the architectural monotony of council housing. These examples were built on the Sandford estate.

c. The results of low-density development in the mid-1930s as seen on the Gipton estate. Groups of houses were frequently set back from the road behind wide grass verges, and sited opposite open spaces where existing trees were retained as landscape features.

d. A typical street scene on the York Road estate dating from the Wheatley era when minimal attention was paid to the aesthetics of council housing, and when building density on council estates was relatively high in comparison to Addison estates and those built after 1933.

bedroom was the same size in both cases, the other rooms were all larger in the Wheatley dwelling than in those built after 1933.[173] On the other hand the later houses incorporated a number of qualitative improvements such as 'back-to-back' fireplaces (which provided heating in the living room and a baking oven in the kitchen), more fitted wardrobes and cupboards and better kitchen sinks.[174]

In Leeds 1933 can be seen as the point at which the trend towards 'building down' was arrested and, on the basis of dwelling size, to some extent reversed. But the improvements in council house design made after this date were in many respects a matter of aesthetics rather than statistics. Both Jenkinson and Livett accepted that the appearance of many of Leeds' existing estates was monotonous and they sought to capitalize on relatively low building costs and economies of scale to avoid this problem on the new slum clearance estates. In 1937 the *Journal of the Royal Institute of British Architects* praised the quality of both materials and construction to be found on Leeds' newer estates, and also the planning philosophy behind them.[175] Livett used architectural variations and lay-out plans to enhance the visual appeal of estates where 'simplification and standardisation' in design was inevitable (figs. 13a and 13b). With building density as low as 9.8 houses per acre on some sites[176] Livett's estates also enjoyed an abundance of open space and street scenes which were in marked contrast to those which characterized earlier developments by the City Council (figs. 13c and 13d).

In assessing the historical significance of the council estate we need to look beyond the (admittedly important) question of housing standards and adopt a broader perspective. We should ask to what extent these estates were more than 'mere aggregations of dwellings' and existed as communities in their own right before 1939; and we should also consider what part they played in shaping the residential pattern of the modern city. In Leeds the term 'council estate' was applied to housing developments of varying size and character. In 1939 there were in all 24 estates in the city, ranging in size from 33 to nearly 3,500 dwellings[177] (fig. 14). On the basis of size the estates can be divided into four groups. The first comprises five estates – Barkly and Grove Hall, Fairfax Road, Headingley, Hillidge Road and Southfield – with less than 100 dwellings each; these were effectively enclaves of council housing within much larger residential areas. Secondly, there was a group of four estates – East End Park and Ivy House, Greenthorpe, Harehills and St Alban's, and Hollin Park – within a range from 216 to 337 dwellings. Thirdly, there were seven estates – Cross Gates, Dewsbury Road, Hawksworth, Potternewton, Torre, Westfield and Wyther – of between 524 and 911 dwellings. Finally, there were eight larger estates – Belle Isle, Gipton, Halton Moor, Meanwood, Middleton, Sandford, Seacroft and York Road – each comprising more than 1,000 dwellings; Sandford was the smallest with 1,060 and Gipton the largest, with 3,478 dwellings. By 1939 this final group dominated council housing in Leeds; together they accounted for 14,461 dwellings, 70 per cent of all council houses in the city. But for the outbreak of war one of them, Seacroft, would have been in a class of its own by the mid-1940s, for although it had only 1,330 dwellings in March 1940 it had been conceived as a 'satellite town', with 11,000 council houses and a population of 40,000.[178] The development plan, eventually completed in the 1960s, envisaged a series of council estates grouped round a 'civic centre' of shops, public buildings, cinemas and other amenities. While there were to be good road and tramway links with the centre of Leeds, the inclusion of a wide range of social amenities, along with a light industrial estate, was intended to make Seacroft a largely self-contained community.[179] At Seacroft council housing in Leeds

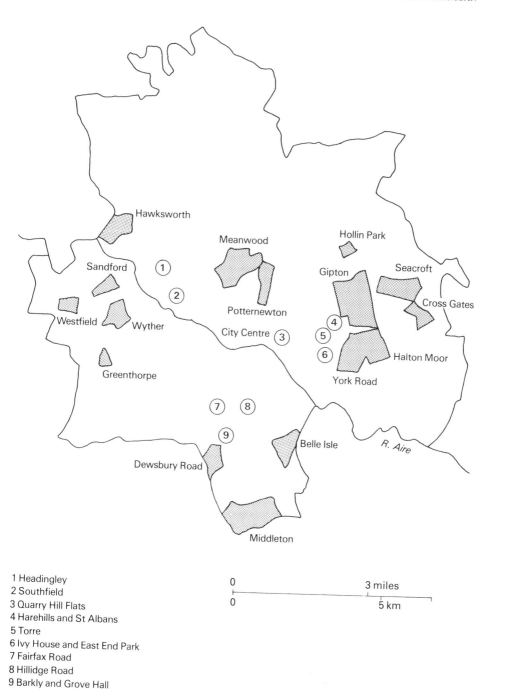

1 Headingley
2 Southfield
3 Quarry Hill Flats
4 Harehills and St Albans
5 Torre
6 Ivy House and East End Park
7 Fairfax Road
8 Hillidge Road
9 Barkly and Grove Hall

Figure 14.   Inter-war council estates in Leeds.

was at last approaching the garden city ideal; the other estates, however, tended to support the view that during the inter-war years 'the image of the nineteenth century garden city was adopted without its substance.'[180]

As we have seen, inter-war council housing reflected one essential of the garden city ideal: 'cottage'-type two-storey dwellings built at low densities. Although here as elsewhere the 'romanticism and individualism' of the garden cities gave way to 'simplification and standardisation', aesthetic shortcomings have to be weighed against the transformation in working-class housing standards brought about by council housing.[181] A more important failing was the lack of amenities, of an infrastructure around which housing estates could evolve as viable economic and social units. Development in Leeds followed the pattern, described in studies of the inter-war suburbs, whereby new estates were essentially residential colonies dependent on the inner city as a place of work and recreation.[182] The implications of this were more serious as distance from the city centre increased. In 1914 almost 80 per cent of Leeds' population lived within a radius of two miles from the city centre [183] and when, after the First World War, small-scale council estates were built within the same radius they were located in established residential areas already well served with local amenities and with easy access to both the city centre and the major industrial zones. By contrast, most of the larger estates were built on sites beyond the radius of residential development as it existed in 1914. In part this reflected a shortage of relatively large building plots within the built-up area, but it was also the consequence of a planning ideal to create new areas of low-density housing on the outskirts of towns and cities. In Leeds, before 1933, this concept found its clearest expression at Middleton; by that date the estate comprised more than 2,300 dwellings and was the largest in the city. In 1925 a deputation from the Garden Cities and Town Planning Association visited Middleton and were told by the chairman of Leeds' Improvements Committee that the estate had been designed with the intention of 'transporting people out of the city to a stretch of country and forming a new town away from the manufacturing centre.'[184] In truth Middleton was yet another dormitory suburb, devoid of many social amenities, whose residents depended heavily on the public transport link with the city proper. It has been argued that by the time of the Addison Act and the planning emphasis on suburban estates 'there was an established tradition of cheap municipal transport to help make such home locations viable.'[185] However, throughout the 1920s a recurrent grievance among council tenants in Leeds was the travelling costs incurred by living on the out-lying estates, which were seen as an unavoidable charge or an 'additional rent'. Moreover, the network of public transport routes was not a major determinant of council estate location in Leeds. Of greater importance was the availability, or otherwise, of building sites of adequate size and thus in many cases, including Middleton, an estate was developed beyond any existing line of public transport and initially tenants were dependent on services which were not only expensive but also slow and infrequent.[186]

The increasing scale and changing purpose of council house building in Leeds after 1933 was paralleled by a growing concern about the inadequate social amenities on suburban estates. Although the political parties disputed many aspects, one point about the slum clearance programme was clear: it would eventually lead to the enforced suburbanization of more than 100,000 people. In 1938 Labour's newspaper, the *Leeds Weekly Citizen*, commented that many of those already rehoused were unhappy with their new life:

Removed from the unhealthy conditions of the congested areas in the central portions of the town, they are at the same time removed from the cinemas, clubs, places of entertainment and the comforting warmth of brightly illuminated shopping centres.[187]

By March 1940 the City Council had rehoused a total of 34,067 people in the previous seven and a half years. Of this total, 62 per cent were to be found on just five suburban estates: Belle Isle, Gipton, Halton Moor, Sandford and York Road. Ten estates each housed less than 1 per cent of the slum clearance population and the mean figure for the remainder was 3.1 per cent.[188] The Gipton estate alone accounted for over 31 per cent of all those rehoused from the slums, and with nearly 3,500 dwellings was the largest single council estate in Leeds at the end of the 1930s. If Middleton typified development in the 1920s then Gipton, built between 1934 and 1938, was its counterpart in the following decade. Gipton was Leeds' first estate to be purpose-built for slum clearance rehousing and as such it embodied the planning ideals of Labour policy, both in relation to housing standards and in the provision of community facilities.[189] The plans for the Gipton scheme included a central shopping area and several secondary groups of shops at various points on the estate; a community centre with a public hall and sports facilities; a cinema, two churches, two hotels and $13\frac{1}{2}$ acres of allotments together with playing fields and other open spaces.[190] In the event only half the number of shops intended for the central area were completed and neither the community centre nor the cinema was ever built.[191] Thus in two key areas, retailing and recreation, the amenities at Gipton were little better than those on the city's older estates, and this was equally true of the other big slum clearance estates in the 1930s. Not until May 1939 did the City Council approve a scheme designed to provide an estate with a comprehensive range of amenities. In that month it was announced that Leeds' first 'model community centre' was to be built to serve the Middleton and Belle Isle estates.[192] Earlier in the year a council report had suggested that twelve estates in all were in need of such centres. The report had been prompted by a growing concern about anti-social behaviour on council estates, among juveniles in particular, which mainly took the form of vandalism.[193]

With the outbreak of the Second World War the scheme for the Middleton community centre was abandoned, and at that point only one municipally operated community facility (other than schools or clinics) had been established on any council estate in Leeds – a community hall and branch library opened at Meanwood in September 1936.[194] The increasing publicity afforded to the social consequences of rehousing on amenity-deficient estates had led one local businessman to salvage something from the Council's grandiose plans. He donated £8,000 to pay for the building of a youth club at Gipton on the understanding that the Council provided the site and assisted in the running of the club.[195] Philanthropic intervention of this kind sharpened the political conflict about social life on the council estates. Labour felt that it was the Council's responsibility to provide a full range of social and recreational amenities on the estates, whereas the Conservatives favoured community development through private enterprise or voluntary agencies and had voted against the Meanwood project on the grounds that it would set a precedent for similar provision on every estate.[196] Historically, voluntary bodies such as the churches or tenants' associations had been the main instigators in establishing social amenities on Leeds' estates, but Labour argued that whenever this was left to commercial interests it usually resulted in 'the erection of a glorified public house, where at the cost of far too great a proportion of the family income expended on making dividends for the brewers, some measure of social life can be obtained.'[197] Indeed, in the absence of municipal initiatives the only widespread amenity, apart from low-order shops, was the public house – to the consternation of the temperance lobby. This fact, together with growing pressure at local and national level for moves to improve the social environment on housing estates, helped to change the attitude of Leeds' Conservative administration and it was they who promoted the Middleton project in 1939.

As in other large industrial cities, Leeds witnessed great social and environmental changes as a result of the housing policies pursued in the later 1930s. To quote Professor Burnett, local authorities in this period 'institutionalised for the working classes the process of suburbanisation which the middle classes had followed since at least the middle of the nineteenth century, but developed what had been a largely unconscious process for the few into a planned process for the many.'[198] For Jenkinson and the Labour Party in general this was, indeed, the purpose of council housing: the removal of almost a quarter of Leeds' population from the congested inner city to new low-density developments in the suburbs. In November 1933 Jenkinson wrote in his parish magazine that slum clearance would 'within a comparatively short period – a few years at most – involve the disappearance of most of the parish as it now is and it will be a great joy to me to be in charge of the job.'[199] Statements of this kind often made Jenkinson appear indifferent to the social upheaval which accompanied the break-up of a long-established working-class community and the movement of people from the familiar to the unfamiliar. Moreover, it was the abundance of social and recreational amenities in these areas which highlighted the shortcomings of the suburban estates. As we have seen, slum clearance rehousing in Leeds occurred predominantly on a small number of outlying estates, and the implications of this are shown in table 10.[200]

Table 10. *Household movements resulting from slum clearance in Leeds, 1936–7*

miles	distance of principal wage-earner from place of work originally (%)	after rehousing (%)	distance between original house and new dwelling (%)
Up to 1	25.5	11.8	7.8
$1\frac{1}{4}$–$2\frac{1}{2}$	51.0	55.8	83.7
$2\frac{3}{4}$–5	9.3	27.4	8.3
Over 5	4.2	5.0	0.2

For the majority of those involved, slum clearance rehousing obviously increased the distance between home and workplace, while at the same time it imposed distance as an obstacle to the maintenance of ties with familiar working-class neighbourhoods. Even among Labour politicians there was a recognition that many people in the clearance areas valued the 'human associations' if not the living conditions offered by their locality. In order to retain these relationships it was advocated that neighbours in clearance areas should be rehoused close together on the new estates.[201] In practice, however, this happened only on a limited scale and the process of rehousing was characterized by dispersal and the destruction of those 'subtle webs of family and friendship.'[202] As table 11 indicates, the population size of clearance areas in Leeds varied considerably, yet even among those with fewer than 100 residents it was usual for the displaced households to be accommodated on a number of different estates. Although the numbers in each 'cohort' were correspondingly greater in the larger clearance areas, so were the number of destinations to which the total population was dispersed.[203]

Table 11.   Population dispersal resulting from slum clearance in Leeds, 1933–40

	no. of persons in clearance area rehoused by City Council			
	Up to 100	101–500	501–1,000	Over 1,000
no. of clearance areas	83	35	8	9
total population	2,503	7,831	5,228	18,059
mean	30.2	223.7	661	2,006.5
av. no. destinations/ clearance area	3.6	7.9	13.4	16.2
mean cohort size (persons)	8.4	28.3	49.3	123.8

Between 1933 and 1940 Leeds saw the removal of almost 34,000 people from one kind of physical and social environment to another as the result of its slum clearance policies. This process aroused remarkably little popular resistance, despite Labour's initial expectation that opposition to the idea of planned suburbanization both from individuals and from communities in the clearance areas was inevitable.[204] Neverthe-less, this prospect had led Jenkinson and his colleagues to make an important depar-ture from their ideal of low-density housing in the suburbs, and to sanction an extensive programme of flat building on sites previously covered by slum property. This was Labour's answer to the problem of maintaining the physical and social fabric of Leeds' central area in the wake of slum clearance. Ultimately it provided the city with a housing estate which became one of the most famous of its kind in the world: Quarry Hill Flats. If the plans of the 1933–5 Labour administration had been completed the Quarry Hill estate would have been just one of several similar developments, for its programme to build 30,000 new council dwellings by 1941 envisaged that 6,500 would take the form of multi-storey flats, or what Livett pre-ferred to call 'grouped dwellings', built on cleared sites in the 'inner ring' of the city.[205] In the past the Labour Party in Leeds had always opposed the idea of working-class flats and Jenkinson himself considered that 'the cottage house is the best dwelling for the normal English family.'[206] But this feeling was over-ridden by practicalities, given that some families would not want to move to suburban estates and that in some areas the numbers would be such that rehousing in flats in clearance areas was 'the only practicable policy.'[207] Moreover, Jenkinson had chosen as Housing Director a man who was firmly wedded to the idea of flat building in the 'inner ring'. (Indeed, a scheme he designed for Manchester Corporation, at Kennet House, can now be seen as a small-scale precursor of the later development at Quarry Hill.[208]) Livett's en-thusiasm derived from both social and financial considerations. He agreed that there would be pressure for rehousing in or near the clearance areas close by workplaces and social amenities. The cost of acquiring these areas and preparing them for redevelopment dictated that the new housing would have to take the form of multi-storey flats built at higher densities than suburban council housing. Livett estimated that whereas an A3 house in the suburbs cost about £350 to build, including a land element of £20–25, a three-bedroom flat in the 'inner-ring' cost £600, including £100 for land. Nevertheless, he argued that to build flats was an 'economic' proposition not only because they attracted a higher level of government subsidy but also because 'inner-ring' developments did not incur the same level of expenditure on providing amenities and services as did suburban house building. Use could be made of existing schools, clinics, recreation grounds, shops and entertainments, and unlike 'outer-ring' schemes they did not require expensive extensions to mains services such as gas, water and sewers.[209] On this count Livett was really more in tune with Conservative thinking, for they had long advocated a greater emphasis on flat building near the city centre.[210] In office between 1935 and 1939, the Conservatives approved further multi-storey developments at Marsh Lane and Sweet Street, comprising altogether 837 flats, while encouraging the Housing Director to prepare plans for the redevelopment of other clearance areas.[211] However, Quarry Hill Flats were the only scheme of this type ever to be completed, and they were very much a product of Labour's housing policy. The redevelopment of Quarry Hill was also a symbolic project, occupying a prime site at the eastern end of the Headrow–Eastgate axis which had been widened during the previous decade to create a major city centre thoroughfare. At the western end were the municipal buildings and the Town Hall, the expression of Victorian Leeds and its civic pride; in the east Quarry Hill Flats were envisaged as 'an architectural ornament to the city'[212] and, by implication, as a testament to the Labour Party's housing reforms (fig. 15).

Having decided to build multi-storey flats Labour were determined that these should transcend the image of the nineteenth-century tenement. They were confident this could be achieved by following the example of continental housing schemes, notably in Vienna. When the first stage of the Quarry Hill estate was opened in March 1938 Jenkinson remarked that its origins dated back to a summer morning in Vienna six years before when he and a fellow Labour councillor had first seen the city's famous workers' flats.[213] What struck them was not the dwellings themselves but the 'unrivalled social amenities' offered by the estates, and thereafter they sought to add these to 'the far superior amenities of the English home' in their plans for Leeds. The execution of this vision was assigned to Livett, himself much influenced by the Modern Movement, as the architecture at Quarry Hill showed. The layout plan of the Quarry Hill site was based on a crescent-shaped 'perimeter wall' enclosing several parallel blocks. The elevations of the buildings, which ranged in height from four to eight storeys, were characterized by flat roofs, strong horizontal lines emphasized by alternating bands of contrasting finishes, and by semi-circular and eliptical archways providing access to the interior of the estate.[214]

A crucial aspect of Livett's design for Quarry Hill was the marriage of a modernistic architectural style to a modern building system. This was the Mopin system which Livett imported from France where it had already been used for public housing schemes.[215] He was drawn towards using it in Leeds for two main reasons. First, it largely removed the need for skilled labour and brickwork, neither of which could be then provided locally on the scale demanded by building the Quarry Hill estate along traditional lines. Secondly, Mopin claimed that his system offered a reduction of 15–20 per cent in building costs when compared to traditional methods, given the promised economies in labour, materials and time.[216] This saving was used to finance two major innovations incorporated into Livett's design, which provided Quarry Hill with amenities hitherto unknown in public sector multi-storey housing. The first was the installation in each flat of the Garchey system of refuse disposal (again of French origin) which carried domestic refuse and sink waste by a combination of gravitation and suction to incinerators at a central refuse-disposal station. Livett considered this to be a simple, hygienic and relatively inexpensive solution to the problem of waste disposal in blocks of flats.[217] The second innovation was the provision of passenger lifts, thus enabling the maximum height of the blocks to be fixed at eight storeys and the total number of flats at 938.[218] Livett firmly believed in vertical as opposed to horizontal development because it maximized the amount of open space within the estate. With blocks of 6 to 8 storeys dwellings could still be built at a density of 40 per acre while leaving 85 per cent of the site free of buildings, thus comparing favourably with the total area of open space on suburban estates, which seldom exceeded 88 per cent of the site; only when housing density fell as low as 9.8 dwellings per acre was this achieved.[219]

In designing the dwellings at Quarry Hill Livett had to try and overcome the problems of privacy and access which had bedevilled the Victorian tenement and fostered the popular prejudice against flats. Labour's policy dictated that the common balcony arrangement would not be used in any multi-storey housing development in Leeds, and at Quarry Hill Livett therefore gave each flat its own private balcony and provided entry to the flats via staircases which served two dwellings at each landing level.[220] The estate comprised five types of accommodation: 80 aged persons' flats, 413 A2 flats, 381 A3s, 22 A4s and 42 A5s. In each case room sizes compared favourably with those found in council houses being built in Leeds at this time.[221] Livett paid great attention to the internal planning and equipment of the flats at Quarry Hill, which Dr Ravetz has described as 'the most advanced dwellings that had then been built for working-class populations.'[222] Jenkinson, together with his allies,

Figure 15.   'An architectural ornament to the city': a view of Quarry Hill Flats from the air.

would no doubt have been gratified by such a comment as they originally promised Leeds would have 'the finest working-class flats in the world.'[223] Even so they never abandoned the notion that a flat was inherently inferior to a house, to which the corollary was an insistence that flat-dwellers should have, by way of 'compensation', access to good social amenities within their estates. This view conflicted with Livett's argument that 'grouped dwellings' in the inner city had the advantage of close proximity to existing amenities and services, thereby reducing the need for new provision. However, Livett's design for Quarry Hill incorporated a number of community facilities, such as a laundry, shops, community centre, clinic and recreation grounds.[224] But from an early stage the Quarry Hill contract was beset by major technical and organizational problems which prolonged building from a planned eighteen months to more than five years. When construction work came to a halt in 1940 only the flats themselves had been completed; subsequently the laundry and a group of nine shops were built, but to the end Quarry Hill was devoid of the range of facilities envisaged in the original plan.[225] In this respect Quarry Hill typified the shortcomings of Leeds' council estates generally during the inter-war years, but at least its residents differed from those on suburban estates in that they lived only a short distance from the amenities offered by the city centre and working-class districts in the 'inner ring'.

Until their demolition in the mid-1970s Quarry Hill Flats stood as Leeds' most dramatic reminder of that process of urban renewal induced by the housing policies of the inter-war years. Today Leeds has only a small reminder of Britain's 'great quinquennium of flat building'[226] during the late 1930s. This is Brontë House, at Potternewton, a block of 22 flats designed by Livett to accommodate single women of working age (fig. 16). Quarry Hill was an exceptional development, and in part this was due to its location in the very centre of the city. It was the only estate of its kind in Leeds to be built before the Second World War and represented less than 5 per cent of the total number of council dwellings built in the city between 1919 and 1939. Indeed, no more than 12 per cent of this total were built within a radius of two miles from the city centre: the area where 80 per cent of Leeds' population had lived in 1914, and where the focus of the slum clearance policy lay. The dominant feature of council housing development in Leeds both before and after 1933 was therefore the suburban estate, beyond the city's existing built-up area. Thus in 1938 the City Council informed the Barlow Commission that its policy 'has been and still is to develop new housing estates of large dimensions in suburban districts leaving many of the central areas thus vacated to be zoned for development as industrial areas.'[227] Clearly, it is to the suburbs that we must turn in order to assess the impact of council housing on the social geography of the city during the inter-war period.

Residential patterns in 1914 were essentially the product of market forces in urban housing. As far as the middle decades of the nineteenth century are concerned there is an as yet unresolved debate about the nature of residential segregation within the industrial city.[228] By the Edwardian era, however, it is clear that the city had become 'a mosaic of territories . . . dominated by the members of a particular class or group and which [had] known if not identified boundaries.' This pattern was the spatial manifestation of the structure of urban society itself, in that social distance between the classes was reflected in, and reinforced by, residential segregation. It separated not only the upper and lower classes but also led to the 'fine grained sifting' of residential areas as the economic and social division of labour became more complex.[229] The interaction of economic development, social change, improvements in transportation and the building cycle created a gradient of housing standards in Leeds as elsewhere which, in 1914, ranged from the slums in the centre of the city to the late Victorian and Edwardian villas in the suburbs.[230]

After 1918 the impact of housing policies was felt at both ends of the urban residential gradient. The inner city was affected primarily by rent control and slum clearance. By providing working-class tenants with an incentive to stay in one house over a long period of time rent control can be held responsible for the dramatic decline in the rate of household movement witnessed after the First World War. Between 1919 and 1939 the rate was little more than 20 per cent of that regarded as the 'norm' in earlier times.[231] With residential mobility both within and between different working-class districts at such a low level the communities in these areas experienced a period of unprecedented stability. Thus when Richard Hoggart reflected on his childhood and youth in a working-class district of Leeds before 1939 and likened such areas to 'small worlds, each as homogeneous and well defined as a village'[232] he was describing a style of family and community life, fashioned by several generations of urban existence, which passed through a 'classic age' between the wars. Ironically, it was at this point that housing policy also began to undermine this way of life. During the 1930s slum clearance did much more than simply remove insanitary dwellings: in the aggregate it decimated established communities and started the long-term destruction of the 'urban mosaic' created by the Victorian housing market. The restructuring of the housing market in the 1920s had already influenced the nature of suburban development. With the decline of the private landlord and the expansion both of owner-occupation and of council housing, tenure itself emerged as a major axis of residential differentiation in the inter-war city. State intervention proved to be as effective as market forces had been in the past at imposing a pattern of residential segregation on the city for 'as long as there were both private and public housing, the boundary of the municipal housing estate would also be a boundary of social class.'[233]

Figure 16.   Brontë House, Potternewton: the only development of multi-storey council flats in Leeds to survive from the 1930s.

Before the First World War housing reformers had seen an end to residential segregation as a prerequisite for the amelioration of class conflict in society, believing that the physical separation of the classes fostered one group's ignorance and fear of another.[234] When it became apparent that the state would promote the process of working-class suburbanization at the end of the war they saw this as an opportunity to promote the cause of class co-operation and social harmony. In Leeds this view was epitomized by Alderman F.M. Lupton, who had chaired the Unhealthy Areas Committee of the City Council in the 1890s. Writing in 1918 about the possibilities offered by the post-war housing programme he contrasted 'the class antagonisms so painfully prevalent in all our large cities' with 'the friendly intercourse so commonly found in smaller places and which naturally arises between people who have always lived next door to each other and been able to share and help each other's troubles.'[235] Like many other people Lupton saw post-war reconstruction as both a physical and a social process. At its heart would be a programme of house building designed to create the kind of environment where social conflict was replaced by co-operation across the class divide. Locally, such hopes were to be held in vain because housing itself became an issue often surrounded by intense political controversy, not least in relation to where council estates were to be built. The sensitivity of this question first came to the fore in 1925 when the Improvements Committee sought to build an estate at Hollin Park close to two prime middle-class residential areas, Oakwood and Roundhay. Although the estate was to comprise high-rented parlour houses, whose occupants would of necessity be relatively 'well off', the proposal disturbed those who already lived in the area. Because the estate was planned at twelve houses per acre, in an area zoned for development up to a limit of eight per acre, it had to be considered by a Ministry of Health local inquiry. The residents' arguments about loss of amenity and reduced property values persuaded the Ministry to reduce the size of the estate from 460 to 360 houses, thereby raising the unit cost and rent of each dwelling.[236] The Council had argued that the residents' real objection was to the kind of housing planned for Hollin Park, which was housing for working-class tenants.[237] Certainly, it is difficult to avoid the conclusion that throughout they saw council housing *per se* as a socially inferior form of housing tenure, and held no brief for the view expressed by the chairman of the Improvements Committee, Alderman Charles Lupton (brother of F.M. Lupton) that there were 'great social advantages' to be derived from the building of working-class housing in what were essentially middle-class residential areas.[238]

In the wake of the Hollin Park controversy Charles Lupton reiterated his belief that 'the city's inhabitants should not . . . be divided into sections, one part being occupied by rich people and the other by the poor, leading to class distinction, which was the cause of so many . . . social evils.'[239] In practice, however, council policy was itself partly responsible for perpetuating residential segregation in Leeds' newer suburbs. To a great extent this resulted from factors beyond the Council's immediate control, and in particular from the structure of land ownership in the city. During the inter-war years the location of council estates in Leeds was effectively determined by a historical pattern of land ownership which imposed geographical constraints on the availability of potential housing sites.[240] Development during the Addison and Wheatley eras was channelled into those parts of the city where relatively large building plots could be purchased and after 1933 a more extensive house-building programme served only to reinforce the existing locational pattern. This pattern comprised four main areas of council housing development. In west Leeds there was a group of five estates in close proximity: Greenthorpe, Hawksworth, Sandford, Westfield and Wyther. To the south the estates at Dewsbury Road, Middleton and Belle Isle formed a second grouping, and in the north the Meanwood and Potternewton estates formed a third. Council house building was most extensive, however, in east Leeds where eight estates were developed along the York Road axis comprising a total of more than 9,000 dwellings in 1939. The geography of council housing in turn reflected the pre-industrial geography of landholding in Leeds. Within the city's boundaries the River Aire formed the dividing line between two distinct regions. To the south and west lay an area characterized by small plots and fragmented land ownership, with more than two-thirds of all holdings amounting to ten acres or less. By contrast, the area to the north and east of the town centre was marked by large plots and compact ownership; almost half the units of ownership extended to more than ten acres.[241] Thus there was good reason why east Leeds in particular should become the 'heartland' of council housing in the city, and why development in the south and west was more dispersed and restricted to the few large sites which became available fig. 14).

A significant feature in the distribution of Leeds' inter-war council estates is the absence of development in the north, beyond a radius of $2\frac{1}{2}$ miles from the city centre. The explanation for this is threefold. First, continuity of land ownership in this area was not as pronounced as in the east, and large holdings were rare. Secondly, north Leeds generally was the area traditionally favoured by voluntary suburbanites and by speculative builders.[242] The fragmented landholding pattern in the locality lent itself to piecemeal speculative development, while the semi-rural environment made districts such as Far Headingley, Lawnswood, Moortown and Roundhay the 'best' residential areas in the city. The third reason why council housing did not intrude into such districts as these was essentially political, for although on occasion the Council came forward with plans to build near 'better-class' property these always provoked an outcry both from builders and from residents in the private sector. The clearest illustration of this came when the Labour council of 1933–5 decided to build an estate of 2,500 dwellings on a 400 acre site at Moortown.[243] To Labour's opponents the scheme was 'a deliberate attack on the property-owners of Moortown' designed to reduce the value of private houses in the area.[244] No doubt Jenkinson and others relished the prospect of council houses costing £300 being built in an area where some houses sold for over £3,000 but the decision to build at Moortown was born of necessity, given the shortage of suitable sites to meet the demands of the rehousing programme. Increasingly the Council was having to consider sites in various parts of the city where the prospect of a council estate being developed would inevitably be controversial.[245] By the mid-1930s, however, these were no longer conflicts fuelled by perceptions of social status; class was now clearly the issue. As the residents of Moortown were aware, council housing in Leeds had become a social service allocated to tenants who were least able to afford adequate housing, including some of the poorest working-class families from some of the most notorious slum areas in the city.

In November 1935 the Conservatives regained control of the City Council, having committed themselves beforehand to abandon the Moortown project. In the following year the Council purchased the Halton Moor site where an estate of comparable size to the one planned at Moortown was built. It was effectively an extension of the York Road estate built under the Wheatley Act and went ahead without any political difficulty since council housing was already the predominant form of tenure in the area. At Moortown the Council had tried to placate local residents by emphasizing the physical distance which would separate them from the council estate[246] and this argument was deployed whenever municipal and private development came into conflict. (Indeed, at Seacroft the Council promised to use tree-planting and other devices to screen the estate from private property in the vicinity.[247]) In 1937 the Conservatives themselves incurred the displeasure of the property lobby when they approved the purchase of a housing site at Beckett Park. Local residents were subsequently reassured by Alderman Blackah, chairman of the Housing Committee, who made this telling remark: 'People in Headingley seem to think we are going to link-up privately owned property with a municipal housing estate. We are not. Several hundred yards will intervene between the two.'[248] Moreover, he noted how building would take place on that part of the site 'which is really Kirkstall', a district having a somewhat lower social tone than Headingley in the 1930s.

The social and physical distance which for the most part separated public and private housing in 1939 demonstrates how the polarization of the housing market during the inter-war years, between owner-occupiers and council tenants, strengthened one of the major features of urban residential development: spatial segregation along class divisions. Twenty-five years after F.M. Lupton had written about these matters it was Jenkinson's turn to consider the prospects for housing policy following the end of a world war. In so doing he reflected on the policies of the immediate past, and expressed his concern about the 'sociological defects' of council housing, and in particular the problems which had arisen with the development of 'welfare housing' in the mid-1930s. Jenkinson noted that after 1933 the larger local authorities such as Leeds had built new housing estates populated almost exclusively by tenants transferred from the slums. Ten years on it could be seen that the consequences had been 'a far slower general improvement than would be the case if estate populations were well mixed with rehoused slum clearance and overcrowded families forming a minority.'[249] In stating a case for 'balanced communities' Jenkinson acknowledged that the improvements in the quality of family and communal life, for which he and others had hoped, had not followed on from environmental improvement. Because of council housing and slum clearance, by 1939 there was no longer a close correlation between income and social class on the one hand and housing standards on the other; many of the very poorest families occupied modern dwellings built to a relatively high standard in suburban locations. But the estates on which they lived were socially and architecturally distinct from contemporary housing areas developed for the owner-occupier. Indeed, from the early 1930s onwards the social composition of council estates became ever more sharply defined as a consequence of housing policy attempting to meet housing need. Increasingly, council tenants were marked out as a class apart: individuals who could not provide themselves with adequate housing without the direct assistance of the state. The growth of council housing between the wars therefore created a new source of social division and helped to perpetuate some of the basic inequalities in urban society.

NOTES

1 I should like to thank both Professor Derek Fraser and my external examiner, Professor John Butt of the University of Strathclyde, for agreeing to read through and comment upon an earlier version of this paper. I should also like to thank Jeanne Bellovics who typed the final version, and Doug Haigh for the photographs which accompany it. Their efforts are much appreciated.
2 Cf. K. Bassett and J. Short, *Housing and Residential Structure* (1980), 101–5.
3 For a comprehensive survey of Leeds' history in this period see D. Fraser (ed.), *A History of Modern Leeds* (1980).
4 Cf. M.W. Beresford, 'The back-to-back house in Leeds, 1787–1937' in *The History of Working-Class Housing*, ed. S.D. Chapman (1971), 95–132, and his more recent article 'The face of Leeds, 1780–1914' in Fraser, *op. cit.*, 72–112 which contains some excellent photographs of nineteenth-century Leeds housing.
5 LCC, *MOH Annual Report* (1920), 101. The number of back-to-backs in present-day Leeds is nearer 20,000; for the recent history of the back-to-back in Leeds see K. Powell, *Leeds: Must Old Still Mean Bad?* (1981).
6 D. Ward, 'The urban plan of Leeds' (M.A. thesis, University of Leeds, 1960), 131.
7 These were defined and described in LCC, *MOH Annual Report* (1920), 101.
8 *Building Societies' Gazette and Land Companies' Record*, XLI (1909), 92.
9 B. Barber, 'Municipal government in Leeds, 1835–1914', in *Municipal Reform and the Industrial City*, ed. D. Fraser (1982), 102–3.
10 *YP*, 11 December 1913.
11 Ward, *op. cit.*, table 15.
12 *YP*, 19 January 1914.
13 T. Paylor, *Leeds for Labour (Tracts for Leeds People, No. 1)* (1905), 6.
14 D. Ward, 'The building cycle and the growth of the built-up area of Leeds', *Northern Universities Geographical Journal* (1960), 56.
15 *Ibid.*
16 LCC, 'Detailed Census Returns, 1901, Relating to Housing Conditions in the Area Controlled by the Leeds City Council'; Leeds Labour Party, *Yearbook* (1914), 53.
17 Beresford, *op. cit.* (1971), 116.
18 *Ibid.*
19 Leeds Labour Party, *Yearbook* (1915), 64.
20 *YP*, 26 January 1914.
21 *YP*, 9 April 1914.
22 *YO*, 17 September 1918.
23 *LWC*, 21 June 1918; M.W. Beresford, *The Leeds Chamber of Commerce* (1951), 187.
24 *YP*, 4 July and 3 October 1918.
25 M.J. Meadowcroft, 'Transition in Leeds city government, 1903–26' (M.Phil. thesis, University of Bradford, 1978), 19.
26 C. Cook, 'Labour and the downfall of the Liberal Party, 1906–14' in *Crisis and Controversy*, ed. A. Sked and C. Cook (1976), 38–65.
27 *YP*, 3 November 1919.
28 Meadowcroft, *op. cit.*, 235.
29 *YP*, 2 November 1926.
30 Ministry of Labour, *Local Unemployment Index* (H.M.S.O., 1932); S. Glynn and J. Oxborrow, *Inter-War Britain* (1976), 145.
31 J. H. Richardson, *Industrial Employment and Unemployment in West Yorkshire* (1936), 63–4, 79; W. G. Rimmer, 'Between the wars', *Leeds Journal*, XXX (1959), 352; J. Thomas, *A History of the Leeds Clothing Industry* (1955), 54.
32 W.G. Rimmer, 'Occupations in Leeds, 1841–1951', *Publications of the Thoresby Society*, L (1967) 162.

33 R.E. Dickinson, 'The regional functions and zones of influence of Leeds and Bradford', *Geography*, xv (1929–30), 553.
34 Memorandum of Evidence submitted to the Royal Commission on the Location of Industry on behalf of the Corporation of the City of Leeds, 1938, Table M (PRO/HLG/27/63).
35 LCC, *MOH Annual Report* (1921 to 1939).
36 *Ibid.*
37 Cf. J. Dale, 'Class struggle, social policy and state structure: central-local relations and housing policy, 1919–39' in *Housing, Social Policy and the State*, ed. J. Melling (1980), 194–223.
38 Cf. J. Butt, 'Working-class housing in Glasgow 1900–39', in *Essays in Scottish Labour History*, ed. I. MacDougal (1978), 143–69.
39 The other cities in this group were Birmingham, Liverpool, Manchester and Sheffield, cf. J.B. Cullingworth, *Housing and Local Government in England and Wales* (1966), 28.
40 LCC, Housing Committee minutes, 15 December 1933; 15 September 1939.
41 LCC, *Improvements Committee Annual Report* (1919–20 to 1933–4); *Housing Committee Annual Report* (1934–5 to 1939–40).
42 This figure was obtained from Ministry of Health, 'Inter-War Years Housing Record Cards' for Leeds, now held by the Dept. of the Environment Headquarters. I am indebted to Mrs Christine Archer, formerly Research Assistant in the Division of Economic Studies, University of Sheffield, for providing this information.
43 LCC, *Development Plan Written Survey* (1951), 10.
44 Cf. M. Bowley, 'Local authorities and housing subsidies since 1919', *The Manchester School*, xii (1942), 57–8.
45 LCC, *MOH Annual Report* (1920), 102.
46 *Ibid.*, 103. Cf. P.R. Wilding, 'The administrative aspects of the 1919 housing scheme', *Public Administration*, li (1973), 307–26.
47 *YP*, 21 February 1922.
48 *LM*, 20 December 1922; *YP*, 21 December 1922.
49 *YP*, 17 December 1924. This was also the way in which Chamberlain himself saw owner-occupation, cf. K. Feiling, *The Life of Neville Chamberlain* (1946), 86.
50 *YP*, 7 October 1926.
51 J.H. Jennings, 'Geographical implications of the municipal housing programme in England and Wales', *Urban Studies*, viii (1971), 121–38.
52 *YP*, 22 October 1932.
53 *YP*, 5 March 1931.
54 Ministry of Health, *Second and Final Report of the Committee appointed by the Minister of Health to consider and advise on the principles to be followed in dealing with Unhealthy Areas* (1921), 6.
55 LCC, 'Report on Slum Clearance presented to the Housing Committee by the MOH' (1932), App. V.
56 LCC, *MOH Annual Report* (1926), 169–70. Dr Jervis served as Leeds' M.O.H. from 1916–47. Cf. O. Hartley, 'The post-war years' in Fraser, *op. cit.*, 445–6.
57 *YP*, 24 May 1923.
58 *YP*, 25 May 1923; cf. Ministry of Health, Memo from Mr W.H. Colin, Supervising Inspector, to Mr E.R. Forber, 12 April 1922 (PRO/HLG/47/371).
59 Ministry of Health, Letter from Deputy Town Clerk of Leeds to Mr J.C. Wrigley, 29 August 1927 (PRO/HLG/47/371).
60 Leeds and District Property Owners' and Ratepayers' Association, *Annual Report* (1924), 21.
61 *YP*, 28 June 1928.
62 P.R. Wilding, 'Government and housing: a study in the development of social policy, 1906–39' (Ph.D. thesis, University of Manchester, 1970), 286.

63 LCC, *MOH Annual Report* (1933), 243; C. Jenkinson *et al.*, *The Minority Report* (1933), 34, 59.

64 Jenkinson, *op. cit.* (1933), 34.

65 *YP*, 26 July 1933.

66 Jenkinson was born in London in 1887 and came to Leeds at the age of forty; he was elected to the City Council for the first time in November 1930. He died in 1949. For a biography of Jenkinson see H.J. Hammerton, *This Turbulent Priest* (1952).

67 For more detail on this period see my essay 'Housing policy in Leeds between the wars' in Melling, *op. cit.*, 120–22.

68 LCC, *MOH Annual Report* (1933), 244; *YP*, 13 January 1934.

69 LCC, *Housing Committee Annual Report* (1934–5), 4.

70 M. Bowley, *Housing and the State* (1945), 155.

71 D.A. Kirby, *Slum Clearance and Residential Renewal: The Case in Urban Britain* (1979), 80.

72 LCC, *Development Plan Written Survey* (1951), 10.

73 LCC, *MOH Annual Report* (1938), 274a; *ibid.* (1939), 102.

74 I have discussed this issue at greater length in Melling, *op. cit.*, 122–5.

75 *YP*, 1 April 1936.

76 *YP*, 25 July 1936.

77 *YP*, 19 December 1936.

78 *YP*, 18 October 1937.

79 *YP*, 23, 28 February, 31 October 1934; *Journal of the Leeds and District Property Owners' and Ratepayers' Association* (February 1934), 17–19.

80 This information was obtained from record cards produced by the Ministry of Health and now held by the DOE; see n. 42 above.

81 Bowley, *op. cit.* (1945), 171–2; S. Merrett, *State Housing in Britain* (1979), 53–4.

82 R.K. Wilkinson and E.M. Sigsworth, 'Trends in property values and transactions and housing finance since 1900', Final Report to SSRC on Grant HR 2030/2(1978), 108; cf. C.A. Archer and R.K. Wilkinson, 'The Yorkshire Registries of Deeds as sources of historical data on housing markets', in *Urban History Yearbook*, ed. H.J. Dyos (1977), 40–47.

83 LCC, *MOH Annual Report* (1927), 198.

84 *Ibid.* (1932), 18–21.

85 *Ibid.*

86 Jenkinson, *op. cit.* (1933), 35–7.

87 J.R. Jarmain, *Housing Subsidies and Rents* (1948), 45.

88 *LM*, 13 October 1920.

89 *YP*, 27 February 1922.

90 LCC, Improvements Committee Minutes, 20 April 1926, 17 May 1927, 4 October 1927.

91 *LWC*, 5 December 1930.

92 LCC, Improvements Committee Minutes, 22 October 1929.

93 LCC, *A Short History of Civic Housing* (1954), 23.

94 LCC, *MOH Annual Report* (1930), 267.

95 LCC, *Report of the Sub-Improvement (Housing) Committee on the Present Position and Future Policy of Housing in the City of Leeds* (1932), 16–17; *YP*, 30 July 1929, 23 November 1932, 22 September 1933.

96 LCC, *MOH Annual Report* (1930), 267.

97 C. Jenkinson, 'Rent differentiation, with special reference to the Leeds policy', *The Municipal Review*, v (1934), 195–6.

98 *Ibid.*; Bowley, *op. cit.* (1945), 161.

99 Bowley, *op. cit.* (1945), 161–2; G. Wilson, *Rent Rebates* (1939), *passim*.

100 Hammerton, *op. cit.*, 114.

101 Wilson, *op. cit.*, 55.

102 Bowley, *op. cit.* (1945), 162–3.

103 Jarmain, *op. cit.*, 218; *YP*, 21 February 1934.
104 *LWC*, 2 March 1934.
105 *YP*, 2 March 1934.
106 *The Times*, 3 April 1934.
107 *YP*, 6 October 1934.
108 *YP*, 22 January 1934.
109 *YP*, 2 March 1934.
110 *YP*, 20 March 1934.
111 *YP*, 30 May 1934, 19 October 1935.
112 Jarmain, *op. cit.*, 138–42.
113 *YP*, 27 November 1934.
114 *YP*, 19 October 1935.
115 *YP*, 25, 28 February 1936; cf. Wilson, *op. cit.*, 21.
116 *YP*, 5 March 1936.
117 *YP*, 28 February 1936.
118 *LWC*, 3 April 1936; *YP*, 5 March 1936.
119 *LWC*, 3 April 1936; *YP*, 5 March 1936.
120 *LWC*, 12 March 1937; *YP*, 20 February, 4 March 1937.
121 LCC, Housing Committee Minutes, 19 March 1937; Wilson, *op. cit.*, 21; *YP*, 20 February 1937.
122 *YP*, 30 November 1937.
123 *YP*, 30 June, 4 October 1937.
124 LCC, *Housing Committee Annual Report* (1939–40), 16–17.
125 *YP*, 22 September 1934.
126 LCC, *MOH Annual Report* (1934), 15.
127 *Ibid.* (1936), 263.
128 *Ibid.* (1928), 221.
129 LCC, *Finance and Parliamentary Committee Annual Report* (1930–31), 70–75.
130 Ministry of Health, *Rents of Houses and Flats owned by Local Authorities (England and Wales)*, Cmd. 5527 (1937).
131 LCC, *Housing Committee Annual Report* (1939–40), 24.
132 *Ibid.*
133 A. Briggs, 'Social history 1900–45' in *The Economic History of Britain since 1700: Vol 2, 1860 to the 1970s*, eds R. Floud and D. McCloskey (1981), 365.
134 Cf. M. Swenarton, *Homes Fit for Heroes* (1981), *passim*.
135 J. Burnett, *A Social History of Housing* (1978), 218.
136 *YEP*, 1 June 1920.
137 LCC, *Improvements Committees Annual Report* (1918–19), 20.
138 LCC, Improvements Committee Minutes, 8 April, 17 June 1919.
139 *LWC*, 7 November 1919; *YEN*, 17 October 1919; *YEP*, 4, 25 September 1919, 1 April 1920; *YP*, 1 April 1920.
140 *YP*, 1 April 1920.
141 *YEP*, 17 December 1921.
142 LCC, *Leeds Tercentenary Official Handbook* (1926), 130; cf. S. Marriner, 'Cash and concrete: liquidity problems in the mass production of Homes for Heroes', *Business History*, xviii (1976), 152–89.
143 *LWC*, 23 January 1920.
144 *YP*, 14 January 1922.
145 LCC, *A Short History of Civic Housing* (1954), 15.
146 Burnett, *op. cit.*, 227–8.
147 LCC, *Tercentenary Official Handbook* (1926), 130; *Finance and Parliamentary Committee Annual Report* (1933–34), 70–74; *Improvements Committee Annual Report* (1923–24 to 1933–34); *A Short History of Civic Housing* (1954), 26.

148 Jennings, *op. cit.*, 127.
149 *YEN*, 23 April 1923.
150 *YEP*, 23 April 1923.
151 E.D. Simon, *How to Abolish the Slums* (1929), 35–6.
152 *YEN*, 23 April 1923.
153 Cf. D.A. Kirby, 'The inter war council dwelling', *Town Planning Review*, xxxxii (1971), 250–66.
154 Bowley, *op. cit.* (1945), 45.
155 Jenkinson, *op. cit.* (1933), 64–5; LCC, *A Short History of Civic Housing* (1954), 23.
156 Building Centre Committee, *Housing: A European Survey*, Vol. 1 (1936), 167.
157 LCC, Report of the Sub-Improvements (Housing) Committee (1932), 16; *YP*, 23 November 1932.
158 LCC, Improvements Committee Minutes, 27 June 1933; Report of the Sub-Improvements (Housing) Committee (1932), 17.
159 *LWC*, 25 October 1929.
160 Hammerton, *op. cit.*, 114.
161 LCC, *A Short History of Civic Housing* (1954), 31; *LWC*, 17 November 1933.
162 Hammerton, *op. cit.*, 85; *YP*, 29 December 1933. Livett was born in London in 1898, and served as Housing Director in Leeds from 1934 to 1946. In 1946 he became Leeds' first City Architect, a post he held until his death in 1959.
163 Jenkinson, *op. cit.* (1933), 1, 18, 23–4.
164 C. Jenkinson, *Our Housing Objective* (1943), 27; *YP*, 1 May, 17, 20, 25 September 1934.
165 H.W. Richardson *et. al.*, *Housing and Urban Spatial Structure*, (1975), 26.
166 Burnett, *op. cit.*, 238–9.
167 C. Jenkinson, *The Leeds Housing Policy* (1934), 21–3; *YP*, 17 March 1934.
168 Cf. *YP*, 16 October 1937.
169 LCC, *Tercentenary Official Handbook* (1926), 130; *Improvements Committee Annual Report* (1923–4 to 1933–4).
170 LCC, *Finance and Parliamentary Committee Annual Report* (1933–4), 70–74; *Housing Committee Annual Report* (1947–8), 7.
171 'Housing and slum clearance in Leeds', *Journal of the R.I.B.A.*, xxxxv (1937), 766–7.
172 *Ibid.*; *LWC*, 19 October 1934.
173 Jenkinson, *op. cit.* (1933), 64–5.
174 *LWC*, 29 June 1934.
175 'Housing and slum clearance in Leeds', *op. cit.*, 765–78.
176 Building Centre Committee, *op. cit.*, 166.
177 LCC, *Housing Committee Annual Report* (1939–40), 30.
178 *YP*, 22, 28 April 1936.
179 'Housing and slum clearance in Leeds', *op. cit.*, 767–70.
180 M. Pawley, *Architecture versus Housing* (1971), 39.
181 Swenarton, *op. cit.*, 191; A.M. Edwards, *The Design of Suburbia* (1981), 103–15.
182 Edwards, *op. cit.*; H.W. Richardson and D.H. Aldcroft, *Building in the British Economy between the Wars* (1968), 300–1.
183 Cf. G.C. Dickinson and M.G. Shaw, 'Coronation Street moves out of town', *Geographical Magazine*, xxxxix (1977) 286–91.
184 *YP*, 25 September 1925.
185 G.C. Dickinson and C.J. Longley, 'The coming of cheap transport: a study of tramway fares on municipal systems in British provincial towns, 1900–14', *Transport History*, vi (1973), 123.
186 Ward, *op. cit.* (1960), 207–8; *YP*, 15 August 1923.
187 *LWC*, 25 November 1938.
188 LCC, *Housing Committee Annual Report* (1939–40), 16–23.
189 A. Ravetz, 'The uses and abuses of the planned environment', *Journal of the R.I.B.A.*,

lxxx (1972), 144–51.
190 'Housing and slum clearance in Leeds', *op. cit.*, 76.
191 Ravetz, *op. cit.* (1972), 147.
192 *YP*, 23 May 1939.
193 *Ibid.*, 28 May 1936, 11 May 1938, 31 January 1939.
194 LCC, *A Short History of Civic Housing* (1954), 45; *LWC*, 21 October 1938.
195 *LWC*, 21 October 1938.
196 *LWC*, 16 November 1934.
197 *LWC*, 25 November 1938.
198 Burnett, *op. cit.*, 230.
199 Hammerton, *op. cit.*, 88.
200 LCC, *Housing Committee Annual Report* (1936–7), 24.
201 *LWC*, 12 April 1935.
202 Edwards, *op. cit.*, 112.
203 LCC, *Housing Committee Annual Report* (1939–40), 18–23.
204 Jenkinson, *op. cit.* (1934), 30–1.
205 R.A.H. Livett, 'Housing in Leeds', *Journal of the T.P.I.*, xxv (1939), 269.
206 Jenkinson, *op. cit.* (1934), 30–1.
207 *Ibid.*
208 A. Ravetz, *Model Estate: Planned Housing at Quarry Hill, Leeds* (1974), 55–9.
209 Livett, *op. cit.*, 269.
210 LCC, Report of the Sub-Improvements (Housing) Committee (1932), 17, 27.
211 LCC, *Housing Committee Annual Report* (1935–6 to 1939–40).
212 *YP*, 24 February 1934.
213 *YP*, 31 March 1938.
214 Ravetz, *op. cit.* (1974), 55–9.
215 *Ibid.*, 52.
216 *Ibid.*, 53.
217 R.A.H. Livett, 'Housing in an industrial city', *The Architect and Building News*, 6 May 1938, 161.
218 Ravetz, *op. cit.* (1974), 56.
219 Livett, *op. cit.* (1939), 270; Building Centre Committee, *op. cit.*, 166.
220 Livett, *op. cit.* (1938), 161.
221 LCC, *Housing Committee Annual Report* (1947–8), 7; 'Housing and slum clearance in Leeds', *op. cit.*, 760–70.
222 Ravetz, *op. cit.* (1974), 65.
223 *LWC*, 31 May 1935.
224 LCC, *A Short History of Civic Housing* (1954), 33.
225 Ravetz, *op. cit.* (1974), 76.
226 A. Ravetz, 'From working-class tenement to modern flat', in *Multi-Storey Living*, ed. A. Sutcliffe (1974), 130.
227 Memorandum of Evidence submitted to the Royal Commission on the Location of Industry on behalf of the Corporation of the City of Leeds, 1938 (PRO/HLG/27/63), 3.
228 Cf. R. Dennis and S. Daniels, 'Community and the social geography of Victorian cities', in *Urban History Yearbook*, ed. D. Reeder (1981), 7–23.
229 R.J. Johnston, *City and Society* (1980), 160, 260; cf. D. Cannadine, 'Victorian cities: how different?', *Social History* (1977), 457–82; M.J. Daunton, *Coal Metropolis* (1977), 124; J.F.C. Harrison, *Learning and Living* (1961), 7–20.
230 Cf. R.M. Pritchard, *Housing and the Spatial Structure of the City* (1976), 188.
231 *Ibid.*
232 R. Hoggart, *The Uses of Literacy* (1958), 58–9.
233 A. Marwick, *Britain in the Century of Total War* (1970), 122.
234 Daunton, *op. cit.*, 125; Johnston, *op. cit.*, 261–5.

235 F.M. Lupton, *Wide Roads and their Influence upon Housing* (1918), 23.

236 *YP*, 21 July 1925.

237 *YP*, 22 May 1925.

238 *YP*, 31 July 1926. Charles Lupton had chaired the Improvements Committee (which was responsible for housing policy until Labour's administrative reforms in November 1933) since before the end of the First World War and retained the position until November 1927.

239 *YP*, 4 June 1926.

240 Ward, *op. cit.* (1960), 206–7.

241 D. Ward, 'The pre-urban cadaster and the urban pattern of Leeds', *Annals of the Association of American Geographers*, LII (1962), 151–2.

242 Ward, *op. cit.* (1960), 194.

243 *YP*, 22 June 1935.

244 *YP*, 4 July 1935.

245 *YP*, 9 October 1935.

246 *Ibid*.

247 *YP*, 22 April 1936.

248 *YEP*, 16 September 1937.

249 Jenkinson, *op. cit.* (1943), 31.

Housing policy
in Bristol, 1919–30

MADGE DRESSER

Housing policy in Bristol, 1919–30

MADGE DRESSER

1 Introduction

a. The background to intervention

Working-class housing in pre-war Bristol was an amalgam of ancient courts and modern speculative development. The latter, which began in earnest in the 1870s, usually took the form of small, plain-fronted houses, built directly on to the pavement, with four or five rooms. A slightly grander version of this dwelling was the five-or six-roomed house which boasted a bay window and a small forecourt. These would be the preserve of the better-off artisan, the foreman or the white-collar worker. Both these house types were mainly concentrated in the eastern and southern suburbs of the city where freehold tenure predominated. Further in stood merchant houses of the late eighteenth and early nineteenth centuries, many divided up into tenements, the preserve of the less prosperous worker or of those such as the boot and shoe workers who needed to live near their work.[1]

In the centre and in pockets in the west and south of Bristol, court housing still persisted, usually on leasehold land still held by various ecclesiastical, municipal and charitable institutions. In these dwellings lived the casual and sweated workers and those who could not afford the rents and fares of the suburban residence. This 'residuum' was small but wretched. There were few 'back-to-backs' in Bristol compared to Leeds and other northern cities, but the courts were densely populated and as unhealthy as they were picturesque.[2]

The diversity of the housing stock reflected the diversity of Bristol's economic structure. As in London, no one industry predominated. The largest industries by the early twentieth century were boot and shoe making, paper and printing, confectionery and a corrugated iron works. Engineering (especially machine making and vehicle construction) and tobacco were also sizeable employers and there was still a large cotton factory in the city and a sprinkling of mines. The municipally owned docks were losing trade to South Wales but the port was still profitable and Bristol was still the nexus of 'a great foreign and coasting trade.' The city boasted a univer-

Figure 17. A slum court in Bedminster, Bristol, c.1928 (courtesy of the Bristol
Environmental Health Department).

sity, two large hospitals, a number of prestigious schools and expanding retailing sector. It supported a sizeable commercial and professional population which lived in the extensive suburbs on the west of the city and on the other side of the Avon Gorge.[3]

Building in Bristol was very buoyant in the last years of the nineteenth century and commercial development proceeded apace until the war (see table 14). House building declined markedly early in the new century in accord with national trends, following a period of marked over-building. In 1901, 9.3 per cent of Bristol's housing stock was comprised of 'voids' or empties, which was a higher proportion than in most provincial cities. Yet even at this point, the supply of *working-class* housing was not adequate. A significant number of the poorest workers, those packed into the courts and tenements in the central areas, were displaced by commercial development and municipal street-widening schemes and many could not afford to move to less populated districts. Their plight was barely touched on by the few philanthropic housing ventures. On the other hand, though prices in Bristol in the late nineteenth and early twentieth century were generally high, rents were relatively low. Thus one author writing in 1897 could comment on the higher standard of accommodation demanded and obtained by a Bristol artisan in comparison with his better paid counterpart in the northern provincial cities.[4]

In 1901, as part of a street-clearance scheme, the City Council made its first tentative venture into municipal housing by providing 70 workmen's dwellings in several grim tenement blocks for some of those it displaced. A few years later four relatively commodious suburban cottages were also erected under the 1890 Act, provoking much opposition on the part of organized ratepayers and cost-conscious councillors.[5]

Density figures for the city as a whole suggested that Bristol did not have much of an overcrowding problem, and most officials and councillors did not see any cause for concern. But by 1904 the slump in house building became more apparent and by 1905, the Council had felt bound to provide temporary accommodation for men newly arrived in Bristol in search of work. This municipal lodgings house was administered by a sub-committee of the Council's Health Committee along workhouse lines. The disciplinarian and pettifogging regime there must account in large part for its under-utilization, a fact taken by some as proof that reports of a 'housing problem' were exaggerated.[6]

The growing housing shortage was soon to undermine such complacency. House closures and demolitions were accelerated by the implementation of the 1909 Housing, Town Planning Act. Between 1909 and 1915 over 1,200 houses in Bristol were closed or demolished without one being replaced. When one considers the ever-growing population and the fact that virtually no working-class dwellings at rents between 4s. and 4s. 6d. 'for what might be termed the decent poor' were erected after 1904, one begins to appreciate the seriousness of the situation.[7]

In 1907 a Labour-inspired local branch of the 'Housing Reform Group' was formed under the leadership of the Labour councillor Frank Sheppard. The group revealed in a pamphlet that official density figures masked acute pockets of overcrowding and ill-health in the central districts and older, less prosperous working-class suburbs. The group, in concert with the local Labour Party, also pressed the need for more municipal housing 'along garden city lines.' Labour advocacy of housing reform took on a more urgent tone. The all-male Council smugly disapproved on moral grounds the petition from the National Union of Women Workers in 1912 for a womens' municipal hostel, but was perhaps less dismissive of Sheppard's warning that the Bristol Dock strike of that year had been fuelled by the housing shortage. In 1913, peaceful but vociferous protests against a clearance scheme in east Bristol were led by the local Liberal association. Liberal women who had founded a garden-suburb scheme a few years before joined with other Liberals in their concern about the low standards of new working-class housing as well as its scarcity.[8]

By 1914, formerly complacent officials were moved to advocate a temporary and very limited role for the local authority as house builder:

> . . . the housing question will very soon become serious if it has not already done so. It would appear that as regards the housing of the poorest of the poor, the most practical solution would be for the work to be taken in hand by the Local Authority, aided by grants from the National Exchequer.[9]

In contrast to this narrow formulation of the 'housing problem', Labour and Liberal housing reformers maintained it was:

> . . . not simply one of slums but also that of narrow mean streets, of jerry built housing; ill-designed and lacking in the 'convenience' which every house should possess. 'Brick boxes with slate lids' was an apt description of these houses.[10]

The reformers seemed to be making headway, aided by the mounting housing shortage. Members of the City Council's Health Committee visited and were impressed by the municipal housing projects at Liverpool and Bath as well as by the developments at Port Sunlight and Bournville. Moreover, trade union pressure mounted for housing in south Bristol, where hardly a single vacancy remained by 1914. A proposal for a £50,000 municipal housing scheme was moved in the Council in 1914. The proposed development was to be located in the inner suburbs of the Bedminster and Stapleton Road areas, in south and east Bristol respectively, and featured a municipal tram line for residents.[11] It seems likely that a £50,000 legacy made to the Council in 1910 by a private philanthropist (the Sutton Bequest) had emboldened the councillors proposing the scheme to suggest a low-density development of 400 semi- and detached cottages.

However, the bulk of Liberal and Conservative councillors were still wary. As one of their progressive colleagues wryly noted, 'The Council all profess to be very anxious to do something about the housing shortage but it must not cost the rate-payers anything.'[12] Some were simply opposed to such costly ventures. The scheme was postponed until the autumn, by which time war had broken out.

During the war, the housing supply deteriorated further. Building dwindled to a virtual standstill which was in part the result of redirecting supplies and labour to the war effort, but was also the outcome of the Increase of Rent and Mortgage Interest (War Restrictions) Act of 1915. It is reasonable to assume that the Act made landlords less willing to rent or repair already existing dwellings because of decreased profit margins. Indeed, the local Liberal daily, the *Western Daily Press*, reported that the Bristol Ratepayers' Association wrote to Dr Addison, the Minister of Munitions, to complain about the plight of landlords and landladies suffering under the new controls.[13]

The one housing scheme partially implemented in the Bristol area during the war was intended to provide accommodation for workers at the strategically important smelter works and docks at Avonmouth. The abortive 'Avonmouth Garden Suburb

Table 12. Subsidized house building and private enterprise building: Britain and Bristol compared

(1) Local authority housing, 1920–30 (absolute numbers)

year	Great Britain	Bristol
1919–20	600	0 (90 Ministry of Munitions houses)
1920–1	15,600	224
1921–2	80,800	651 (+141 converted Army huts)
1922–3	57,500	250
1923–4	14,300	140
1924–5	20,700	389
1925–6	44,200	1,013
1926–7	74,100	1,244
1927–8	104,100	1,138
1928–9	55,700	457
1929–30	61,800[a]	822

[a] 1,600 built under 1925 Act

(2) Subsidized private housing, 1920–30 (absolute numbers)

1919–20	100	no figures
1920–1	13,000	20
1921–2	20,000	35
1922–3	10,300	38
1923–4	4,300	34
1924–5	47,000	281
1925–6	62,800	613
1926–7	79,600	489
1927–8	74,600	632
1928–9	49,100	558
1929–30	50,200	261

Scheme', sponsored both by Progressive Liberals and by Labour activists such as Ben Tillet, Ernest Bevin and Frank Sheppard, was in part inspired by the original Bristol Garden Suburb Ltd of 1909. But the Avonmouth proposal was much more innovative than its predecessor. It incorporated transport, sports grounds and social centres and shops in its plans and also included communal laundries, kitchens and nurseries for working women. The scheme was conceived as a co-operative, and encountered difficulties with the acquisition of land and raising of capital.[14]

The housing shortage was made more acute both in Bristol and the nation as a whole by the increase in the number of households with the trend towards earlier marriages and the spate of war weddings. In Bristol, the increase in separate households meant that by 1921 there were 11,773 more families than there were dwellings. The housing shortage formally estimated in 1918 at 5,000 dwellings was actually far worse. Both Bristol's Chief Inspector of Housing in 1921, and the Secretary of the city's Housing Department in 1928, argued convincingly on the basis of census data

(3) Unsubsidized private enterprise house building, 1919–30

year	Great Britain		Bristol
1919			12
1920			11
1921	No figures	53,800[a]	14
1922			5
1923			73
1924	67,500		275
1925	69,200		403
1926	66,400		384
1927	63,900		413
1928	60,300		452
1929	64,700		577
1930	90,100		805

(4) Total private enterprise house building (with and without subsidies), 1919–30

1919			12
1920			11
1921	No figures	97,500[a]	14
1922			40
1923			111
1924	71,800		309
1925	116,200		684
1926	129,200		997
1927	143,500		902
1928	134,900		1,084
1929	113,800		1,135
1930	140,300		1,066

[a] Including, says Bowley, houses built by unsubsidized private enterprise up to October 1922, estimated by the Ministry of Health as 30,000.
Source: National figures from M. Bowley, *Housing and the State* (1945), p. 271. Bristol figures from City Engineer's Reports.

that the real need was closer to 15,000 dwellings. The pre-war 'problem' had, by the war's end, become a full-blown crisis.[15]

b. Bristol's housing policy 1919–30: an overview
It was in the decade after the First World War that Bristol, like most other authorities, saw the development of its first state subsidized housing estates, as well as the revival of its private house-building market. In Bristol, well over 9,000 dwellings were added to the existing housing stock by 1931. Almost half of these were corporation houses[16] (see table 12). How did Bristol respond to the vagaries of national housing policy? What factors were involved in the relationship between local and central government and between local government and its electors? And to

what extent did the housing built during this period – especially the subsidized housing – meet the need of Bristol's working-class population?

A brief survey of house-building activity for the period under review is a first preliminary to more detailed considerations regarding the provision and management of subsidized housing in Bristol. The progress of Bristol's municipal house

Table 13. Statistics concerning houses and other buildings^a built, 1897–1930 (Bristol)

year	other buildings	houses
1898	73	581
1899	77	1,157
1900	83	1,591
1901	72	1,570
1902	105	1,551
1903	168	1,240
1904	95	1,176
1905	129	1,206
1906	119	1,372
1907	121	1,239
1908	147	859
1909	146	454
1910	157	386
1911	182	297
1912	181	204
1913	143	218
1914	—	132
1915	—	98
1916	—	89
1917	79	42
1918	90	25
1919	56	72
1920	124	101
1921	156	248
1922	199	832
1923	261	361
1924	258	449
1925	320	1,073
1926	295	2,010
1927	185	2,146
1928	310	2,222
1929	258	1,592
1930	304	1,888

^a Other buildings include: warehouses, offices, factories, shops, and stables and sheds.

Source: City Engineer's *Annual Reports*.

building over the 1920s is broadly typical of the national pattern, following as it does the ebb and flow of Exchequer subsidies.[17] Thus as fig. 18 and table 12 show, there was a peak of corporation housebuilding in 1921–2 which fell sharply thereafter – victim of the Geddes axe. The trough of 1923–4 reflected the 'policy vacuum' succeeding the axe, and the slow and limited take up of the Chamberlain subsidy by local authorities. The sharp rise in activity in 1925–6 is accounted for by the introduction of the Wheatley subsidy and the increased exploitation of the Chamberlain subsidy for council house building.

By 1926, however, national and local patterns of municipal house building began to diverge slightly. Council house building nationally began to climb decidedly in 1926 and 1927, reaching its peak early in 1928. In Bristol, on the other hand, house building climbed very sharply in 1926, peaked in 1927, declined slightly in 1928, and fell off steeply the year after. The Council's conservatism may lie behind this divergence from the national pattern.

Bristol Corporation's achievement in terms of municipal housing provision varied in relation to that of other corporations according to which subsidy is considered. The 1,189 Addison Act houses built in Bristol worked out at 3.3 houses per 1,000 inhabitants, well under the national average of 4 houses. Bristol's activity under the 1923 and 1924 subsidies was somewhat higher. Taking into account the 5,000 Wheatley and Chamberlain houses built by 1931, Bristol's performance (of 23.1 houses per 1,000 population) exceeded that of Leeds (12.8) or Manchester (22.9). Of this total, 1.615 were built under the Chamberlain Act, 3,406 under the Wheatley Act. There

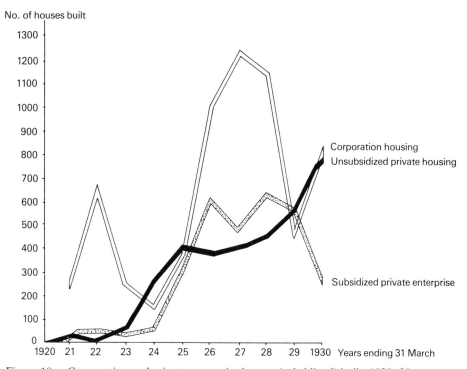

Figure 18.   Corporation and private enterprise houses (subsidized) built, 1920–30.

was an intensive use of the Chamberlain subsidy for local authority house building in Bristol, accounting for 13.8 per cent compared to the national average of 6.7 per cent of houses built. This is explained by the lower rate contribution it entailed – a point much appreciated by the largely Conservative city council.[18]

Table 14. *Numbers of corporation houses built in England and Wales and in Bristol under the three major Housing Acts*

	England and Wales	Bristol
Addison Act (1919)	170,101	1,189
Chamberlain Act (1923)	73,902	1,615
Wheatley Act (1924)	283,800	3,406 (+1,060 under contract)

The private housing sector in Bristol tells an altogether different story. Whilst the 1930s can be characterized as the decade of the unsubsidized building boom, the 1920s were certainly the age of subsidized private housing. In Bristol, fully 46 per cent of the 6,600 private houses built by 1930 were subsidized. Although less than 100 of these were assisted under the Additional Powers Act of 1919, over 2,800 utilized the Chamberlain subsidy. Most of this subsidized housing took place after 1925, as prices and labour costs fell (see fig. 18). The dip in subsidized house building activity in 1927 is possibly due to the threatened subsidy cuts but must also have been due to the competition for labour and materials, engendered by corporation schemes.[19] Its final collapse in 1929 was due to the cancellation of the Chamberlain subsidy.

Table 15. *The population of Bristol, 1920–30* (City area, estimated by City Engineer: 18,445 acres)

1920	375,000	
1921	376,975	
1922	381,700	
1923	383,900	
1924	385,600	
1925	386,200	
1926	385,700	
1927	383,300	
1928	385,700	extension of city boundaries: Sea Mills, Henbury, Portishead added: 241 acres
1929	390,700	
1930	391,300	

An inverse relation between private and corporation house building is exhibited in a more consistent and marked manner by the course of unsubsidized house building. As subsidies declined and costs continued to fall, the time was ripe for unsubsidized house building for owner–occupation. By 1928, a number of Bristol's newer industries (artificial silk, metal-window manufacturing, aeroplanes, aluminium) were expanding. Retailing was another growth area, and building was reported to be 'swimming in the waters of prosperity.' Inter-war Bristol, with its large proportion of middle- and lower-middle-class inhabitants, was able to take advantage of building society mortgages by the late 1920s, as indicated by the growth of north and west Bristol. Conversely, the availability of private housing was said to have been an important factor in attracting new industry to Bristol during this time.[20]

A consideration of the changing composition of, and political factions within, the City Council, will establish the context for a subsequent discussion of the Council's performance as house provider and housing manager. This first section will pay particular attention to the development of the housing committee and the changing role of the Labour group within the Council. The investigation of the Corporation's achievements as house builder will also be considered thematically, looking first at housing finance and the acquisition of sites, then at the part played by contractors in the building process and at the adequacy of the supply of labour and materials. An evaluation of the origins and results of experimental building schemes will follow, to be succeeded by an analysis of changing council house standards and amenities provision. A critical account of the Corporation's housing management concludes this study and deals with rent policy, the development of the housing bureaucracy and its assumptions about the corporation tenant. From this last section, it should emerge that the growth of state subsidized housing has helped to change the scope and exercise of state power in ways we are only just beginning to appreciate.

c. Political tensions and vested interests

Bristol's City Council was distinguished by its Conservatism. In 1918, the Conservatives held a controlling majority with a very large Liberal opposition and a tiny Labour enclave. By 1923, a growing Labour presence had precipitated an alliance between Conservative and Liberal councillors under the aegis of the 'non-political' Citizens Party. Progressive Liberals inside the Council seem to have faded away and tensions between the Citizens Party (which appears to have generally followed the Conservative Party line) and the Labour group increased steadily, reaching a crisis point just after the General Strike when an open power struggle for aldermanic and committee posts erupted.[21]

From this point, the Citizens Party which had traditionally managed the exclusion of 'socialists' from most key positions in the Council became openly antagonistic. Labour councillors fought back, gaining both in numbers and influence as the decade progressed. By the end of our period, Labour councillors and aldermen were a powerful and fully fledged opposition party on the Bristol Council.[22] They were also on the whole a less radical group than they had been in 1919, and one which became increasingly identified – at least in the case of housing policy – with a somewhat narrow and bureaucratic 'labourism'.

While there is no comprehensive study of the social background and outside interests of council members in this period, my own research indicates that the vast majority were business and professional men of some considerable local prominence at the beginning of the period with a growing number of smaller businessmen and skilled workers, and a few women, by the end of it.[23] Certainly the composition of the Housing Committee in the Council seems to confirm this observation. The constitution of this committee also suggests a close relationship between outside business interests and committee membership. Of the 32 people serving on the Housing Committee between 1918 and 1930, at least three were members of the local building contractors' association, the Bristol Master Builders, which was renamed the Bristol Association of Building Trades Employers in 1919; one was a wallpaper and paint manufacturer; another owned a quarry supplying granite chippings for roads; at least one belonged to a family with extensive land holdings in the city; three were on the boards of building societies, including the locally based Bristol and South Wales Permanent Building Society.

When first formed in 1918, the Committee contained seven Conservative, six Liberal and two Labour members. It was very much an employers' body, with its eight industrialists, five professional men and two trade unionists. By 1924, its composition had, along with that of the Council, changed noticeably. Its Conservative chairman, Ernest Savory, had been replaced by the Labour alderman, Frank Sheppard, and there were now four active Labour members, each with strong trade union links.[24]

How important was this change in composition, and more particularly in chairmanship, for the implementation of housing policy in Bristol? Both chairmen were active and committed men, and their respective political differences were, as we shall see, readily apparent in their approach to housing provision. But, generally speaking, central government policy left them little room for manoeuvre, and what began as differences in policy objectives ended more as differences in political style.

The initial differences between the Labour members and Progressives on the one hand, and the Conservatives and right-wing Liberals on the other, were based on contrasting conceptions of the proper role of central and local government. Nowhere were the contrasting notions more apparent than in the area of housing policy. Basically, Conservatives and their allies on the Council were for minimal state provision of services, especially when the cost of that provision had to be borne by the local authority. When, because of what it saw as exceptional circumstances, the central government provided Exchequer assistance to the local authority for such provision, these councillors were more ready to embrace 'collectivist' policies. When the central government threatened to limit or withdraw such assistance, as in 1921, 1926 and 1928, many Conservative-dominated local authorities, including Bristol, initially urged its maintenance but subsequently minimized the need for such provision.

Thus it was that Bristol councillors who had been staunch opponents of a municipal housing programme before the war agreed to combine to pressure central government for continued subsidy assistance after the Addison subsidy had been withdrawn. They did this partly in response to pressure from below, for local authorities were subject not only to the constraints of central government policy, but also to local pressure from ratepayers' groups, trade unions and other members of the 'grass roots'. By 1922–3 the housing shortage had occasioned a widely based coalition of charitable, religious, educational and political groups from all parties to form a 'House Famine Campaign' under the auspices of the University of Bristol Settlement.[25] Much of this pressure was defused by the introduction of the Chamberlain subsidy in the summer of 1923. But in that year a partial decontrol of rents was also effected, and a growing number of evictions resulted. The reluctance of the private sector to build under the new subsidy, despite the plight of the homeless and overcrowded, made it politically inexpedient to oppose collectivist provision in 1924. However, once the Wheatley programme got under way and rates expenditure increased, attitudes changed. When the Conservative government announced impending subsidy cuts in 1926, there was a resurgence of anti-collectivist sentiment, in the guise of 'retrenchment fever'.[26]

The expense of the municipal housing programme was firmly identified with local Labour Party policy – even if the benefits were not. Resentment at the behaviour of some Labour council members during the General Strike precipitated a backlash against council housing in general and the Labour-led Housing Committee in particular. In 1926, the right-wing chairman of the Council's powerful Finance Committee, Sir William Howell Davies, succeeded in gaining the power to vet Housing Committee proposals before they were formally put to the Council. Labour members saw this as an attack on the powers of the Housing Committee and accused Howell Davies of trying to establish a 'House of Lords' Finance Committee.[27]

At the same time, the continuing housing shortage, rising unemployment, evictions and council house arrears meant that Conservatives could not restrict municipal housing strictly to the rehousing of slum clearance families. Instead, they adopted national Conservative party rhetoric about housing the 'low-paid workers'. This notion seemed to assume that aside from a small minority of *particularly* low-paid workers, who might justly claim the help of the state, most workers could and should become owner-occupiers. As Bristol's Liberal weekly, the *Bristol Observer*, proclaimed: 'it *should* be everyone's ambition to become an owner instead of a tenant.'[28]

Yet by the late 1920s only a very few Bristol workers could raise the deposit on a mortgage. Moreover, the identity of the deserving 'low-paid worker' was ambiguous and confused. Tenants at one council estate were deemed to be 'low paid' in comparison with fellow tenants at another estate, while corporation tenants as a group were often distinguished from those 'low-paid' workers who could not afford the high costs council house living entailed. At other times, the term 'low-paid worker' was used to denote those living in slum conditions, a usage which obscured the fact that there were many people 'living in reasonably decent circumstances' in apartment, who could afford neither a suburban corporation house nor the down payment on a mortgage. Finally, the term 'low-paid worker' glossed over the point that many low earners were irregularly employed by virtue of the casual nature of their jobs, and would have trouble keeping up regular payment of rent, municipal or private, without recourse to sub-letting or extended credit.[29]

This lack of definition enabled the Conservative government to wax eloquent about the need to house those it vaguely classified as deserving, without offering adequate financial assistance to local authorities to do so. In the face of such rhetoric, it is hardly surprising that most Labour members of Bristol Council were forced into increasing accommodation with a residualist housing policy. Sheppard, for example, ended up advocating lower standard housing and slum clearance policies. He and most of his Labour colleagues supported the sale of council houses and assumed that most working men would prefer to own their own homes. It is apparent that although Labour councillors displayed a sincere and committed desire for housing reform, they lacked a coherent economic analysis with which they could effectively counter the parsimonious complacency of their opponents. The left-wing socialism of such councillors as W.H. Hennessy and Lilian Pheysey seemed, in the context, increasingly utopian as the war years receded. The pragmatic labourism of Sheppard and his allies was rapidly eroded by compromise, accepting as it did many of the assumptions of neo-classical economics.[30]

There were a number of other respects in which the increasingly narrow and bureaucratic tenor of Labour housing policy in Bristol became manifest. First, in a debate with Hennessy in 1929 Sheppard contended that the responsibility for the increasing number of homeless should be left with Poor Law Officials rather than with the Housing Committee. Secondly, in the admittedly vexed question of slum clearance, Sheppard showed himself to be high-handed and misleading about the impact such clearance schemes might have on the area's poorer inhabitants. Could all the scheme's opponents be so glibly dismissed as 'property jobbers' and slum landlords? Or was there something more to one resident Liberal politician's argument that 'people were not feelingless pieces of furniture to be moved about here or there at will'? Thirdly, the repeated complaints made by tenants about the poor standards on one estate built by direct labour were deflected by the Labour councillors involved with defensiveness and complacency. Fourth, the patriarchal assumptions of traditional trade unionism increasingly informed housing policy after the Armistice. The suggestions made by Sheppard, Bevin and Tillett in 1916 for communal kitchens and nurseries had disappeared. The woman's place was again assumed to be firmly back in the home. Women's needs both as workers and as mothers were simply ignored. Finally, the administration of the housing estates was bureaucratic and undemocratic. This last development stemmed not so much from the explicit assumptions of labourist or socialist ideology but from the inability of its proponents to recognize, account for or control the negative aspects of bureaucratic development.[31]

In one sense, the major problem confronting local Labour politicians in 1918 was whether they should base their housing demands on what was possible or on what was desirable. Thus just after the war Labour councillors pushed for high-standard 'Tudor Walters' parlour houses at low rents, and to this end also agitated for cheap loan capital, higher wages and control of the building industry. By the mid-1920s, however, the majority of Bristol Labour councillors seemed to have accepted that they would have to work within a system which would not make the revolutionary changes in financial and industrial organization which well-built housing at low rents demanded. These councillors still, however, clung to the idea of universalist state provision. As a result, by the end of the decade, they were implicated in a housing programme which had already abandoned many of the ideals of the immediate post-war period.

2 The Council as builder

a. Finance

Subsidized housing in the 1920s made unprecedented financial demands on local authorities. For one thing, capital had to be borrowed on a massive scale at a time of high interest rates.[32] For another, changing government policies ensured that an ever-increasing proportion of the annual losses made on housing schemes had to be met by rates contributions and council house rents (see fig. 19).

In Bristol, the Council, confronted by an acute housing shortage, periodically attempted to reduce the cost of the assisted schemes by cutting standards and attempting to sell off council houses. Such moves, though they were in keeping with national Conservative policy, could not effectively transform the housing programme into something approaching a self-financing enterprise. By 1930, Bristol's municipal housing scheme constituted the city's largest single item of capital expenditure, and some local politicians implied that municipal housing was creating an intolerable burden on the rates.[33]

The initial problem facing local authorities at the outset of the first (Addison) housing scheme was the raising of loan capital. This task was made much more difficult and expensive for them by Treasury policy, as Bristol's experience illustrates.[34] In the autumn of 1919, just as Bristol was attempting to lure smaller builders into tendering for council house contracts by offering them cash advances, a freeze was declared on low-interest government loans. No large authorities would be able to borrow money from the Public Works Loan Board for house-building purposes. At the same time, the Bank of England raised its borrowing rate from 5 to 6 per cent. Housing reformers in Bristol were quick to deplore the Government action on loans, and the Council itself protested formally to the government at a meeting convened by one of its Labour members. Bristol councillors feared that a general scramble for capital by housing authorities would further drive up interest rates and make the housing programme prohibitively expensive. After all, the local Housing Committee had by then already been forced to borrow £2m from the banks as a temporary measure in order to avoid further delays on the housing scheme.[35]

The Treasury, in anticipation of the possible ill-effects of mass borrowing from the banks, decided early in 1920 to endorse a National Bonds Campaign as an alternative method of raising housing capital. Local authorities were left to launch the scheme in their own areas. Bristol appears to have responded to the call with more promptitude than most, opening a campaign early in April 1920. In a florid display of civic solidarity, trade unionists joined with Merchant Venturers, Druids and Rotarians, to support the scheme. Appealing to the 'patriotism and good English common business sense' of local citizens, the city offered bonds in multiples of £5 at a promised return of 6 per cent. Unfortunately, that same month, interest rates rose to 7 per cent.[36]

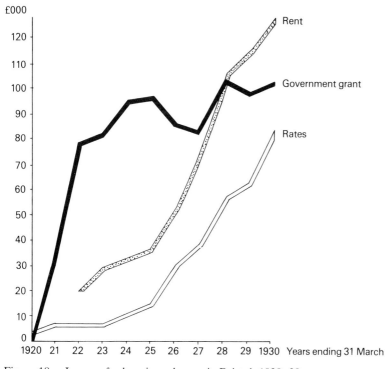

Figure 19.   Income for housing schemes in Bristol, 1920–30.

A great deal of publicity was devoted to the campaign, and one half-page advertisement in the *Bristol Observer* declared that every citizen was expected to 'do his share to solve the housing problem.' Great emphasis was in fact placed on the contribution which the working man was expected to make. The Bonds were 'available at Stockbroker, Banker, Solicitor, Friendly Society Lodge, Trade Union Branch . . .' and could be paid for in 5s. instalments. Given the high unemployment and low wages suffered in Bristol as the slump succeeded the post-war boom, it is hardly surprising that the campaign failed to engender a new breed of worker-investor. Bristol's performance in the campaign was unimpressive but better than that of many authorities, raising less than half of the anticipated £800,000, and less than a fifth of the £1.84m spent on the Addison scheme. The bulk of the capital was ultimately raised through the issue of stock, and to a lesser extent through the granting of mortgages. The initial response to the first issue of Bristol stock was disappointing. Less than a third of the £1.5m issued was bought, which was characteristic of the experience of most participating authorities. The second issue was more successful and £1.4m was raised by March 1921. The bond scheme was not repeated again during the decade, and the piecemeal approach to raising loan capital at a time of dear money must have done much to discredit the idea of collective housing provision in the eyes of a council which had been traditionally averse to incurring large debts.

Borrowing under the 1923 and 1924 Housing Acts was also financed from the private sector, but at a time when interest rates were somewhat lower than they had been earlier in the decade. Two issues of stock brought out by Bristol Corporation in 1925 and 1928 offered 4.75 and 5 per cent respectively. Cheaper mortgages were also made available and were an important secondary source of loan capital. In addition, the Corporation also began to borrow sizeable amounts from the bank and from private individuals. At the end of the decade, the interest rate fell further, but it was not until the late 1930s that 'borrowing became relatively cheap.'

For most of the decade, excepting the period of the 'policy vacuum' of the early 1920s, assisted housing schemes constituted the largest single item of Bristol Corporation's capital expenditure for non-trading services (table 16). In the year ending 31 March 1921, when building costs and interest rates were at their highest, nearly two-thirds of the city's capital expenditure went on the Addison scheme. Although this proportion soon fell, capital spending on housing climbed from 1925 and reached as high as 42 per cent of the city's total expenditure in 1927 (table 16, fig. 20).[37]

Only a very small part of Bristol's capital expenditure on housing was financed by the sale of council property such as building sites on council estates and council houses. The greater part of the capital was borrowed, and the oustanding loan debt on housing increased over the decade from a mere £14,300 in 1920 to £1.8m in 1921 and £4.0m by 1930. Most of the loans obtained for this purpose were long-term loans ranging from 20 to 80 years, and by 1930 only 12 per cent of the £5.2m originally borrowed for housing schemes had been repaid. Much of this loan debt was incurred under the Addison Act (table 17) and ultimately shouldered by the taxpayer. It is probably true to say that it was the special open-ended subsidy afforded by the Addison Act, rather than any profound conversion to collectivism, which had convinced most Bristol councillors initially to support the municipal housing programme. By modern standards, Bristol was not 'seriously burdened with debt.' However, local authorities were always happier to off-load expenses on to taxpayers rather than ratepayers, and once the burden was shifted back on to the ratepayer by the 1923 and 1924 Housing Acts, old objections to deficit spending reasserted themselves. Influential councillors began to express concern both at the amount of capital borrowed for housing schemes and the implications this had for the rates.[38]

Table 16. Capital expenditure in Bristol: Total capital expenditure compared with capital expenditure on assisted housing schemes, 1919–30

year (ending 31 March)	capital expenditure on housing (assisted schemes) (excluding Small Dwelling Acquisition Act) (£)	total capital expenditure (£)	total capital spent on housing (assisted schemes) (%)
1920	225,871	667,845	33.8
1921	651,598	1,004,124	62.2
1922	542,794	1,249,127	43.5
1923[a]	141,098	782,935	18.0
1924[a]	116,223	718,360	16.2
1925[b]	332,565	1,145,724	29.0
1926	823,304	2,029,057	40.6
1927	901,982	2,126,587	42.4
1928	727,022	2,268,993	32.0
1929	309,838	1,451,811	21.3
1930	618,233	2,289,291	27.0

[a] In these years housing comes third on the list of capital expenditure, after highways and electricity.
[b] Housing is a close second to highways as far as items of expenditure are concerned (£342,131 on highways, £324,043 on housing).

Table 17. Capital expenditure in Bristol under each Act

Act	capital expenditure	houses provided
1919	£1,293,146	1,189
1923 (corp. houses)	£856,742	1,615
1923 (private enterprise subsidies)	£259,500	2,741
1924 (corp. houses)	£2,120,214	3,406 (1,060 under contract)
(Sutton Trustees)		176
1925 (slum clearance)	£166,475	194
	£4,696,077	9,401[a]

[a] 6,485 by Corporation, 2,917 by private enterprise.

Source: Housing Department Booklet, 1919–30, 68.

Table 18. *Rate in the £ of net cost of housing under assisted schemes (1919, 1923, 1924 Acts) and actual net cost after income and government grants deducted Bristol, 1920–30*

year ending 31 March	rate in the £	net cost
	d.	
1920	0.78	£5,831
1921	1.0	£7,659
1922	1.0	£7,804
1923	1.0	£7,908
1924	1.4	£11,673
1925	1.8	£15,118
1926	3.65	£30,329 (£15,872[a])
1927	4.6	£39,511 (£13,674[a])
1928	6.6	£57,195 (£11,193[a])
1929	7.4	£65,429 (£12,195[a])
1930	7.7	£77,239 (£14,050[a])

[a] Net cost of Addison Act houses.

Indeed the Bristol ratepayer *was* paying more and more for the financing of council houses (table 18). In 1923, rates contributed just under 5 per cent to the city's Housing Revenue Account, but by 1930 they contributed 18 per cent. Between 1926 and 1930 the rates bill for housing had quadrupled and by 1930 Housing and Town Planning took over 5 per cent of total rates expenditure. Although council housing was never the largest drain on the rate fund, and was consistently exceeded by the cost of education, highways, poor relief, public health and policing, it was perhaps the most visible and the most controversial.[39]

Moreover, although the local authority was in theory obliged to make an annual minimum rates contribution of only £6 per house for 20 years towards the Chamberlain Act houses (reduced to £4 after October 1927) and £4 10s. per house for 40 years towards the Wheatley Act houses (reduced to £3 15s. in 1927), in practice Bristol's contribution exceeded that minimum. In this context, the more generous subsidies afforded under the 1923 and 1924 Acts, for slum clearance schemes – up to 50 per cent of losses incurred – had a special appeal for rates-conscious councillors. It is also true that the rates, being a particularly regressive form of taxation, did cause hardship, particularly by the end of the decade. In March 1929 one paper reported that over 1,100 Bristolians, mainly from working-class areas, had been charged with defaulting on the rates in the previous year.[40]

However, all this should not obscure the seldom acknowledged fact that Bristol's council tenants paid rates as well as rents. Indeed, it was asserted that the rating of Bristol's council houses was inordinately high, a charge which gains credibility when one considers the exclusively right-wing composition of the Council's Rating and Valuation Committee which successfully resisted the inclusion of Labour members throughout the 1920s. It should be emphasized that rents from council houses constituted an increasing proportion of the income in the Housing Revenue Account, reaching 54.5 per cent of the total by 1930 as opposed to 18 per cent contributed by the ratepayer and 27.4 per cent from the Treasury (see fig. 19). Although the municipal docks were increasingly less profitable as the decade proceeded, Bristol still enjoyed a substantial cash surplus on her trading services for much of the period. Thus Bristol, enjoying a diverse industrial base, an above-average proportion of middle-class inhabitants, and a high rateable value in relation to her population, was better able to finance her rate fund expenditure than were many other authorities.[41]

b. Land

Most of the land purchased by the Corporation for municipal housing was situated on the outskirts of town where land prices were lower. In 1918, the Council bought a total of 700 acres of land in several sizeable parcels, the most notable of which were the Bedminster, Fishponds, Sea Mills, Speedwell and Horfield sites. Another major site, Shirehampton, was also purchased on account of its proximity to the Avonmouth Docks. These estates were only partially developed under the short-lived Addison scheme and so by 1923 some 500–600 acres were still available for future building. Of these, less than 25 acres were let for 999 years to private developers by 1928. The remainder was exploited by the Bristol Housing Committee for many years to come. Towards the end of the period, in 1929, another major land purchase of 700 acres was made by the Corporation. Half of the land then bought adjoined the existing Bedminster/Knowle estates on the south of the city. The remainder was at a new location on the less populated northern side of Bristol. This

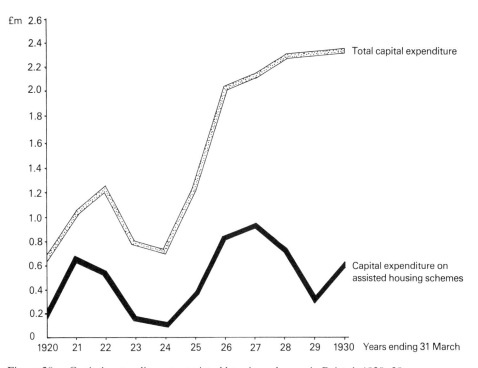

Figure 20.   Capital expenditure on assisted housing schemes in Bristol, 1920–30.

new estate, called Southmead, was developed throughout the 1930s and after the war.[42]

The vendors of the suburban sites included large and small landowners. The Sea Mills and Shirehampton sites had been largely owned by Sir Napier Miles, while much of the Bedminster and Knowle estates was carved from the extensive Smyth (or Ashton Court) estate. The Southmead site had been part of the Hardwicke estate. These substantial landowners stand in stark contrast to the very small owners of property in central Bristol who were forced to sell out in the slum renovation and clearance schemes. In between these extremes there existed a range of small to medium-sized vendors from whose property were pieced together the Fishponds, Speedwell and Horfield Estates. Of these, perhaps the largest was the Bristol and West Building Society which sold nearly 80 acres at Horfield to the Corporation between 1919 and 1928. This society had on its board not only Frank Cowlin, the prominent local builder, but also three councillors, including one Tory member of the Housing Committee.[43]

Over the decade under study, an increasing proportion of the money spent on housing schemes was devoted to land purchase. Whereas only 2.2 per cent of the capital invested in the Addison scheme was spent on sites, this rose to 5.7 per cent of the cost of the Chamberlain scheme and nearly 13 per cent of the cost of the Wheatley scheme. This rise occurred despite the fact that many of the 1923 and 1924 Act houses were erected on sites purchased in 1919 (table 19).[44]

Table 19. *Breakdown of capital outlay per Act in Bristol according to three categories of sites: erection of buildings, roads and sewers*

Act	sites	erection of bldgs.	roads and sewers	total
1919	£28,678 2.2%	£1,151,145 89.0%	£113,324 8.8%	£1,293,147
1923	£49,728 5.8%	£679,679 79.0%	£130,995 15.2%	£860,402 (£259,500[a])
1924	£17,926 10.8%	£148,226 89.0%	£323 0.2%	£166,475

[a] Subsidies to builders.

Source: Compiled from 'Housing: Analysis of Capital Outlay', *Abstract of Accounts 1929–30*, 232–3.

Site prices were influenced by two concurrent but contradictory trends affecting demand. The first was the fall in prices due to the trade depression which depressed prices for agricultural land. The other trend was related to the expansion of Bristol. During the 1920s Bristol enjoyed a fairly steady population increase and by the mid-decade had increased private building development (see tables 13 and 15). Land in the central areas became increasingly scarce and this tended to push up site values in direct proportion to their proximity to the city centre. Also, prices varied with the quality of the particular parcel of land in terms of drainage, proximity to other sites and similar factors.[45]

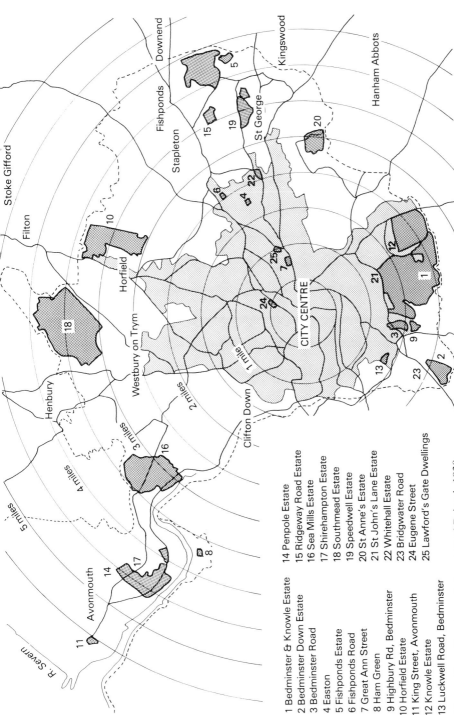

1 Bedminster & Knowle Estate
2 Bedminster Down Estate
3 Bedminster Road
4 Easton
5 Fishponds Estate
6 Fishponds Road
7 Great Ann Street
8 Ham Green
9 Highbury Rd, Bedminster
10 Horfield Estate
11 King Street, Avonmouth
12 Knowle Estate
13 Luckwell Road, Bedminster
14 Penpole Estate
15 Ridgeway Road Estate
16 Sea Mills Estate
17 Shirehampton Estate
18 Southmead Estate
19 Speedwell Estate
20 St Anne's Estate
21 St John's Lane Estate
22 Whitehall Estate
23 Bridgwater Road
24 Eugene Street
25 Lawford's Gate Dwellings

Figure 21. Housing estates around Bristol, 1930.

By 1926, there is a suggestion of profiteering by some landowners on sites adjoining already established estates. Land on the Fishponds estate, for example, cost under £70 per acre in 1919, but extensions to the estate purchased in 1926 cost about £300 per acre. According to its Labour vice-chairman, the Allotments Committee 'was able to buy [land] at about half the price the Housing Committee was invariably called on to pay and this indicated that the landowners grasped the last farthing directly they knew the land was wanted for housing.' On the other hand, land bought at Horfield from the Bristol and West Building Society kept at a fairly constant price throughout the decade, at about £220–£240 per acre, presumably because Horfield, and still more so Southmead which cost £128 per acre in 1929, were in less developed areas. The 387 acres purchased in 1928 on the more densely populated Bedminster side of Bristol seems reasonable at £227 per acre, until one considers that 100 acres of this was not suitable for housing and was to be used as an open space. But even this did not represent an increase in price over land in the same area which was purchased in 1920.[46]

High land costs were most significant in central Bristol and were largely responsible for the high cost of municipal flats built under the 1923 and 1925 slum clearance subsidies. The two largest slum clearance schemes, at Lawford's Gate and Eugene Street, cost over £67,000 for 86 flats on two compact sites, a quarter of this total being spent on the purchase of land. Yet despite the high prices paid for the central sites, many property owners received minimal compensation. Under the provisions of the 1919 Act, owners of compulsorily purchased properties were entitled to compensation at site value only. Not all the owners so affected were absentee landlords. A number were working people who had spent their meagre savings and war pensions to buy homes in the Eugene Street area from unscrupulous landlords who had known the area was to be scheduled for compulsory purchase, and according to Ministry records, site value compensation was as low as £15–£30 per property.[47]

c. Contractors

The conventional picture of the role which local contractors played with regard to inter-war housing policy has up to now been based largely on local and central government records and newspaper accounts. Little attention has been paid to the records of the building contractors themselves. Yet there existed at this time a National Federation of Building Trades Employers whose records contain much relevant information about the actual implementation of municipal housing schemes. Much of the following section has exploited the minutes and reports of the Bristol Association of Building Trades Employers which was affiliated to the National Federation.

Contractors built the vast majority of council houses during the 1920s, and in Bristol, contractors were particularly influential in the outcome of the Addison and Chamberlain programmes. Bristol contractors, like their colleagues elsewhere, were not at first very interested in building municipal housing, a fact which had an immediate impact on the Addison programme. The Bristol Association of Building Trades Employers (BABTE), to which virtually all of Bristol's largest builders belonged, was assiduous in protecting what it perceived to be the interests of its members in the difficult days just after the war. In 1919, for example, BABTE established minimum price increases on materials used in repair work; refused to employ craftsmen black-listed by the Federation of Furniture Manufacturers; and acted as a negotiating body both with the building unions and with Bristol Corporation's newly established Housing Committee.[48] In the spring of 1919, Bristol's Housing Committee had begun to negotiate with BABTE in an effort to launch the Addison scheme. After initial discussions, it was decided to invite separate tenders from individual contractors, but these turned out to be alarmingly expensive, as much as £1,500 for a parlour house. Bristol's Housing Commissioner rejected the tenders as the 'highest he'd ever seen' and advised the Council to invite fresh ones.[49] The Council at the same time attempted to attract unfederated builders by offering them cash advances but this had only limited success. Tender prices began to fall slightly by the autumn but were still prohibitively expensive. Meanwhile, no houses were being built and as the *Builder* explained at the end of 1919:

> The housing problem in Bristol is now worse than it was 12 months ago and as much as £100 is being now paid in excess of the price asked a year ago for the smallest type houses. Much dissatisfaction is being felt at the poor results [of the municipal scheme].
>
> The root of the difficulty is that every private builder has more orders than he can possibly execute, and is indifferent to accepting any work which is not distinctly remunerative. All the local builders are fully occupied with local repair work.[50]

The Housing Committee, like many others around the country, was by then desperate and had virtually to threaten the contractors into building municipal houses. The president of BABTE, F. N. Cowlin, told his members that December:

> they would have to interest themselves in the matter [of council houses] or the Government would step in and close down all other classes of building [under the 1919 (Additional Powers) Act] and it was therefore necessary for them as an association to cooperate with the Authorities and get the houses erected as speedily as possible, although he did not think it was possible to put up the number required, 1,500, within the twelve months.[51]

The Corporation's strategy had the desired effect, and BABTE representatives met with the Town Clerk and later the Housing Committee to renegotiate terms. The tendering system was dropped and tough discussions ensued with a view to formulating a mutually acceptable contract.

Most councillors on the Housing Committee were unfamiliar with the industry and in the words of their own City Engineer 'inexperienced in estimating expense.' The only two councillors who did have relevant expertise were BABTE members and so had divided loyalties. Although the local Housing Commissioner did his best to keep contract prices down and even threatened to invite large contractors from outside Bristol, his powers were limited. The contractors on the other hand could point with some justice to the rapid wage and price rises when they pushed for high contract prices. After much negotiation, BABTE representatives managed to secure a form of contract which included the so-called 'elastic clause'. This clause allowed contractors a guaranteed minimum profit even if the final cost of a house exceeded the sum originally agreed. It is significant that the contractors accepted this particular contract in preference to another offering a larger lump sum per house, precisely because 'it did not necessitate the keeping of strict accounts of costs in accordance with a system prepared by the Commissioners.' Furthermore, no provisions were made for auditing contractors' accounts until after the Addison programme was axed. One should not ignore the temptations that the combination of the elastic clause and unaudited accounts must have posed to builders. Of course, contractors may have preferred these contracts simply because they entailed less paperwork, and perhaps it is true, as Marriner concludes, that builders rarely earned more than 5 per cent profit from these Addison contracts, and indeed often went bankrupt.[52]

When audits were finally introduced in Bristol in 1922, they did reveal a massive difference between the initial contract price and the actual cost of the houses built. In one such case, a Bristol builder who ultimately charged £160 more per Addison house than originally agreed, was charged with jerry-building some of these houses. This raises the possibility that some contractors may have raised prices on the grounds of higher costs, whilst actually skimping on materials or exploiting the lack of cost-accounting procedures. It could, of course, be argued that contractors may have charged high prices but made low profits because they were inefficient. This may well have been the case with smaller builders but seems less likely in the case of a firm like William Cowlin & Son Ltd. At best, the elastic clauses encouraged 'extravagance' on the part of building contractors, as Bowley has asserted. Such extravagance helped to discredit the Addison scheme and with it the notion of well-provisioned subsidized housing. Moreover, it is doubtful whether the federated contractors had the capacity to build half the 980 houses they contracted for by March 1920. Only a few months prior to securing the contract, the chairman of BABTE confided to his members his doubts that they could build 500 houses. BABTE was careful to retain the right to distribute the council work amongst its members itself. The one large builder actually brought in by the Housing Committee from 'abroad' (John Knox of Evesham) was co-opted into BABTE so that he did not compete with the locals. Apart from the undertaking of Bristol's two largest firms (William Cowlin & Son and Wilkins & Son) to build 300 corporation houses each, and the 150 house contract taken up by John Knox, the rest of the contracts were small, between 20 to 50 houses per builder.[53]

Just over a year after these contracts had been negotiated, Addison resigned from the Ministry of Health and a change in policy was soon very apparent. By mid-April, the Ministry of Health rejected the latest offering of BABTE members and through the Housing Committee advised them to return to a tendering system. The Association was also informed, on instructions from the Housing Commissioner, that no further contracts were to be placed with them until there was a 'very considerable reduction in their prices.' Gilbert suggests that the Cabinet Finance Committee had by then determined not to contract for any more houses. This certainly seems to have been the conclusion drawn by BABTE members, who at a meeting that same month expressed the view that:

> the Ministry did not wish to let more contracts and were adopting the method of fixing an impossible price as their maximum to prevent builders from tendering with any hope of getting the work.

A week later BABTE members learned from a colleague on the Housing Committee that the government was expecting to get a price of £200 below the previous basic price of £889 plus £46 profit per house. The general conclusion of the contractors was that 'it was hopeless' for builders even 'to entertain the idea' of taking on houses under such conditions. Thus, two months before the formal axing of the Addison

Act, Bristol builders described the municipal scheme as 'practically closed down'; operatives' wages suffered a 2d. per hour reduction; and reference was made to the 'near cessation' of housing schemes all over the country.[54]

In the months after the cuts in municipal house building, unsubsidized private enterprise building began to recover. Builders especially preferred more lucrative non-residential contracts. This explains why Bristol builders were at first disinclined to take up the 1923 subsidy offered on private house building. Less than 100 houses had been built between 1919 and 1923 under the special Addison subsidy for private houses. Yet the Conservative chairman of the Housing Committee in 1923 was enthusiastic about the prospects of the Chamberlain scheme to remedy the rapidly deteriorating housing shortage. Savory's 'strategy' was that private contractors would build on municipally owned sites, despite the limited profit which the small houses specified by the 1923 Act would afford them. The local Liberal paper, the *Western Daily Press*, on the other hand, estimated that builders would receive only £40 profit on a £400 house, and doubted that this would be a sufficient incentive. The authority also had high hopes that the Bristol Garden Suburb Company, a public utilities society sponsored by local philanthropists, would set the example to others in the private sector by contracting to build Chamberlain houses, despite the fact that only 89 houses had been built under the more generous 1919 subsidy to private builders.[55]

Savory chaired a meeting with local building contractors in the summer of 1923 and offered them a special subsidy of up to £120 per house for houses not subject to price and rent controls. These, as Savory himself claimed a few months later, were terms more generous 'than any other city in the Kingdom' and yet only a negligible number of the 500 houses envisaged were contracted for by the year's end. Although very disappointed, Savory still attempted to reconcile the interest of private builders with the interests of those needing cheap housing. A new public utilities company, replacing Bristol Garden Suburb Ltd was launched by the Council with the active assistance of Frank Cowlin, Bristol's largest builder, former BABTE chairman and Sheriff of the city. Only a modest number of houses were built, while the Sutton Trust also erected 193 houses under the Chamberlain Act at Brislington. But by this time, unsubsidized non-residential building was increasing. The reluctance of builders to build private houses under the 1923 Act helps to explain why Bristol built an above average number of corporation houses under this Act. Almost half of the first 500 council houses constructed under the 1923 Act were built by direct labour at Speedwell, and most of the contracts were for less than 30 houses.[56]

With the easing of labour and material shortages, falling costs, and more generous financing from building societies, subsidized building for private sale became much more attractive especially to the small builder, and the numbers of subsidized private houses built rose sharply by 1925. Certainly, contractors preferred to build private subsidized houses. According to one Labour member of the Housing Committee, this was because the contractors could pocket the subsidy instead of passing it on in the form of a lower purchasing price. When corporation housebuilding under the more generous Wheatley subsidy was finally begun in 1925, BABTE refused to tender against unfederated builders and thus succeeded in restricting competition. This not only kept contract prices higher than they might have been, but limited the number of houses built. When, in 1926, the Housing Committee chairman tried to build 1,000 houses on the Sea Mills estate, he found that 'there was no desire on the part of any of the important builders in Bristol to undertake the responsibility of building those houses in anything like the numbers required.' It seems likely that at this point unfederated builders began to win more corporation contracts, since building continued at high levels until the subsidy reduction in 1927, and the Bristol branch of the National Federation of House Builders, a rival to the National Federation of Building Trades Employers, was founded in 1928. It seems ironic that just as the local cartel of BABTE was challenged, moves to end the Chamberlain subsidy and cancel the Wheatley subsidy were announced by the government.[57]

In retrospect, the contribution of Bristol's contractors to municipal housing schemes of this period was ambivalent. On the one hand, the houses they constructed were generally built to a high standard. On the other hand, the federated builders in particular were partly responsible both for the delays which helped to dampen public support for municipal housing, and for the expense which helped to undermine it. The contractors were acting in accordance with accepted business practice when they combined to fix prices and limit competition, and, in contrast to the homeless and overcrowded, they had the power and organization to protect their own interests.

d. Labour

It is difficult to assess the precise nature of the shortage of skilled building labour in Bristol just after the war. The categorization of skilled and unskilled building trade operatives in the 1911 census is not comparable with that employed in 1921. Although, for example, we can tell from the census that the number of masons fell from over 1,100 in 1911 to 450 in 1921, we cannot draw similar conclusions about the number of skilled bricklayers or plasterers. However, it is clear from the available qualitative evidence that in Bristol as elsewhere a scarcity of skilled labour did exist and that it impeded progress on the first municipal housing schemes.

In 1920, contractors joined with city councillors to discuss the shortage with representatives from the Ministry of Labour. Bricklayers and plasterers were reported to be in particularly short supply, and the local chief housing inspector complained that those skilled men still in Bristol preferred to work on the more remunerative repair jobs than on municipal housing sites. Since very little other building was undertaken before 1922, it may be safely assumed that there was an absolute shortage of skilled men, the seriousness of which was underlined by the reports of the poaching of operatives from the housing schemes by private industrialists, and by the complaints of rural housing authorities that Bristol was poaching from them. Bristol building operatives in this happy position enjoyed the high wages generally characteristic of the immediate post-war period, earning less than their colleagues in London but the same as workers in Birmingham, Nottingham and most other large provincial cities.[58]

The building workers employed on Bristol's housing scheme in this period were represented by the National Federation of Building Trade Operatives (NFBTO) and through this negotiating body secured a guaranteed 44-hour week (except for December when they worked $41\frac{1}{2}$ hours) and nationally negotiated wages. Bristol operatives joined their fellow federation members elsewhere in continuing to press for the payment of walking time and wet time. After an unofficial strike and a lockout on the housing schemes in Bristol, operatives were awarded walking time to the suburban estates by the newly established South West Conciliation Board, much to the irritation of the contractors who had to pay.[59]

Meanwhile, there had been mounting criticism of the building operatives' productivity. Late in 1919, Raymond Unwin, then with the Ministry of Health, told Bristol housing officials that:

180

he did not know if all the best men in the building trade had been killed, whether those who were now employed were suffering from war weariness, or whether there was an organised restriction of output, but what took 40 hours to do before the war now took 74.[60]

The members of the Bristol bourgeoisie echoed these charges with apparent enthusiasm. Contract labour on the municipal sites was charged with card-playing and absenteeism, and special venom was reserved for those operatives on the small direct labour scheme at St. John's Lane. One grocer was reported to have bet his colleagues £10 that anyone visiting this site: 'would see there 50 or 60 or perhaps 70 men at work (a voice: "At work"?) – Well, on the ground; and they would see 50 per cent of these men not at work.' A more dispassionate view of the evidence suggests that workers were being very careful, to use the words of one official report, 'not to work themselves out of a job.' At the same time and for the same reason the NFBTO steadfastly resisted repeated government attempts to dilute labour in the building trades.[61]

The precariousness of the building workers' position was rarely if ever mentioned by the national or local press. But the memory of the pre-war slump in the building industry must have been still fresh to the operatives themselves. The cyclical pattern characteristic of the industry persisted throughout the inter-war years. The industrial strength of building workers declined radically between 1921 and 1923, and although their wages were never to fall in money terms to pre-war levels, few other industrial workers suffered as great a reduction of wages. As the demand for labour subsided with the demise of the Addison scheme, wages plummeted from 2s. 4d. per hour commanded by the skilled operative in 1921, to 1s. 7d. in 1923. Unemployment amongst building workers rose to a national figure of 100,000 and the right to the 44-hour week was lost. By the time the Chamberlain subsidy was introduced in the summer of 1923, unemployment in Bristol generally had risen, and employers were willing to take up their full quota of apprentices allowed by the unions, yet operatives were still being pressed to accept unemployed, unskilled servicemen on to their apprentice schemes. As late as May 1923, the Dean of Bristol was able to suggest that unions held the key to the housing shortage and should take on unemployed men who would be 'partly subsidised by out-of-work pay.'[62]

When the Chamberlain scheme was launched in Bristol, shortages of bricklayers and plasterers again became a cause for concern. The Conservative Housing Committee chairman saw the skilled labour shortage as the major impediment to the success of the housing scheme and suggested experimental building and the dilution of labour. If some local operatives' representatives agreed that the problem was serious they certainly denied that this shortage was the deciding factor in the slow progress of the Chamberlain programme in Bristol. Operatives laid the blame at the door of the contractors, and promised Labour councillors 'to supply all the labour necessary if our Corporation will put in hand 1,000 houses to be built by direct labour.'[63] Employers and many councillors were, however, equally adamant that a shortage of skilled men due to the restrictive practices of the unions was largely responsible for the slow take-up of the Chamberlain subsidy by private contractors. The truth was that there were enough skilled men to enable contractors to effect a revival in non-residential building and a modest rise in the pace of middle-class housebuilding, but there do not appear to have been enough bricklayers and plasterers to man those 'Assisted Schemes' which contractors found less financially attractive. Priorities as well as numbers were responsible for the shortage of skilled labour on subsidized housing schemes.[64]

Savory advocated experimental building as a way to circumvent the scarcity of skilled labour without recourse to municipalization. His scheme raised intense opposition and was largely responsible for his resignation from the chairmanship of the Housing Committee in December 1923. One of the first actions his Labour successor, Frank Sheppard, took as chairman, was to call a meeting with operatives' representatives on the labour supply problem. The union delegates were clearly predisposed to co-operate with a Labour chairman and assured him that municipal housing schemes would not be delayed on account of an insufficient number of skilled men. As part of these negotiations, Sheppard sought permission from the government to begin a direct labour scheme for 250 houses. He obtained it and by doing so secured a minor victory for a 'Labour approach' to the manpower problem. For although a direct labour scheme had already been implemented back in 1920, this earlier scheme had been approved more as a test case against the high prices charged on contracted schemes, than as a challenge to contract labour itself.[65]

Wheatley's famous 'gentlemen's agreement' with the operatives entailed that the unions allowed a shorter training period for skilled labourers (especially masons, plasterers and bricklayers) and an increase in the number of semi-skilled men, in return for a guarantee that local authorities would employ more apprentices on their housing schemes.[66] The effect of this agreement was not immediate but it did help to ease the shortage, although a national shortage of plasterers and plumbers persisted until 1926. In Bristol, the shortage of bricklayers on municipal housing schemes began to ease by October 1924, and the shortage of plasterers was reported to be coming to an end. Since non-residential building had not been curtailed, we may conclude that there was an absolute increase in the numbers of skilled men. Of course, the worsening employment picture may well have ensured a flow of skilled workers back into the building industry. In the twelve months since January 1924, the number of unemployed insured adult males in Bristol had increased by over 4,000 to 16,000, but even so, some credit for the improved supply of building workers must surely be due to the negotiations that took place in both Bristol and London.[67]

Certainly Sheppard seems to have enjoyed the confidence and goodwill of Bristol's operatives, even during the national building dispute in the summer of 1924. Throughout the seven week strike, members were allowed by their federation to continue working on the direct labour scheme in Bristol on the understanding that the Corporation would award them whatever new concessions were obtained as a result of the action. However, the City Council blocked the Housing Committee's attempts to caution contractors employing non-union labour on municipal schemes, and sided with contractors objecting to the retrospective pay rise awarded at the dispute's end.[68]

With the shortage of skilled labour easing significantly by 1926, an unprecedented number of corporation houses were built in Bristol before the subsidy cuts announced by the Conservatives took effect early in 1928. As house building began to decline after that date, operatives' wages were cut to 1s. 7½d. and 1s. 2¾d. per hour for the skilled and unskilled worker respectively. By the end of 1928, municipal house building had fallen dramatically and was not to recover until the implementation of the Greenwood Act in 1930.[69]

The declining numbers of houses constructed between 1928 and 1930 were built mainly by contract labour, but one additional direct labour scheme, at

Shirehampton near the Avonmouth port, was also launched in 1929. The corporation-owned site, already laid out in 1927 as part of an unemployed relief scheme, was to be developed to provide workers' housing for the National Smelting Company at Avonmouth, so as to 'keep industry in the area.' The estimated capital cost of the proposed 250 dwellings was just under £106,000 of which the company was to contribute only £13,000. Here was a clear case of the municipality subsidizing industry and one which excited no opposition from erstwhile advocates of 'free enterprise'.[70]

Direct-labour schemes were not as important in Bristol as they were, say, in local authorities in County Durham. They were initially accepted by a predominantly Conservative City Council as a way to avoid high prices and delays associated with contracted schemes under the Addison Act. Although the Council had been pressured by trade unions to build with direct labour, it was probably more influenced by pressure from the Ministry. Councillors were very worried that the unprecedently high costs of house prices in this early period might jeopardize their entitlement to the Addison subsidy when accounts were finally reckoned. Addison himself did nothing to assuage the Council's anxieties when the chairman of Bristol's Housing Committee queried him on this point. Thus the houses built in the first direct-labour scheme (at St. John's Lane) were conceived of as a 'control group' in a prices experiment. But although labour groups claimed these houses were about £50 cheaper than houses built by contract labour,[71] the Council continued to assume that contractors would build the bulk of corporation housing. The direct labour scheme adopted in mid-decade by Sheppard was allowed by the Council as a solution to the labour scarcity problem and is evidence of growing Labour influence. Throughout the decade direct labour was condemned by those outside the Labour Party on the grounds of waste and low productivity. The final direct labour scheme in 1929 was supported by Labour as a work-relief scheme, but was passed by the Council largely because it serviced the needs of private industry.

Direct labour and contract labour were not the only alternatives available to local authorities in 1920. In the first half of the decade, Labour councillors attempted to build houses by another form of labour organization called Building Guilds. These locally organized 'quasi-syndicalist' co-operatives based on the concept of workers' control were a post-war phenomenon. They were affiliated in 1921 to the NFBTO, which saw in the guilds a way to provide more and cheaper municipal housing without surrendering to the government's proposals for dilution.[72]

By 1922 there were some sixteen local authorities contracting with Building Guilds to work on housing schemes. Guilds seemed an alternative worth trying at a time of high contract prices, and there seemed to be no inherent structural problems in employing local guilds given the fact that the building industry of the time was itself based on small locally oriented units. However, central government was sceptical, and Addison had himself told the National Guild Federation that they would have to 'prove themselves' before they could expect the Ministry's support. After the axe, although the Ministry was still approving a very limited number of housing contracts, it appears to have operated a virtual embargo on those contracts proposed by the Building Guilds.[73]

Bristol's Housing Committee formally protested in October 1921 against the Ministry's rejection of a guild contract for a pair of houses approved by the Committee. The price offered by the guild was £695 per house which was lower than the contractors had up to that point been willing to offer. Officially, the Ministry claimed that it wanted still lower prices for houses, but there also seems to have been an element of discrimination exercised against the guild. Councillor Tothill (Labour) moved the protest against the Ministry's 'refusal to allow contracts . . . with the Building Guilds,' and as late as 1924, W. J. Baker, one of Bristol's two Labour M.P.s, vainly attempted to get the government's attitude towards building guilds clarified.[74]

The motives behind the central government's attitude are revealed in the *Report of the Committee Appointed to Investigate the High Cost of Building Working-Class Dwellings.* The committee professed sympathy for the guilds, stating there was 'much to recommend them,' but in the end expressed grave reservations because they would upset vested interests in the building industry.

> We do think, however, that the differentiation in wages and conditions of payment by the guilds is undesirable in that it is likely to cause unrest in the building trade. The enabling provisions of the contract whereby the guilds are able to give to their employees terms by way of payment for wet time and sick time and holidays which are not recognised in the industry as a whole we think must have a disturbing influence upon building labour, which is such a large factor in considering the question of costs.[75]

There is not enough evidence to ascertain whether, with support from the Ministry of Health, the Building Guilds would have proved viable and cost effective. But it is clear that they were never given the chance to prove themselves.

e. Materials

The high price and inadequate supply of house-building materials were recurring problems which dogged municipal housing programmes for most of the 1920s. In Bristol, these problems seemed particularly acute and the evidence indicates they could only have been effectively addressed by a national policy of government control. The wartime dislocation of brick and tile manufacturing and inadequate transport facilities were the most immediate difficulties facing the local authority. But in Bristol there is also evidence to suggest that profiteering went on at every level of the materials market: from the manufacturers themselves through to the builders' merchants and the housing contractors. Moreover, it appears that no government during this period felt willing or able to tackle the problem effectively.

Before and after the Armistice, Bristol had repeatedly urged the government to ensure an adequate supply of building materials for the new Addison houses. But not only was the Carmichael plan for the reconstruction of the building industry jettisoned, the prices of most building materials were decontrolled early in 1919. This move, accompanying as it did the launching of the new housing programme, permitted serious inflation. It is true that in the West Country price rises were initially limited as the Ministry of Reconstruction had been empowered to buy building materials for resale to local authorities, and local authorities were required to purchase their bricks from the Ministry's Department of Supply. But it was soon apparent, in Bristol at least, that the Department was able neither to guarantee sufficient quantities of bricks and tiles nor to ensure that what was delivered was of adequate quality. Consequently, prices for bricks and other building materials climbed to unprecedented heights and continued to do so until 1921, when changes in government policy, along with the slump, served to reduce demand. In other words, prices continued to rise even after most building materials' manufacturers had had sufficient time to recover from the war.[76]

The Housing Committee, Town Clerk and City Engineer in Bristol all worked hard to secure building materials at reasonable prices. Early in 1919, they conferred with both federated and unfederated brick and tile manufacturers in the region about supply and prices. The Bridgwater firm from which the city obtained the necessary tiles was having a difficult time recovering from the war as it could not obtain a government loan to help expand its capacity and the price of tiles supplied to Bristol Corporation fluctuated violently, rising by nearly 50 per cent between October 1919 and April 1921.[77] Bricks (which account on average for over two-thirds of the materials cost of a house) were also supplied by the same Bridgwater firm and later by a firm in the Bristol area. The results were disappointing. Huge price rises (from 63s. per 1,000 bricks in October 1919 to 82s. by May 1921) were further aggravated by extra haulage fees (as much as 12s. extra for every 1,000 bricks delivered). Moreover, the City Engineer complained that the inadequate number of bricks which were finally delivered after protracted delays were of poor quality. The Addison programme in Bristol was further hampered by shortages of cement, pipes, guttering and baths.[78]

Local builders' merchants also combined informally to pressure Bristol councillors not to use 'foreign materials' on the Addison scheme. In one case, the Corporation retracted part of its order for window frames with Critall's of Braintree in order to place it with a local firm (Gardiner's) on allegedly less favourable terms. Trade unions in Bristol also played some part in discouraging the use of both imported and local goods which used non-union labour. Trade union pressure was much more 'public' than pressure from local businessmen to limit competition, which must have been largely informal in a city where so many councillors were in the Chamber of Commerce. Labour and Liberal councillors in Bristol as elsewhere made repeated allegations of price-fixing and profiteering from the autumn of 1919 onwards. Although the Conservative Housing Committee chairman gave a cool reception to such direct accusations, he did support a Cardiff City Council resolution in December 1919 which called on the government to reduce the cost of building materials and to prohibit luxury building. Apart from sponsoring a rather cursory investigation of the high price of building materials in 1920, the government declined to take action. When the Addison programme was formally axed it is interesting to note that Conservatives and right-wing Liberals preferred to dwell on the high wages and the restrictive practices of labour, while those on the left focused their cricitism on the high cost and restricted supply of building materials.[79]

When the Chamberlain programme was launched in the summer of 1923, materials supplies seemed adequate whereas prices were still high, though they had fallen from the peak reached in 1921. Bristol socialists renewed the campaign to highlight profiteering. Although the building supplies industry was generally able to meet the increased demand stimulated by the Chamberlain subsidy, local shortages began to recur early in 1924. Bristol was one of those authorities unlucky enough to suffer from a shortage of bricks as well as from particularly inflated prices in a wide range of building materials. The brick shortage delayed progress on 1923 Act council houses and this situation was exacerbated by the increased demand occasioned by the implementation of the Wheatley Act.[80]

Wheatley had attempted to obtain a 'gentlemen's agreement' with federated building supplies manufacturers analogous to that which he obtained from building operatives. The new Minister reckoned, as he explained to the Commons, that it was 'easier to deal with a ring rather than with unfettered private enterprise.' Manufacturers' representatives, including E.G. Vevers from Bristol, were more than anxious to avoid the imposition of legal constraints and pledged themselves to 'a policy of non-exploitation of the government Housing Schemes.' But the agreement allowed manufacturers to raise their prices whenever their costs increased by another 'elastic clause'. This proviso was exercised with such abandon in Bristol that the efficacy of Wheatley's gentlemanly approach soon proved questionable.[81]

In 1924, Bristol's Housing Committee conferred with both the Ministry of Health and, on the Ministry's advice, with local brick manufacturers about the price and supply of bricks. Vevers himself promised full co-operation with the Corporation. Despite the 'record number of bricks produced in Bristol' that year only one brick manufacturer felt able to supply the authority. It was only when the committee decided to start building in concrete that the manufacturers discovered they could after all meet the Corporation's demand for bricks at a somewhat more reasonable price.[82]

Wheatley's Bill introduced in June 1924 to regulate materials supply was defeated despite the particularly vigorous support in the Commons of Bristol's two Labour M.P.s (W.H. Ayles and Walter Baker). As the municipal house-building programme began to rise sharply in 1925–6, brick prices in Bristol also rose: from 62s. 6d. per 1,000 in May 1924 to 67s. in June 1925, to 80s. at the height of house building in November 1926. Bristol and Birmingham led the prices for Portland cement that same year, and early in 1927 a local price ring affecting the price of sinks supplied to Bristol's municipal estates was exposed.[83] That June there was yet another call, this time by the Regional Conference of the Housing and Town Planning Council which met in Bristol, for investigation into the cost of building materials. But no government action seems to have been taken. By the winter of 1927, the subsidy cuts began to depress the rate of corporation house building and costs of materials began to fall. There was yet another shortage of bricks in 1929, necessitating the roughcasting of some council house exteriors. But overall, the price and supply of building materials, never effectively controlled by the government, was finally controlled by the market.[84]

f. Experimental building

Why were experimental construction techniques employed on the first municipal housing schemes? Was the adoption of such techniques motivated, as Herbert Ashworth suggested, 'largely by the desire to apply engineering principles to building', and 'alleviate the housing shortage in the quickest possible time'?[85] It is surely wrong to contend that these were the only important motives, or to imply that experimental building schemes were politically neutral.

The idea that experimental buildings would be cheaper than conventional ones was important to policy-makers at both local and central levels. Even if the new methods and materials did not in fact turn out to be cheaper, it was initially hoped they would be. As one Bristol politician had reasoned early in the decade 'the only way to secure cheap housing was by mass production.'[86] One must also remember that delays in municipal housing schemes were not merely the products of conventional building processes, but of shortages of cheap capital, materials and skilled labour. Experimental building was one way to circumvent such problems without resorting to comprehensive government control of the building industry. In Bristol, building experiments were attempted on municipal schemes throughout the decade under study. They were always deployed with the permission and, to varying degrees, the encouragement of central government. They were particularly favoured

Figure 22.   a. Fishponds Estate at its bleakest, c.1928 (courtesy of the Bristol Environmental Health Department).

b. A rare interior view of a slum dwelling: no date but probably c.1936 (courtesy of the Bristol Environmental Health Department).

as a way to get house prices down without increasing subsidies. In Bristol at least they did not seem particularly successful from either a functional or an aesthetic standpoint.

Bristol's Housing Commissioner had originally recommended experimental methods as a means of combating the high tenders first offered by contractors in 1919. As a result, 250 Dorman Long houses were built at the Sea Mills Estate under the Addison subsidy. These steel-frame and concrete houses were erected by William Cowlin & Son Ltd, a firm long associated with an innovative approach to concrete construction techniques. Although praised by *The Builder* for their rapid construction, easy maintenance and ingenious design, these houses were less favourably viewed by consumers. At a contract price of just under £800 per house they were not the hoped-for cheap alternative to brick. In the long term, the houses proved difficult to maintain and this, along with their thin party walls, made them unpopular with tenants. The remainder of Bristol's 1,189 Addison houses were built in brick by conventional methods.[87]

By early 1923, the housing shortage had worsened to such an extent that unless a larger number of houses were quickly and cheaply built, the Housing Committee Chairman believed that Bristol would be heading for 'housing bankruptcy'. Even assuming the full co-operation of the existing labour force, Savory did not think the acute need for accommodation could be met with sufficient speed if bricks were used. He saw alternative construction methods as the only way to overcome both the time factor and the vexed problem of lack of skilled labour.[88] Savory was an enthusiast who turned his own hand to devising the 'Bristol chalet' and later the 'Bristol bungalow' as an alternative to conventional Tudor Walters-inspired housing. A fine-arts publisher by profession, Savory saw these chalets and bungalows as a brave new experiment when he proposed to the Council in 1923 that 1,500 chalets be built under the new Chamberlain subsidy. The chalet was at best spartan, with its exposed interior steel beams and corrugated iron roof, which even one of its advocates confessed made it 'vulnerable to the extremes of temperature.' Much smaller than the Addison houses, the chalets possessed only partitions, which did not quite reach the ceiling, to separate the bedrooms and bath from the living room.[89]

Savory and his allies had not reckoned on the ferocity of Labour's opposition to the scheme. During the local election that November, socialist candidates were scathing about 'Savory's kennels', attacking them as 'hen roosts' which were expensive and 'not conducive to family life.' The Labour movement appeared to be most offended by the lack of truly separate bedrooms. In the following weeks, most Labour councillors, the pragmatic Sheppard excepted, declared themselves opposed to any experimental building techniques on municipal housing schemes. By December 1923, not only was Savory's scheme defeated, but Savory himself resigned as Housing Committee chairman amid much acrimony.[90]

Before his departure, Savory had managed to push through another experimental scheme, whereby 300 otherwise conventional houses were to be erected in concrete under the 1923 Act. The shortages of brick and other materials, and the support of the new Labour government for experimentation, meant that Savory's successor as chairman, Sheppard, carried on the concrete building programme. It is significant that once the 300 concrete houses had been built, by the end of 1924, the previously reluctant brick manufacturers began to canvass the housing department for orders.[91]

The exploitation of new building materials and methods was encouraged with renewed vigour once the Conservative government was returned to power.[92] In

Bristol, plaster substitutes were tried out during the shortage of skilled plasterers but were soon abandoned when the shortage eased in 1925. Steel houses were also encouraged. The major advantages of these were discussed with Bristol Housing Committee representatives at a number of meetings held by the Ministry of Health and at a special conference promoting the new systems in 1925. By the summer of the same year, Bristol arranged for the erection of 38 steel-frame houses, four of which were to receive a special £200 lump sum subsidy from the Exchequer and the rest to qualify for assistance under the Chamberlain Act. The Council soon found, however, that the houses were not the cheap and easy solution to the skilled labour shortage that had been hoped.[93] Furthermore, it transpired that tenants heartily disliked the steel houses. The malfunctioning fireplaces in one scheme had reduced tenants to burning their gas lights for heat, while Sheppard himself complained of the condensation problems, the high cost and the generally unattractive appearance of steel-frame houses.[94] The official Bristol Housing Department report in 1930 stated that although the period of experimentation had 'served useful purposes', the department contemplated no further departures from ordinary brick construction in the future. Such bland pronouncements obscured the fact that steel houses had proved to be a minor disaster whilst only the concrete houses had been a qualified success.[95] In short, experimental building methods, based as they were on a tangle of economic miscalculation, unexamined political value judgments and technological enthusiasms, were no substitute for a comprehensive housing policy.

3 The Council as landlord

a. 'Hutches for heroes':[96] standards and amenities

Generally speaking, there was a progressive decline in Bristol's standards of corporation house design and amenity provision from 1921 to 1930. This decline must be considered in conjunction with concurrent policy trends favouring the increasing privatization of housing provision. The preference for residualist slum clearance and rehousing programmes and the enthusiasm for assisting the private sector to provide 'general needs' or 'universalist' housing were continuing themes in Conservative housing policy throughout the decade. 'Residualist' housing policy before 1946 advocated state provision only for the very poorest, whilst 'universalist' policy advocated state provision for the working class generally. This set of policy assumptions greatly influenced the 'non-political' Citizens Party majority on Bristol's City Council.

In assessing the evolution of corporation housing standards, we shall first consider what was assumed to constitute 'good' housing. Since before the war, the notion of centrally located tenements was condemned by Bristol Labour councillors, and some Liberals, as a cheapjack approach to municipal housing. This was largely because the advocates of such dwellings were usually opponents of universalist provision. In this way, the debate about the respective merits of centrally located flats and suburban cottages became divided along political lines, with the unfortunate result that the integrity of poor neighbourhoods and the convenience of centrally located dwellings tended to be underrated by the very people most concerned to secure 'good' public housing for the working class.[97]

Soon after the war, local women's groups along with community and labour organizations (which often had a high proportion of women members) were quick to lobby the local council for housing along the lines proposed by the Tudor Walters Report of 1918. Suburban parlour houses with adequately sized living rooms and large cupboards were favoured by such groups along with generous gardens and plenty of public amenities. Women in particular emphasized the need for convenient, easy-to-clean interiors, and a petition from 1,700 'working women' in Bristol demonstrated both the high level of interest exhibited in the housing question and the way in which local feminists channelled their energies into a form of 'welfare feminism' which pushed for improved conditions for women in the home, but left the ideal of female domesticity unquestioned.[98]

Within the Council, Labour members were particularly assiduous in pushing for low-rent, high-standard suburban cottages with parlours. In fact, Labour councillors wanted all houses to have parlours though the committee finally resolved that only 60 per cent be so equipped. This emphasis on parlour development derived from the popular conviction that a parlour denoted respectability and dignified living conditions. Indeed, one local survey undertaken in 1939 seemed to suggest that corporation tenants considered a parlour more of a necessity than a bathroom. The labour movement in Bristol fought for provision of parlours and, like suburban development, parlour housing had become a politically charged issue.[99]

In 1919, the Housing Committee held a competition for the best housing design submitted by local architects. The winners were to have their houses built on an experimental basis before they were erected on a large scale. The winning designs were originally reproduced in the *Builder*. The designs were clearly determined by the *Manual of Guidance to Local Authorities* issued in 1919 by the Local Government Board, which was itself based on the principles of the Tudor Walters Report. The layout plans which were used for Fishponds and Sea Mills estates were similarly inspired, and are full of curving lines, cul-de-sacs and plenty of open spaces.[100] The house designs themselves were redolent of some pre-industrial patriarchal idyll and are all illustrated in sylvan settings, with hens scratching at the lawn and trees in profusion. These 'Addison cottages' were unlike modern houses in that there was no kitchen, but rather a scullery with a cooking range provided in the living room. They were originally intended to be built in blocks of two or four, and in most respects the houses erected in Bristol were typical Addison houses. The newly appointed Housing Committee was anxious to provide good standard housing under the generous 1919 Act subsidy. Their efforts were closely vetted by the Bristol Women's Advisory Committee, a local branch of a nationally recognized consumer group.[101]

Generally, the standards of the first Addison houses were very high, especially when compared with pre-war private and municipal working-class housing in the city. The only exception was the 141 army huts in Shirehampton, converted under the 1919 Act. These had no baths, though a communal bathhouse was built. However, a 500-strong delegation from the Inter-Allied Housing and Town Planning Conference, which inspected the first houses in 1920, criticized the small sculleries and internal fittings and joinery work on the conventional houses, and was even less fulsome about the experimental Dorman Long houses. They did on the other hand commend the high quality of the materials used. The Addison houses were notoriously expensive, built as they were by an inexperienced council at a time when labour, materials and loan capital were scarce and costly. They were Bristol's most expensive corporation houses in the 1920s, costing on average £1,089 per house, almost 90 per cent of which was expended on the building itself as opposed to the sites and services. The cost was in part attributable to the high proportion of parlour houses built as well as to the good standards of construction and generous layouts employed. However, in view of the mounting criticisms of the cost of these houses, culminating in the report in 1921 of the committee investigating the high cost of working-class dwellings, Bristol's Housing Committee was forced to reduce standards on the new estates. In order to effect a saving of an estimated £25 per house, cheaper damp courses, less substantial foundations and similar economies on construction costs were made. Semi-detached houses were increasingly replaced by blocks of four and even eight houses.[102]

After the cancellation of the Addison subsidy, the Ministry of Health advised authorities to lease the empty sites on corporation estates to private contractors. The Corporation decided, in the words of its City Engineer, to let private enterprise 'fill the gaps'.[103] In July 1922, Wm Cowlin & Son became the first contractor to build privately on a Bristol Corporation estate. The 14 plots let to the firm on a 99-year lease at Sea Mills had been already prepared at the city's expense. Purchasers were difficult to find for these houses, but as building costs continued to fall Cowlin secured a dozen more leases (this time for 999 years) for houses and shops. By granting such long-term leases, Bristol was undermining its own planning safeguards on future housing development. The tenants' group at Hillfields Park Estate (Fishponds) opposed this practice, fearing the intrusion of private developers would ruin the garden-suburb character of their estate. They did not, said one of their spokesmen, want 'Hillfields Park to degenerate into a cross between Clifton [a wealthy private suburb] and the slums.' As building plots continued to be let, tenants kept up their protest, complaining in 1923 that private contractors would not preserve uniform road frontages or build high-standard housing. The introduction of the Chamberlain and Wheatley Acts marked a time of further disillusionment in terms of municipal house design. Local authorities were given no new directives on housing design and layout. There was simply not the same interest in high standards as there had been just after the war: no design competitions were held and the topic had disappeared from the popular magazines and newspapers.[104]

Under the two Acts, standards began to decline further. On the estates in Bristol, fewer parlour houses were built and frontages and internal layouts were more cramped, but at least fixed baths were a statutory requirement. Some Chamberlain houses no longer had water supplied to their upper storeys and on one site cooking grates were sacrificed on grounds of expense and women were banished, amid the protests of the Women's Advisory Committee, to the scullery.[105] The tenements built under the slum clearance provision of the 1923 Act were far less lavish. The first block at Lawfords Gate featured a large proportion of three-roomed flats and separate bathrooms were not provided. Frank Sheppard (Labour), by this time Housing Committee Chairman, blamed these cuts in conveniences on rising building costs and the Ministry of Health. Committee members, he pointed out, 'were not free agents', but were dependent on government approval, and the government allowed only those things 'which were regarded as essentials.'[106]

Corporation house building in Bristol under the above-mentioned Acts finally began to take off in 1925–6. Still faced with a serious housing shortage, Sheppard and his committee were emboldened to propose a scheme early in 1926 for building 800 houses per year for a period of several years. They hoped to begin with the erection of 1,000 houses on the Sea Mills site.[107] Pressure to reduce housing standards had already been mounting since the beginning of the year when one Citizens Party councillor called for the development of existing estates at a higher density of 20 houses instead of the established 12 per acre. Although some Conservatives on the Housing Committee opposed higher densities, this attack on Tudor Walters standards was in line with Conservative Party policy. Only a fortnight before this issue was first raised in Bristol Council, the Central Council of the National Association of Conservative and Unionist Associations had passed a resolution 'regretting' the tendency of some authorities to build houses only of the larger type 'which the poorer wage earners could not afford.' The Central Council also urged that 'a much greater proportion' of money be devoted to slum clearance, and backed a declaration made at the meeting by Chamberlain himself, that 'cheaper building was the crux of the whole problem.'[108]

The squeeze on standards worsened after the intention to reduce housing subsidies was made known in 1926. Indeed, as unemployment intensified, some Housing Committee members were won over by the view that cheaper dwellings, as opposed to higher wages or more generous subsidies, were needed 'in order to provide dwellings at a lower rental.' At the same time that compromises on housing standards were approved, the Council redoubled its efforts to sell off council houses. In keeping with this, the Committee Secretary, A.W. Smith, successfully proposed that advances on mortgages on houses sold should be made by the Corporation itself, so that the proceeds of the sale of these council houses could be 'applied towards the cost of erecting others.' It was also hoped, in the expectation of declining government subsidies, that the private sector would help in the provision and financing of housing on a philanthropic basis.[109]

Although they had favoured the very financial constraints which necessitated the monotonous replication of skimped designs, shrinking grass verges and treeless streets, right-wing councillors attacked the new corporation houses on aesthetic grounds. They complained, for example, about the uniformity of the houses at Sea Mills, and the 'wilful multiplication' of 'one of the ugliest house types in Bristol.' This had the unfortunate effect of polarizing opinion over the aesthetics of corporation estates. Those attempting to maintain a universalist provision were on the defensive and could hardly be expected to dwell on the unattractiveness of corporation estates. In such circumstances, it is plain to see how aesthetic considerations could increasingly come to be seen by champions of a collectivist housing policy as an impractical luxury, or even an insidious diversion. When the subsidy cuts were actually implemented, they hit Bristol at a time when the prices of building materials had reached abnormally inflated levels. These prices offset the reduction in the price of housing tenders which initially followed the announcement of the subsidy cuts. Material costs, plus the problem of finding suitable sites, exacerbated the problems of building new houses which could cater for the 'lower paid' worker without occasioning a further increase in rates.[110]

Caught between the inability of *most* workers to pay more than 10s. a week inclusive rent, and the unwillingness of the Council to make up for subsidy reductions by sufficiently increasing the rates, the Housing Committee had to make increasing accommodation to the logic of a residualist housing policy. In July 1927 they announced that it could no longer construct houses for the 'ordinary' worker and had decided to concentrate on a slum clearance and rehousing scheme of a thousand dwellings. The Citizens Party on the Council continued to press for 'smaller but not less convenient dwellings' to be erected as part of the slum clearance programme. The move to downgrade standards was given a prestigious boost by Kingsley Wood,

Chamberlain's Parliamentary Secretary, who came to open the new Church Tenements' Association flats. Kingsley Wood tactfully remonstrated with the Housing Committee for having 'aimed a little too high' with regard to the type of housing they provided. On the other hand, Kingsley Wood made much of the very modest achievements of the Church Tenements' Association, thus pressing the government preference for private provision.[111]

In 1928 still further cuts were threatened by Baldwin's Ministry. Sheppard, opposed only by a few left-wing councillors, suggested that bungalows rather than cottages should be built at one of the new suburban sites intended for rehousing slum families. These bungalows were to cost £505 each or about £15 less than the standard Wheatley Act cottages. Because they were built under the 1924 Act, the cost on the rates would be substantially less, and because they were clearly different from the standard design a lower rent could be charged for them without tenants on other estates protesting. Meanwhile, the slum rehousing scheme in central Bristol continued despite left-wingers' complaints about the 'barrack like' tenements.[112]

In the face of the continuing housing shortage, the Housing Committee was loath to restrict its activities to slum clearance schemes. At least 10,000 houses were estimated to be needed in order to replace unfit stock and keep up with the enlarged population.[113] Not all of these houses could be built under the provisions of slum clearance legislation, yet the large-scale programme under the Wheatley Act was considered to be too costly, particularly if rents were reduced to levels more people could afford. A way out of this impasse was suggested in a report submitted to the Housing Committee by its Secretary, A.W. Smith, in November 1927. Smith held that the only way to implement a long-term building programme of low-rent houses was to build more cheaply. In order for a house let at 10s. rent per week inclusive of rates to be economic, the building costs would have to be limited to £200. But the average capital cost for houses built in the two years preceding the report had been £520. Smith proposed the erection of 5,000 smaller dwellings on less centrally located and less expensive sites, at a cost of £430 each. In addition to this long-term scheme, which would be financed under the 1924 subsidy, he proposed a comprehensive slum clearance programme which would include the replacement of 5,000 unfit dwellings.[114]

The committee approved Smith's proposals and arranged for a discussion of the report with the Council. In the summer of 1928 the committee formally requested the Council to approve the acquisition of several hundred acres of land at Southmead and additional sites adjoining the existing Bedminster Down and Knowle Estates. The Bedminster/Knowle sites were not as good in terms of value for money as the Southmead site; but they were purchased after 'pressure [had been] . . . brought to bear on the Committee to provide houses [there] . . . especially as it was an industrial district.'[115] The land was to be utilized for up to 10,000 houses over the next fifteen years, though it had been acknowledged that the Southmead site could not be immediately used for building as it was 'too far out' and on the opposite side of most of the city's industrial development. The Finance Committee did not oppose the purchase of the land at £150,000; the land at Southmead was the cheapest ever secured since the Corporation began to buy housing sites. Indeed, it was so cheap that the potential problems of transport to and from the more centrally located industrial areas were not fully considered. Many on the Council thought they had gone a long way towards laying the groundwork for an adequate housing policy for Bristol. One Conservative Housing Committee member, for example, told electors that with the erection of 8,000 to 9,000 houses on the new sites, the 'Council felt that they had met the requirement of the working classes for some considerable period ahead.' However, by then the 'requirements of the working classes' had been redefined. The period 1919–30, which had begun with the implementation of the Tudor Walters report, ended with Tudor Walters himself advocating a downgrading of standards for the sake of lower rents.[116]

High-rise flats with doormen, functioning lifts and a variety of other well-maintained communal facilities currently command high rents on the private market. Publicly owned dwellings with inadequate custodial care, broken lifts and a dearth of communal facilities are one of today's great planning disasters. Such disasters have prompted critics to point out that public amenities are not optional extras but essentials for a successfully functioning housing estate. Such insights are not new. Ebenezer Howard himself recognized that attention to amenities, including transport, was central to good planning. In Bristol, similar concern was shown before and during the war by housing reform groups. The very title of the Housing Extension and Town Planning Committee formed in 1918 implied official recognition that the committee's brief included more than just the erection of dwellings. In the words of one official policy review, the Housing and Town Planning Act, by encouraging the acquisition of large sites, 'afforded [the Corporation] ample scope for good planning'.[117]

Yet, as early as 1920, before Bristol's first corporation houses were completed, the Housing Extension and Town Planning Committee announced that it was concentrating on 'housing first then, town planning'. In April of that same year, the Ministry of Health refused to approve Bristol's request for the inclusion of recreation grounds and the implementation of road improvement plans at a number of estates. By 1922, Savory, then Committee Chairman, admitted that his members had 'done little' in respect of town planning and soon after the Housing Committee divested itself of such planning functions. Responsibility for planning was hived off to a separate committee which was mainly notable during the rest of the decade for its inactivity.[118]

The increase in the number of houses on corporation estates after 1925 produced more pressure from tenants for such basic public facilities as schools, playgrounds and shops. Such amenities as were granted were provided on an *ad hoc* basis, usually as a result of campaigning by tenants. In 1926, however, plans for building shops on empty sites at one estate were deferred and a request for provision of a hall at another was denied, 'in view of the urgent need for houses.' In 1928, a second request for a recreation ground at Horfield was turned down on similar grounds. The same year, tenants began to campaign for the provision of electric lighting to their homes and this was promised, albeit on a seven-year installation plan. Ironically, the Housing Committee had intended to supply the first corporation houses with electric lights but had been prevented from doing so by Ministry officials who judged that the gas light already supplied was sufficient for tenants' needs.[119]

The work involved in building houses stretched the resources of the Corporation – in both financial and administrative terms – as never before. Given the difficulties of coping with this unprecedented responsibility at a time of severe overcrowding, it was all too easy for councillors and officials to see town planning as a luxury for later. Administratively, there was little formal contact in Bristol between corporation committees with regard to the provision and co-ordination of estate facilities. The main exception to this state of affairs was the negotiation between the Education and Housing Committees whereby the former purchased Housing Committee land on two estates with a view to erecting schools. There must have been a measure of informal contact also between the Housing Committee and the Education, Libraries, Health and Electrical Committees because several members of the Housing Committee were also members of these other bodies. However, each committee had a separate budget and a carefully defined brief, which discouraged more extensive co-ordination and liaison. Finally, the financial uncertainty bred during the post-1921 period by retrenchment policies was exacerbated by the repeated threats of housing subsidy cuts. In such a climate, local authorities were not encouraged to take a long-term and comprehensive view of the needs of those living on suburban corporation estates. For example, although the need for a cheap and adequate tram service to the estates was glaringly apparent, the Council chose not to municipalize the tram service under the terms of its option in 1929. This was because Conservative councillors expected that such a purchase would burden the rates at a time when the demands of the Poor Law were particularly pressing. Of course, the municipalization of the trams would not inevitably have meant that the public would have benefited. But it is notable that Bristol was one of the few large cities which did not own its tram service, and such ownership might have facilitated a more integrated development of housing and transport services, had the political will to do so existed.[120]

Public amenities on Bristol's corporation estates were, as table 20 shows, extremely limited and on some of the estates there were virtually no shops, libraries, community halls or pubs for several years after the first tenants had moved in. Roundsmen were left to supply residents of these suburban estates with consumer goods, and Jevons and Madge describe the extra expense and inconvenience entailed by the lack of permanent shops. One informant has contended that this lack of shops encouraged high-pressure salesmen to inveigle tenants into expensive hire purchase agreements they did not fully understand for furniture and other consumer durables. It has also been pointed out by Jevons and Madge that the relatively small number of shops which were eventually built on the estates could not provide as cheap or as varied a service as did stores in more central shopping areas. No research has yet been done on inter-war private housing developments in Bristol, so one cannot compare the provision of amenities on such estates with those on corporation estates. But Jackson's research on speculative development indicates that private housing estates in London also tended to suffer from lack of such communal facilities as libraries, sportsgrounds and community halls, though they tended to be better served by shops than their publicly owned counterparts.[121]

It should also be remembered that during the entire period there was not one cinema or social centre provided on a corporation estate in Bristol. The open-air schools seriously proposed for tenants' children do not seem to have proved viable substitutes for sheltered provision. At Sea Mills four classes were taught in the one-room ex-army hut that doubled as church and social hall. Nor does provision for medical services seem to have been adequate since it appears to have been customary for non-resident doctors to take rooms in a corporation house for use as a surgery. This led to overcrowding, and according to an official report: 'During epidemics and often in normal times, patients have had to queue for attention, sitting on the stairs in some instances, or even out in the garden.' The distance from hospital facilities must also have caused residents concern, particularly before the widespread installation of public telephones and in the absence of cheap and frequent transport to the city centre.[122]

Table 20. Estate amenities, 1930

	schools	creches	shops	medical	churches	social centre halls	sports grounds	pubs	library	cinema
Sea Mills	1	none	none till 12 built 1927–9	dentist in 1922 (1 day p.w.) 1 surgery	3	1 ex-army hut	rec. ground by 1930, probably earlier	none	none until 1934	none
Fishponds (Hillfields Park)	site bought in 1924, school erected by 1930	none	4 after 1925. No post office till at least 1925	? surgery	2 built in 1925 and 1928	none, requests in 1922 and 1926 turned down	10-acre open space granted in 1929	none	?	none
Horfield	1 school begun 1928, completed by 1930	none	? none recorded	? surgery	?	none	none–request for one in 1928 denied	none (at least until 1929)	none till 1930	none
Knowle	none until after 1926, 1 school recorded by 1930	none	none	? surgery	1 temp. church	none	cricket grounds	none	none	none

196

Although we know remarkably little about the structure and internal ecology of working-class life in early twentieth-century Bristol, some recent research, based on oral interviews with Bristolians recalling the pre-1924 period, suggests that informal support networks of relatives, neighbours, workmates and local shopkeepers were an important and all-pervasive feature of everyday life, particularly in Bristol's older and poorer areas. With this point in mind, we might better appreciate why those who found themselves stranded on isolated, under-resourced estates might disagree with those who argued in the name of economy that public amenities were an 'optional extra.'[123]

b. Rents

Three factors prevented Bristol's Housing Committee from developing a consistent rent policy during the period under study. The first factor was the erratic and unpredictable nature of Exchequer assistance and the objectives of the subsidies themselves. The second, perhaps no less important factor, was the very limited earning power of the majority of corporation tenants, which made it impossible to charge rents acceptable to the Ministry of Health without forcing a large number of tenants into sub-letting, protest, arrears or hardship. The third was the difference of opinion within the Council itself, about the acceptable level of rate fund expenditure, a debate which rested on different conceptions of the role of public housing provision.[124]

Jevons and Madge likened the Addison subsidy to agricultural grants 'given to stimulate production.' A subsidy was given for each house built, and 'whether one family benefited more than another was considered as of secondary importance.' This is a broadly correct, if somewhat crude, characterization of the rent policy implied in the 1919 Act. The open-ended Addison subsidy was intended to ensure that local authorities would not feel tempted to meet the abnormally high building costs of the time 'by charging high rents for the houses.' Since the government had assumed that the high costs were temporary and that market rents could be resumed in 1927, there was seemingly no call for councils to adopt a long-term rent policy in 1919. The level of rents to be charged was to be based on three considerations: the controlled rents of working-class houses; the superior amenities of the new houses; and the estimated capacity of working-class tenants to pay.[125]

The chairman of Bristol's new Housing Committee, Ernest Savory was careful to point out that the working class eligible for the new houses included 'bank clerks as well as navvies.' He assumed that it would be 'the self-respecting artisan rather than the slum dweller who would take advantage of the new houses.' The rents first proposed for the new houses appeared to reflect this assumption. They were high, ranging from 7s. 6d. per week for a two-bedroom house without parlour, to 14s. 0d. per week for a four-bedroom house with parlour. The bulk of the houses were to have three bedrooms and a parlour and were to be let at between 12s. and 14s. per week, exclusive of rates and water charges.[126]

These high-rent houses were supported in the Council by an unusual alliance of Labour and non-Labour politicians. It is at first glance surprising that a Labour member like Frank Sheppard was anxious to push the scheme through since the rents were so high. The truth was that he was anxious to get the public housing scheme 'on the books' and did not think it opportune to quibble over rents at that point. He was supported by some non-Labour members of the Council 'for business as well as moral reasons', the location of new factories at Avonmouth depending, it seemed, on the prompt provision of public housing there. Those councillors opposing the housing scheme justified their position on the grounds that the rents were too high. However, their arguments must be evaluated in the light of their long-standing opposition to universalist housing provision.[127]

The rents, as Savory later admitted, were considerably in excess of those adopted for similar houses' elsewhere in the country, and he soon began to wonder about the ability of tenants to pay. By the end of 1919, Savory wrote to Addison to seek assurance that the city would still receive the subsidy even if working-class tenants could not pay the rents and members of higher income groups were admitted. Addison would not commit himself on this matter, and as slump succeeded boom in mid-1920, the Housing Committee's worries were confirmed by the discovery that many of the people selected from the housing waiting list of almost 3,000 were 'unable to avail themselves of the accommodation offered' because of the high rents. As a result, the committee resolved in June 1920 to reduce the scale of rents. The Ministry, however, did not approve this initial request, protesting that the revised levels, shown in table 21, were too low. The Housing Committee stood firm, maintaining that 'the rents proposed are the maximum which the tenants can be expected to pay.' Whilst the Ministry wrangled with the Housing Committee over this issue, something had to be done to assist the tenants to meet the rent payments.[128]

Table 21.   Revised rent levels in Bristol, June 1920

house type	economic rents	original rents	revised rents
Type One (2 bedrooms without parlour)	25s.	10s. plus	7s.6d.
Type Two (3 bedrooms without parlour)	27s.6d.	12s.6d.	8s.6d.–9s.6d.
Type Five (3 bedrooms with parlour)	30s.	15s.	10s.–11s.6d.

Rents exclusive of rates.

Sources: BHCM, 27 March 1920, 282, no.0879; 26 April 1920, 300, and Report of the Secretary to the Housing Committee in *BHCM*, 5 September 1921, facing 115. Economic rents taken from *BCM*, 14 December 1920.

In September 1920, the previous ban on sub-letting Corporation houses was lifted. When the houses had been first erected, this practice was strictly forbidden, and one tenant had been formally threatened with eviction for taking a lodger. Now the Housing Committee defended its turnabout on the grounds that the majority of the families on the waiting lists were small families and so 'the accommodation provided could not be utilised to the fullest extent if one house was allotted to each family.' Sub-letting was permitted only 'as an emergency measure', each case to be subject to the formal approval of the Housing Committee. Of the 722 families housed by the Corporation in 1921, most wage-earners were reported to enjoy average incomes of over £3 per week. Many of those renting the parlour houses appear to have been clerks and supervisory manual workers earning over £4 10s. a week. There was even a sprinkling of teachers and reporters. However, as the slump intensified, the Secretary of the Housing Department, A. W. Smith, reported that 'tenants are suffering through trade depression and it is undoubtedly a struggle for many to meet the weekly sum due.' The Ministry of Health, having declined to approve the reduced scale of rents proposed by the committee, referred the matter to a Rents Tribunal. Early in 1922, the Housing Committee decided to send a deputation to the Ministry to press their case, but the matter took several more months to resolve. In the interim, the Housing Committee insisted on charging the reduced scale of rents even when the Ministry withheld just under £2,500 of its £79,000 grant as a sign of official displeasure.[129] The Housing Committee also attempted to get the Overseers and Assessment Committees to reduce the rates payable on the corporation houses, which were among the highest charged in the country as a whole. But these committees refused to do so, saying that appeals would be heard on an individual basis only.[130]

Tenants on the newly occupied estates at Fishponds and Knowle formed the first Corporation Tenants' Associations precisely in order to press for rent and rates reduction. In March 1922, the Hillfields Park Tenants' Association was founded as a result of a mass meeting of 300 tenants over the rents question. According to the Rev. Patterson, who was reported to have addressed the meeting, conditions were bad. 'The trade depression now rampant everywhere had resulted in much unemployment on the estate and he himself . . . had come across some harrowing cases of poverty and actual starvation.' He went on to observe that many men working full time were earning as little as £2 15s. 9d. per week and had to pay almost £1 in rent and rates.[131]

A committee of twenty members (including five women) was formed to represent the tenants in a campaign which was primarily to press for rent reductions but also for the provision of amenities on the estate and for the right of tenants to buy their own houses. This last demand confirms that at least some tenants were in a high enough income bracket to consider owner-occupation. The Housing Committee plainly sympathized with the tenants who petitioned them, but could hardly press for a further reduction of rents when most of the rents currently being charged had not yet gained Ministry approval. Nor could the Housing Committee persuade the Assessment Committee to reduce the rates. By July, however, the situation had altered. The Overseers Committee had received 26 individual appeals for rates reductions within one month and were sufficiently impressed by the evidence presented to them to recommend a 20 per cent reduction in the rates to the Assessment Committee. Rates had formerly added between 6s. and 8s. per week on top of rents. The reduction meant that inclusive rents which had ranged from 13s. 6d. to 18s. fell to between 12s. and 17s. 2d. The Hillfields Tenants (Fishponds) formally thanked the committee for their role in pressing for the reduction in the rates and expressed the hope that the rents themselves would also be further reduced. Early that autumn, the Ministry of Health finally approved the Committee's unilateral revision of the rents and forwarded the £2,500 in subsidy money which they had held back.[132]

However, rents were still beyond the means of many tenants, and Hillfields Park Tenants' Association continued to lead a movement for further rent reductions. There was by 1923 'scarcely a single house' on any of the estates where unauthorized sub-letting did not occur.[133] Table 22 shows the widespread existence of rent arrears. The particularly high percentages of tenants in arrears at Fishponds and

Shirehampton is attributable to the fact that a relatively high number of lower paid workers were living there. Shirehampton housed most of the dockers and labourers who were tenants in 1921.

Table 22. Rent arrears on Bristol estates, May 1921

	no. of houses occupied	arrears	% in arrears
Fishponds	730	134	18.3
Sea Mills	250	22	8.8
Knowle	90	8	8.8
St John's Lane	154	40	25.9
Shirehampton	141	46	29.0
Easton	9	1	11.1
Luckwell	28	—	—

Source: BHCM, 5 May 1921, 144.

The Chamberlain and Wheatley Acts provided specific, fixed, grants for each house built. The Chamberlain Act had been aimed mainly at assisting private enterprise to build houses for sale, so there was not a specific rent policy for the minority of corporation houses built to let under this Act. The local authority had to decide for itself how much should come out of the rate fund and how much from the rents in order to finance Chamberlain houses, and in Bristol their rents seem to have mirrored those charged for Addison houses.[134]

Before the passage of the Chamberlain Act in 1923, the Housing Committee had expressed itself as 'deeply concerned' to provide accommodation for those 'who are not in a position to occupy houses in the outlying estates' but was divided largely along party lines as to how this might best be done. Sheppard stated publicly that the Corporation as well as the government should bear the losses in order to build houses at sufficiently low rents. Savory and his Conservative and Liberal allies attempted to meet the need for lower rents by cutting down building costs and by focusing their efforts on rehousing slum dwellers under the special provisions of the 1923 Act, whereby slum clearance and rehousing schemes qualified in approved cases for a 50 per cent subsidy on the losses incurred.[135]

The Wheatley Act, introduced in 1924, aimed at the provision of lower rent housing, but its rent policy was open to widely differing interpretations. The rents were to be fixed by authorities in relation to controlled rents but this was only a guideline, not a rule. Bowley explains that the only specific constraint on local authorities was that they had to 'contribute a minimum of £4 10s. per house for 40 years in an effort to prevent the *average level* of rent for new working-class housing rising above the level of similar pre-war houses. They were under no obligation to contribute more than this.' Within this limitation, rents would be fixed as the individual authority wished. Bristol's rents were higher than those charged by Birmingham and Bradford, but generally lower than those charged in Manchester and Leeds.[136]

The Bristol Housing Committee foresaw difficulties in building lower rent Wheatley Act houses on the same sites as the more expensive Addison and Chamberlain houses. Tenants, they felt, would resent paying higher rents for broadly similar housing. The committee therefore applied to the Ministry of Health for protection against financial loss incurred by standardizing the rents on the older houses at the level of the Wheatley rents. This was refused and the committee thus decided to build the first 1924 Act houses on undeveloped sites at Horfield and Bedminster Down.[137]

The exclusive rents for a non-parlour house with three bedrooms thus varied from 7s. 6d. per week for a Wheatley house at Horfield and Bedminster down to 9s. 6d. per week for a similar Addison or Chamberlain house at Sea Mills, Fishponds or Knowle. Parlour houses with three bedrooms varied from 8s. 6d. for a Wheatley house to 10s. for an Addison or Chamberlain house. The Housing Committee's fears about tenant reaction proved correct. Tenants at Knowle and Fishponds campaigned in 1927 to press the Housing Committee to reduce their rents to the level of those charged at Bedminster Down.[138]

With the industrial repercussions of the General Strike affecting jobs and wages, the position of corporation tenants took a turn for the worse in 1926. The amount owed in arrears tripled in the six months after September 1925, and according to the *Bristol Observer*, 812 or 45 per cent of corporation tenants were in arrears, 14 per cent for four weeks or more. Unauthorized sub-letting was flourishing, much to the Housing Committee's annoyance, and it seems to have been tacitly, if grudgingly, tolerated for the rest of the decade.[139]

The main response to the cuts was a renewed concentration on slum clearance schemes under the terms of the 1925 Act, and a renewed attempt to find ways to cut building costs. Even slum clearance and rehousing schemes were problematic. The rents charged at Lawford's Gate and Eugene Street were less remunerative than the rents of Wheatley houses, but they were often a good deal higher than their inhabitants had previously paid for slum dwellings. On the other hand, rehousing slum dwellers at lower rents in cottages was problematic as well, as Sheppard explained to the Council in 1927:

> Supposing the houses to be created . . . were let at rents 2s. to 3s. a week below what was being paid for houses on the Bedminster Down Estate, they would immediately get a demand from the people occupying the latter for a corresponding reduction in their rents [and] . . . if the Committee endeavoured to solve it by adopting the tenement system, under which the rents would be 5s., 6s. or 7s. per week all in, the loss to the Corporation would be greater than it was from the provision of self-contained houses – there would be a loss whichever way they looked at it.

Tenants on the ordinary corporation estates continued, as the decade neared its end, to find the rents a strain on their resources. A considerable proportion of the 1,100 families who left the corporation houses by 1928 did so because they had difficulty in paying their rent. Tenant pressure for further rent reductions continued.[140]

It had long been recognized that low wages were at the root of the rents problem. But, short of a revolution in wage rates, what could be done? The government was hardly likely to increase Exchequer aid; in fact it was intending the opposite. Despite falling costs, it was estimated that a 1s. reduction on corporation rents per week would have meant almost 2d. more on Bristol's rates. Even under the more generous provision for rehousing slum dwellers under the 1924 Act, the government seemed loath to approve truly low rents. Sheppard was particularly frustrated by the Ministry's refusal, in 1929, to approve low rents of 9s. per week inclusive for houses built under the Wheatley Act at Bedminster Down. 'What was the good of the Government one moment telling them to house the people and the next that they must charge a higher rent than the nine shillings they proposed?'[141]

The local housing authority had a number of options when handling the non-payment of rent. It could evict tenants, it could take them to court, it could threaten them with such actions, or otherwise attempt to persuade them to fulfil their obligations. In Bristol, each case of rent arrears appears to have been considered on an individual basis by the Housing Department, which evicted only the very worst offenders.

Tenants were evicted for arrears amounting to as little as £10; a few were given the 'opportunity' of transferring to less expensive and less spacious corporation property. For example, one tenant was transferred to one of the converted army huts at Shirehampton, whilst two others were promised bungalows elsewhere on condition that they promised to keep the property in good condition. In the case of the death of the breadwinner, and in other unspecified cases, a significant minority of arrears were written off, though it is unclear whether the families involved were able to continue to stay in their dwellings. The large number of rent arrears cases occurring in the wake of the General Strike were dealt with at the discretion of the Housing Department Secretary. In other cases, there is limited evidence to suggest that court action was taken to recover monies owed in rent. But according to one retired official working in the Department, as unemployment persisted the Corporation preferred to exhaust methods of persuasion and exhortation before resorting to legal proceedings.[142]

A Bristol Labour councillor reported in 1929 that there was evidence that some tenants were starving themselves to pay their corporation rents. A researcher studying local housing conditions complained in 1930 that whilst the demand for the high-rent subsidy houses, let to clerical workers or well-paid artisans, was almost satisfied, there still remained 'a large unsatisfied demand for houses at 11s. 6d. per week (inclusive) or less.'[143] Yet the Government was bent on a course of further reducing subsidies. The General Election of 1930 finally saw the institution of a rent policy based on tenant need under the Greenwood Act, but there was no standardized comprehensive rent policy throughout the inter-war period.[144] Certainly, during the eleven years after the passage of the Addison Act, the chopping and changing of government subsidies, and the dominance of the retrenchment ethos, prevented the formulation of a coherent and workable strategy. During that period, there was no rents policy, only a rents muddle.

c. Housing management and the tenant
The foundations of Bristol's modern Housing Department were laid in the twelve years after the First World War as the Housing Committee's need for an administrative support system became obvious. The implementation of the 1919 Act also had a wide-reaching effect on the corporation bureaucracy generally, expanding as it did the work load of the City Engineer's Department and the City Treasurer's Office.[145] By 1930, the Housing Department employed under 30 people, whose duties focused on the maintenance, allocation and letting of Corporation dwellings. Such a department seems small and unsophisticated when compared to its modern counterpart which commands a trained staff of over 500 working in a wide range of specialized areas. However, the significance of the early Housing Department cannot be measured solely in terms of size or structure. We must ask what an examination of its early development can reveal about the assumptions behind local provision and management policies. In attempting to assess the development of the Housing Department in these terms, one is led to examine the way in which staff were

selected. Was there a long-term plan of staff development? Or were new staff hired on an *ad hoc* basis as the need arose? What aspects of housing management were developed most intensively? What type of candidates were preferred for which posts? How did Bristol's Housing Department compare with the size of similar departments elsewhere?

The evidence relating to these concerns is scanty, but suggestive. The build-up of staff does seem to have been pursued in its earliest days in a mostly *ad hoc* manner, reflecting the inexperience of the Corporation in housing matters and its unease about the financial commitment involved in public housing provision. The first applications for corporation houses were made before the establishment of the Housing Department and were personally screened by the chairman and vice-chairman of the Housing Committee. The first corporation rent collectors were co-opted on a temporary basis from the Medical Officer of Health's housing inspectorate in April 1920, only weeks before the first houses were let. It was not until July that A.W. Smith was appointed from the Town Clerk's Office to act as 'Secretary to the Corporation Housing Estates.'[146]

Smith appears to have been a hard-working administrator who was keen to build up his staff. He pointedly reported to his superiors on the Housing Committee on the organization of Birmingham's Housing Department which boasted 56 members on its payroll, including a prestigiously titled Director of Housing, a deputy director, a quantity surveyor, an accountant and a resident architect. By contrast, Bristol had to make do with an architect acting in an advisory capacity, one administrative assistant and servicing from the departments of the City Engineer and the City Accountant. Smith's request in 1921 for permanent central offices was at first unsuccessful, although a parlour in one of the Hillfields Estate houses was allocated as the first estate office that same year. By 1923, Smith had one room in the top of the Council House and a staff of six, including one deputy, two rent collectors, a maintenance supervisor, a general clerk and a shorthand typist. The rent collectors do not appear to have been given any specialist training although their duties included the investigation of applications as well as estate administration. Indeed one of the collectors had been recruited from the local taxation department whilst the other was retained from the staff of the Medical Officer of Health. By 1923 the Department employed thirteen people including six at head office and two each at the Fishponds, Knowle and St. John's Lane sites and one at Sea Mills. Such appointments were hardly in the tradition of Octavia Hill. Rather the emphasis was on numerate, hard-headed men who could 'manage' the houses in the narrow sense of ensuring repairs was made, rents were paid, and records were kept.[147]

By 1925, however, Bristol's Housing Officers were having to deal not only with a small proportion of tenants from slum clearance areas, but also with an increasing number of 'ordinary' tenants distressed by the unhappy combination of high rents and low wages. It was in this same year that the Department began to utilize the 74 workmen's dwellings erected in 1901 under the 1890 Housing Act for families 'not in a financial position or *otherwise unsuitable*' for accommodation in the new corporation houses. However, the problem of the dirty tenant continued. Rabbits, it was revealed, were being kept in the bathrooms of certain houses and some properties were being reduced to 'slum standards'.[148] It was in response to such problems and to the failure of an *ad hoc* property-oriented style of housing management to cope with them that several corporations had begun by 1927 to consider the employment of a female housing manager trained in the Octavia Hill tradition. In Bristol, Sheppard favoured the idea of a woman manager, and Miss E. H. White (Citizens Party) echoed his suggestion, asking the Housing Committee to appoint a 'lady social worker', to 'hint' to residents about clean housekeeping standards. Although it was suggested that this would cause resentment amongst many of the housewives so advised, Sheppard was adamant. 'Supervisory workers', he said, 'were regrettably necessary; some tenants needed to be disciplined to do what they ought to do.' In due course it was decided to advertise for a 'Lady House Visitor', to deal specifically with tenants rehoused in the new tenements. In January 1928, one 'Mrs' (actually Miss) Baskett was given the six-month appointment. Thus Bristol became one of the first authorities to recruit a woman trained by the Association of Women House Property Managers, an institute founded by a former pupil of Octavia Hill.[149]

The assumptions behind this appointment appear to have been of a contradictory nature. On the one hand, the Association was the only body which offered specialist training in housing management. In this sense the Corporation ostensibly hired a woman because in terms of qualifications she was professionally superior to her male counterparts. On the other hand, dealings with slum clearance tenants on a personal basis was thought to involve such specifically 'female' qualities as 'an enormous amount of personal attention to detail, tact, discretion, common sense and sympathy.' Neville Chamberlain remarked in 1927 that because the management of small-house property required these personal skills as well as technical knowledge, 'it is admirably performed by trained women and I am convinced that in this direction there is room for an interesting and valuable extension of the sphere of women's usefulness.' It is significant that despite the higher professional qualification of the said appointee, her salary was, at £150 per annum, £20 less than that of the most junior male rent collector. This differential, when considered in conjunction with the fact that the post was seen as specifically suitable for a woman, suggests that the welfare side of housing management commanded less professional prestige than did the technical side.[150]

Furthermore, the element of social control implied by house visiting was recognized and resented by at least one Labour member of the Housing Committee. The personalized approach to housing management had after all been first employed by Octavia Hill to ensure the profitability of her patron's investment. On the other hand, it could not be denied that Octavia Hill's close involvement with her tenants made her, in some respects at least, more sensitive to their needs. Something might have been learned from the value Octavia Hill placed on establishing an integrated approach to housing management, where the tenant was not seen merely as a rent-payer or a husband of property but also as a person with a variety of needs and problems. However, perhaps because the housing service was operating under so many constraints already, some Housing Committee members in the Labour Party preferred to stick to a more property-oriented approach. The segregation of 'house visiting' from the rest of the duties of those engaged in estate management may have been administratively convenient, but it led to a narrowing of vision on the part of those who could leave the welfare work and personal interaction to their female colleagues.[151]

Once the Housing Department was firmly established under the aegis of A. W. Smith, it took over from the Housing Committee the administration of allocation and transfers. Since the overwhelming majority of houses were three-bedroom houses, few if any transfers seem to have been made by families seeking larger accommodation. Furthermore, because of the limited number of corporation houses available, those nearest to the city centre were much sought after, a fact which further inhibited the frequent transfer of tenancies. Apart from the cases in connection with arrears, there is little written evidence on the subject of transfers. According to one former official in the Housing Department, those applications which were made were considered on an individual basis at the discretion of the Department.[152]

It is certainly true that even the Wheatley Act could not provide houses at rents the poorer Bristolian could afford, or in sufficient numbers to supply those who could afford corporation houses but could not afford to own their own home. One should not, however, conclude that corporation housing in the 1920s catered only for the relatively affluent. Although the Addison tenants were originally selected on the basis of their ability to pay, the post-war slump destabilized matters. Sub-letting was said to be nearly universal by 1923, which indicates that the position of even the best paid worker was not always secure. By 1930, the majority of corporation tenants in Bristol were said to be unskilled workers, and the average family size of these tenants exceeded the average for Bristol as a whole. The social and occupational structure on corporation estates had begun to change even before large-scale rehousing of slum dwellers under the 1930 Act began. It should also be kept in mind that even the better paid workers may have been living in intolerably overcrowded conditions before they secured a council house. Over half of the tenants housed by 1928 came from the traditionally overcrowded areas in south, central and east Bristol.[153] In response to the justified criticism that those most in need of housing had not been rehoused, Sheppard pointed out in 1927 that three-quarters of the 20,000 rehoused came from living in 2.25 rooms per family. In 1930 the Housing Department was careful to state that 75 per cent of the families living in Corporation houses had previously lived in two rooms or less.[154]

The selection of tenants was, at first sight, a straightforward enough procedure. There was not a formal points system employed during our period, but rather a set of qualitative criteria. Top priority was given to families headed by ex-servicemen, particularly those men affected by shell shock and poison gas. Special consideration was also accorded to those applicants with a large number of children, to expectant mothers and to those under medical care (especially those suffering from tuberculosis). In addition, note was taken of the state of the applicant's present accommodation, the availability of the type and location of house desired and the date of registration with the Housing Department. By 1930, formal mention was also made of the ability of tenants to pay. In practice, the guidelines remained essentially the same throughout the period.[155]

Implied in this seemingly neutral selection procedure were certain assumptions about acceptable or deserving tenants. The level of rents and their weekly collection clearly implied that the acceptable tenant was prompt and regular in his rent payments. Arrears of even one week were a matter of concern and thus a wide range of people in casual and part-time work was less likely to have access to corporation housing. The payment of rent was perhaps the most important criterion of the good tenant for, baldly stated, the corporation and the ratepaying public were keen to see their capital investment in housing well looked after. From this perspective, the needs of the tenant become less central. The principle of the ability to pay also reflected the Corporation's hope that by housing the better paid worker, the housing needs of the lower paid could be solved or ameliorated by the 'trickle down' process, by which it was anticipated that those who could afford to move into corporation houses would free accommodation in the private sector for the less well off.

However, since the families of Addison tenants were on average smaller than those of Bristol families overall, and since it appears that a number of Addison tenants had been sharing dwellings before moving into corporation dwellings, the 'trickle down' process did not work as anticipated. Housing officers saw at first hand the difficulties experienced by tenants in large, expensive suburban housing. But they also accepted that the houses had to be run along lines approved by the Ministry of Health and by a less than indulgent Council. Conservative and mainstream Liberal councillors were at best uneasy about the notion of publicly funded housing, particularly given the vagaries of Exchequer aid, and therefore wanted it run as 'efficiently' and cheaply as possible. Labour councillors, having fought so long for public provision, were inclined to adhere to a similar norm of efficiency, in order to prove the viability of universalist provision.[156]

The very nature of the accommodation offered, as well as the criterion of family size, excluded the 7.6 per cent of the population who, in 1921, lived alone. In 1930 there were no single people living in corporation housing, a fact deplored by Jevons and Madge as late as 1946, and less than 5 per cent of the tenants in 1930 were childless couples. Publicly owned housing had been justified both nationally and locally in terms of national efficiency. It is at least partly for this reason that tenancies were intended for families with children. It was also assumed that, apart from a tiny number of war widows, the 'normal' tenant would be a male head of family who was also assumed to be sole breadwinner. Yet by 1931, there was an 'excess' of 27,000 women in Bristol, and 31,000 of single people between the ages of 20 and 40 years of age were female.

It is true that the suburban location of the estates made it difficult for many women to find waged work but a number of women did find employment at factories in Bedminster, notably at W.D. & H.O. Wills. Other women were reported to have resorted to taking in laundry in order to 'keep up with the children's appetites', and the expensive corporation rents. It should be remembered too that the widespread practice of sub-letting, usually in the form of taking in boarders or lodgers, must have entailed work for the women of the family. One lady who grew up on the Sea Mills estate in the late 1920s recalled that her dresses and jumpers were both made by female neighbours in their homes. These ladies took payment and supplied other neighbours, but were not classified as 'working' by the interviewee. The network of other necessary services, both paid and unpaid, such as child-minding for female neighbours working outside the home, is not documented locally for this period, and awaits the collection of oral evidence from original tenants and their families.[157]

What is also implicitly assumed in this connection, by the ban both on unauthorized sub-letting and on the conducting of private business from the home, was that the separation between 'work' and 'home' was desirable. In this way, those women who did not fit into the implied norm were either suspect or ignored. Even the otherwise sensitive study by Jevons and Madge noted the correlation between poor housekeeping and women in part-time waged work without explicitly questioning the basic assumption that women were to be solely responsible for housework and child care in a privatized context. Nor did Sheppard or the Bristol Women's Housing Advisory Committee appear to question this basic division of gender roles. The woman of the house was not accorded recognition as a 'worker'; as a 'housewife' she became invisible in official literature, her identity merged with that of the house itself. In this way commonly accepted gender roles were further reinforced by the institution of corporation housing.[158]

The application procedure makes no mention of considering the 'housekeeping standards' of prospective tenants and their families, but official literature shows that the Department was clearly concerned to protect corporation property. There was deep anxiety that tenants would not 'measure up' to their new environment. The Inspector of Housing warned in 1919 that 'habits ingrained by years make many of these people very undesirable as tenants and they would soon render the best type of house into slum like conditions.' There were indeed problems; even in the first Addison Act houses, deposits for repairs had to be quadrupled to £2 a year after the first tenants moved in. The appointment of a Lady House Visitor in 1928 to inculcate good housekeeping standards has already been discussed, but it is worth pointing out that the women whose housekeeping was to be judged were not the legal tenants but merely the wives of tenants. Housing officials were anxious to assure dubious members of the Council and the public that the majority of the 'tenants' had shown themselves worthy of the corporation houses. The terms in which such assurances were made are interesting. A. W. Smith reported in 1930 that 'contrary to the prophecies of pessimists, picture rails are used, and baths are not misused. Gardens are generally very well cultivated and prove of great service to the tenants. Horticultural societies have been formed on the large Estates, and the results obtained are most gratifying.' This emphasis on the state of tenants' gardens is significant. Nowhere, it seems, was the transforming power of the garden more taken for granted than by those involved in corporation housing. The garden was seen implicitly as a major moral regenerator, and a well-kept garden was repeatedly assumed to be the sign of a 'good' tenant. Housing Committee members held garden competitions and Sir John Swaish exhorted tenants to:

> live up to the new conditions in which they find themselves. If they will treat their dwellings, garden, privet hedges and grass verges with proper respect, life would be that much more pleasant for them and they will save the Housing Committee much anxiety and a great deal of money.

The importance of the garden is widely acknowledged to be deeply rooted in British society and is often thought to transcend both class and cultural boundaries. The recent influx of New Commonwealth residents into Britain has, however, underlined the fact that criteria for a properly kept garden are culturally specific. Indeed, the very concept of a garden with cherished ornamental privet hedges and lawns is considered in some cultures to be a profligate waste of water and time. Jevons and Madge found that it tended to be the low-paid tenants who worked at heavy manual jobs who found the upkeep of the relatively large corporation gardens the most burdensome. The ideal of the thrifty artisan or labourer supplementing his diet from a lovingly tended garden did not always correspond with the actuality, nor were gardens the universal indicators of social virtue that was so often assumed. Indeed, most working-class housing in Bristol either had a small yard or patch, apparently used for keeping pigeons or rabbits, for growing a few vegetables, or for nothing at all. The acquisition of a large garden must have proved daunting to those who were not enthusiasts.[159]

Despite the confidence expressed publicly by the Housing Department and Housing Committee members in the majority of tenants, there appears to have been a deliberate policy of discouraging the provision of licensed premises on the corporation estates. Certainly the objections voiced in response to applications for such premises at the Sea Mills and the Horfield Estates throw light on the nature of middle-class anxieties about giving corporation residents ready access to drink. In 1929, neither estate had a pub or off-licence, and tenants had to resort to vans selling alcoholic drink which plied the area. It was felt by professional people living near the Horfield Estate that as many of the corporation tenants had 'come from districts which were slums or not so nice as that district . . . if drink were [to be] brought into the area, conditions would deteriorate.' It was also maintained that the people at Horfield 'could not afford to spend their money on drink.' The low wages which many of the tenants earned, it was argued, meant that 'anything spent in drink was bound to come out of the necessities of the home.' One suspects that it was for these reasons that the Council did not consider the provision of licensed premises on estates to be expedient on moral and social grounds. There were no pubs on corporation estates until the 1930s.[160]

A Housing Committee ruling also banned, shortly after the General Strike, a local branch of the Labour Party from holding 'political meetings on the land under their control.' This ruling does not appear to have been rescinded during the next four years and represented a real restriction on the civil rights of tenants on corporation estates. Throughout the inter-war period the Council appeared reluctant not only to provide venues for public meetings, but also to allow tenants a significant measure of control over the public facilities which were provided. It is interesting that Citizens Party politicians who had proved themselves so hostile to the Labour Party after the General Strike were also those who justified the return to a residualist slum clearance policy on the grounds that slums caused political unrest as well as industrial inefficiency. In any case, petty regulations barring the freedom of individual expression, be it to decorate a house or hold a meeting, derived from a concern to safeguard 'public' property, and a conviction that housing administrators knew what was best for 'their' tenants.[161]

In retrospect, it seems that the corporation tenant was to be diverted from the pub, protected against agitation, advised on housekeeping and tempted into horticulture. The model of a clean-living and right-minded family man, implied by formal and informal procedures and rulings, tells us as much about the values of the housing bureaucracy as about the tenants it administered.

4 Conclusion

By the beginning of 1930, many aspects of Bristol's housing problem remained unsolved. Few of the city's most notorious slum areas had been improved: the few clearance schemes actually implemented displaced more than they rehoused. It had been estimated that as much as 12 per cent of the city's housing stock, or 10,000 dwellings, was unfit for human habitation by the end of the decade. Although the 1931 census showed a substantial decline in the percentage of Bristol families living in overcrowded conditions, from 6.9 per cent in 1921 to 5.3 per cent in 1931, the small proportion of families living in the worst conditions (of three or more persons to a room) had not declined.[162]

Not only did corporation housing fail to cater for those in the worst conditions, it also failed to meet the housing needs of the ordinary working-class population. Not enough council houses were built by 1930 to meet the demand, as evidenced by the 5,000 'live' applications still then on the books. Those houses which were built were generally too expensive, especially when their suburban location is considered, for most unskilled workers to afford. To some extent, these deficiencies were redressed in the succeeding decade. Bristol's relatively buoyant economy during the 1930s, along with the private house-building boom, combined to ease the overcrowding problem and improve the housing stock. Building under the Wheatley Act continued until 1933 to supply 3,700 more houses for general needs. The generous Greenwood subsidy instituted in 1930, augmented by additional slum clearance legislation in 1936 and 1938, supplied another 3,500 dwellings. Falling costs enabled the local authority to reduce council house rents, but it is calculated that 80 per cent of these rents were still beyond the reach of about one-third of Bristol's working-class population by 1938.[163]

It would be ungenerous to paint a completely negative picture of Bristol's performance as a house-provider. Of the nearly 14,000 corporation dwellings built during the inter-war years, most appear to have been better constructed, roomier and more salubrious than pre-war working-class housing had been. But the long-term social and political impact of the under-resourced, isolated and bureaucratically administered estates has yet to be adequately assessed.

NOTES

1 Board of Trade, *Report of an Enquiry into Working-Class Rents, Housing, Retail Prices and Standard Rate of Wages in the United Kingdom 1908*, PP 1908 (Cd. 3864, 115–17; F. W. Lawrence, *Local Variations in Wages* (1899), 82–3.
2 *Enquiry into Working-Class Rents*; The Report of the Medical Officer of Health and the City Engineer in the *Minutes of the Sub Committee on the Housing of the Working Class*, February 1896.
3 D. J. Weber, 'The changing industrial geography of the Port and the City of Bristol', M.A. thesis, University of Bristol, 1966; S. J. Jones 'The growth of Bristol', *Trans. and Papers, Inst. of Geographers* (1946); H. Meller, *Leisure and the Changing City 1870–1914* (1976).
4 Bristol City Engineer, *Annual Reports*, 1898–1914; S. B. Saul, 'Housebuilding in England 1890–1914', *EcHR*, xv (1962), 128; Lawrence, *op. cit.*, 82–3; *Enquiry into Working-Class Rents*, xxxiv.
5 According to the *Report of the Joint Select Committee on the Houses of the Working Classes* (1902), 325, Bristol Council cleared 116 houses with 380 people and provided 70 dwellings for 298.
6 *Enquiry into Working-Class Rents*, 117; Bristol City Engineer, *Report*, 1905; City Accountant's Report and Financial Statement for 1910, in *Minutes of the Sub Committee on Housing for the Working Classes* (1910).
7 Bristol Housing Reform Committee, *Report*, 1907, 19 and 15; Bristol City Engineer, *Reports*, 1904–14.
8 Bristol Housing Reform Committee, *Report*, 1907, 4–6; *Bristol Labour Herald*, 2 April 1910; F. Sheppard, 'Labour unrest and some of its causes' (1912), in Sheppard Collection, BCRO; *Minutes of the Sub Committee on the Housing of the Working Classes*, 30 September 1912, 21 October 1912, 24 January 1913, 13 May 1913, 10 March 1914, 8 June 1915; 'A Garden Suburb for Bristol' (*c.* 1907), in papers of Bristol Garden Suburb Ltd, Bristol Central Reference Library; E. Sturge, *Reminiscences of My Life* (n.d.).

9 Bristol City Engineer, *Report*, 1914; *Report of the Bristol Medical Officer of Health*, 1914; *Minutes of the Sub Committee on Housing*, 16 January 1914.

10 *Bristol Labour Herald*, 2 April 1910.

11 *Minutes of the Sub Committee on Housing*, 29 December 1910, 24 November 1913, 30 October 1913.

12 J. Moore, 'Housing', in *Facts of Bristol's Social Life* (1914), BCRO, Bristol Trades Council Collection.

13 *WDP*, 11 December 1916.

14 *The Labour Woman*, September 1918.

15 M. Bowley, *Housing and the State* (1945), 7–10; *Report of the Medical Officer of Health for Bristol*, 1919; A. W. Smith's memorandum in BHCM, 1928.

16 Bristol Housing Department, 'Bristol housing 1919–1930' (*c*.1930), 1–4, 62ff.; Bristol City Engineer, *Report*, 1930; R. Jevons and J. Madge, *Housing Estate: a study of Bristol Corporation policy and practice between the wars* (1946).

17 Bowley, *op. cit.*, 101–6; 'Housing reports', in *Ministry of Labour Gazette*, 1925–30.

18 For comparative figures, see J. Melling (ed.), *Housing, Social Policy and the State* (1979), 115–16, 210–13, M. Dresser Summerbell, 'Bristol's housing policy 1919–1930', M.Sc.(Econ.) thesis, University of Bristol, 1980, table K. 258.

19 H. W. Richardson and D. H. Aldcroft, *Building in the British Economy between the Wars* (1968), 230–6.

20 'Commercial review supplement', *BTM*, 1 January 1928.

21 The Citizens Party in Bristol was part of the National Citizens Union, founded in the early 1920s. According to one founding member, the Citizens Union was founded specifically 'to fight communism . . . to fight corruption and to reorganise the housekeeping of the nation'. See Benwell, Community Development Project, *North Shields: Working Class Politics and Housing 1900–1977* (1978), 21. BCM, 9 November 1924, 9 November 1930; *WDP*, 15 December 1926, 17 December 1926, 8; *BTM*, 29 October 1926, 8.

22 Only 3 out of 22 members of the Finance Committee were Labour members. Labour members were also under-represented on the Rating and Assessment, Sanitary and Dock Committees: *BTM*, 23 October 1926, and committee lists in BCM, *passim*. *WDP*, 15 December 1926, 9; 16 December 1926, 5; 17 December 1926, 8; 18 December 1926, 8; *BO*, 12 February 1927, 4; *BTM*, 23 and 30 October 1926, 13, 2 November 1926, 5.

23 Derived from a survey of the BCM and *Kelly's Bristol Directory*, 1919.

24 Derived from a survey of the BHCM membership lists; *Kelly's Bristol Directory*, 1919–30; 'Bristol personalities' (extracts culled from *BTM*, 1922–32), Bristol Central Reference Library; BABTE *Minutes*, Research Department, Head Office, Bristol and West Building Society.

25 Biennial Report for 1921 to 1923, Records of the University Settlement at Barton Hill; 'Bristol's house famine' (1923), in Sheppard Collection, BCRO; BCM, 29 May 1923, 196–7; *WDP*, 15 May 1923, 5.

26 *The Times*, 8 April 1924, 7 and 19 June 1926, 12; BCM, 9 November 1923, 6; *Report of the (Bristol) Medical Officer of Health* (1923), 48ff.; *BO*, 11 September 1926, 9.

27 *BO*, 12 February 1927, 4 and 7; *BTM*, 23 October 1926, 13; 10 November 1926, 8; *WDP*, 10 November 1926, 9; 17 December 1926, 8.

28 BHCM, 16 November 1927, 631ff.; *WDP*, 12 June 1927, 7; *BTM*, 19 October 1927, 8; 14 February 1928, 9; *BO*, 16 July 1927, 5; *BTM*, 12 February 1927, 10; 18 October 1927, 9; *WDP*, 1 December 1926, 8; *BO*, 26 March 1927, 5; 12 March 1927, 5; *BO*, 26 March 1927, 5; 12 March 1927, 5.

29 Bowley, *op. cit.*, 169–72; *BTM*, 14 April 1926, 8; 21 October 1927, 8; *BO*, 24 April 1926, 7; 23 October 1926, 7; 12 February 1927, 7; 16 July 1927, 5; 23 July 1927.

30 *BO*, 17 April 1926, 7; 12 February 1927, 7; *BTM*, 14 April 1926, 8; R. Skidelsky, *Politicians and the Slump* (1967), 10–14, 24–5, 27–31, 43–6.

31 BCM, 11 October 1927, 345; *BTM*, 14 February 1928, 5; 12 June 1929, 8; 11 December

1929, 9; 17 December 1929, 8; see O. Banks, *The Faces of Feminism* (1981), 171, 178, for the ambivalence of the organized Labour movement in the 1920s towards the role of women in society.

32 *Statistical Abstracts, 1930*, table no. 18, 180–1. D. Chester, *Central and Local Government* (1951), 48; Board of Trade, *Statistical Abstracts* (1935), 202–5; J. Clarke, *Housing Problems* (1921), 413ff.

33 City of Bristol, *Abstract of Accounts, 1920–1930*; BHCM, 21 June 1920, 325; 7 December 1925, 260; BCM, 8 February 1927, 129; *BTM*, 9 February 1927, 8; Housing Reports in *Ministry of Labour Gazette*, 1925–9; *BTM*, 15 July 1925, 7; 10 March 1926, 9; 18 October 1929, 9. There was officially estimated to be a shortage of 5,000 dwellings in 1919. The shortage grew worse by 1923: *BO*, 23 January 1926, 7; memorandum of A.H. Smith in BHCM, 16 November 1927, 631ff.

34 S. Marriner, 'Cash and concrete. Liquidity problems in the mass production of "homes for heroes', *Business History*, xviii, 2 (1976), 152–89; B. B. Gilbert, *British Social Policy* (1970), 144–50.

35 BHCM, 8 September 1919, 168; BCM, 19 September 1919, 194; 3 December 1919, 39; *BO*, 29 November 1919, 10; 6 December 1919, 8; Marriner, *op. cit.*, 154; Gilbert, *op. cit.*, 148–50.

36 Marriner, *op. cit.*, 154; Gilbert, *op. cit.*, 150; M. Swenarton, *Homes Fit for Heroes* (1981), 119–21; *WDP*, 14 April 1920; see also *The Times*, 4 May 1920, 17.

37 *BO*, 17 April 1920, 6; 1 May 1920, 3; 17 July 1920; 7; 10 July 1920, 6; *WDP*, 14 April 1920; Marriner, *op. cit.*, 155–7; Swenarton, *op. cit.*, 120–1; BCM, 8 March 1921; *Abstract of Accounts, 1921*, 79; Bristol Housing Department, 'Bristol housing 1919–1930' (*c*.1931), 38; W. L. Abernethy and A. R. Holmes, *Housing Finance and Accounts* (1957), 173.

38 *Report of Bristol Housing Department*, 1928; *Abstract of Accounts, 1920–1930*; Bristol City Treasurer, *Annual Report*, 1929–30; U. Hicks, *The Finance of British Government* (1938), 119, 124; *BTM*, 15 July 1925; 7 and 16 July 1925, 7.

39 Calculated from the *Abstract of Accounts, 1920–1930*. This follows the national trend in local authority housing finance, according to Hicks, *op. cit.*, 119.

40 'Bristol housing 1919–1930', 4 and 69; Bowley, *op. cit.*, 42; *BO*, January 1930, 8 and 17 January 1929, 10; *BTM*, 14 March 1928, 13 February 1927, 9; *BO*, 22 December 1929, 9; 11 March 1922, 7; BHCM, 5 December 1921, 172; 24 April 1922, 214–15; 12 June 1922, 232–3, 691–2.

41 M. Dresser Summerbell, thesis, 117–19 and 138; *Abstract of Accounts, 1920–1930*; A.E. Davies, *Public Ownership: Points from Prospectuses* (Fabian Tract, 224, 1928), 5.

42 BCM, 14 May 1918, 128–9; 19 March 1919, 89; 31 July 1928, 311–12; BHCM, 8 April 1918, 15ff.; *Builder*, 24 May 1918, 312; *WDP*, 12 March 1919, 3; *Bristol Housing Department Report*, 1928, 11; *BTM*, 1 August 1928, 8.

43 BCM, 14 December 1920 and 16 July 1918; BHCM, 15 September 1924, 211; information kindly provided by the Research Department, Head Office, The Bristol and West Building Society.

44 Compiled from the Housing Accounts, *Abstract of Accounts, 1919–1930*.

45 A. Shannon and E. Grebenik, *The Population of Bristol* (1943), 11.

46 BCM, 14 May 1918, 14 December 1920, 31 July 1928, 311; *Bristol Housing Department Reports for 1928 and 1931*; *BTM*, 14 April 1926.

47 *Housing Accounts*, especially 'Analysis of capital outlay for 1920–1930' in *Abstract of Accounts*; PRO, HLG 47/285/105/1–2, Ministry of Health Minute Sheet, Report of meeting with deputation from Bristol housing committee (*c*. April–November 1925); BCM, 10 March 1925, 97.

48 BABTE *Minutes*, 13 August 1919.

49 *Builder*, 24 October 1919, 419; *BO*, 11 October 1919, 12; BHCM, 21 August 1919, 159; F.E. Fremantle, *The Housing of the Nation* (1927), 34, 37.

50 *Builder*, 5 December 1919, 572; Swenarton, *op. cit.*, 116–17.

51 BABTE *Minutes*, 16 December 1919, 17 December 1919; BHCM, 28 August 1919, 163; 8 September 1919, 168; 14 October 1919, 188.

52 BABTE *Minutes*, 26 February 1920, 15 March 1920; Marriner, *op. cit.*, 163.

53 BHCM, 7 February 1921, 39; 4 September 1922, 263; 22 September 1922, 263; 20 November 1922, 293; Bowley, *op. cit.*, 34; BABTE *Minutes*, 22 March 1920; BHCM, 1 March 1920, 258; 22 March 1920, 272; BCM, 24 March 1920.

54 BABTE *Minutes*, 13, 21 and 28 April 1921, 22 May 1921, 26 May 1921, 20 June 1921; BHCM, 18 April 1921, 67; Gilbert, *op. cit.*, 149; *BO*, 27 January 1921, 5; 7 May 1921, 9; *Builder*, 20 May 1921, 663.

55 Richardson and Aldcroft, *op. cit.*, 237–9; *WDP*, 9 May 1923, 5; 26 May 1923, 7; 30 May 1923, 7; *Builder*, 8 June 1923, 936; *BTM*, 11 July 1923, 6; 'Bristol housing 1919–30'.

56 *BTM*, 11 July 1923, 6; 19 September 1923, 8; 30 October 1923, 6; BCM, 9 November 1923, 36–40; 10 March 1925, 110; 'Bristol's housing famine', in Records of the Bristol Garden Suburb Company, 7 November 1923, Bristol Central Reference Library, B. 20757; *WDP*, 7 September 1923, 5.

57 *BO*, 23 January 1926, 7; *Builder*, 12 February 1926, 292; 10 February 1928; *BTM*, 10 March 1926, 9.

58 *Annual Report of the Bristol City Engineer* (1919–21); BABTE *Minutes*, 4 May 1920, 21 March 1921, 21 April 1921; BHCM, 12 April 1920, 284; 25 October 1920, 404; 18 November 1920, 420; Report of the Chief Inspector of Housing in the *Annual Report of the Bristol Medical Officer of Health, 1919*; *BO*, 15 May 1920, 5; *The Report of the Inter-Departmental Committee on the High Cost of Building Working-Class Dwellings* (1921), 26 and 31; *Builder*, 24 May 1918, 321; 23 May 1919, 519; 21 May 1920, 616; BCM, 9 December 1919.

59 BABTE *Minutes*, 7 January 1919, 24 April 1919, 29 May 1919, 11 February 1921, 14 February 1921, 21 February 1921, 28 February 1921; BHCM, 12 April 1920, 329; 28 April 1920, 304; 30 August 1920, 375; 25 October 1920, 406–7; 21 May 1921, 78; 25 July 1921, 109–10.

60 *BO*, 13 December 1919, 10; *Builder*, 24 October 1919, 419.

61 *BO*, 12 June 1920, 11; *Report on the High Cost of Building Working-Class Dwellings* (1921), 26, 31.

62 *Builder*, 29 June 1923, 1063; T. Austrin, 'Industrial relations in the construction industry' (Ph.D. thesis, University of Bristol, 1978), 30–2, 60–7; Aldcroft and Richardson, *op. cit.*, 130–1; *BO*, 5 May 1923, 10; 2 June 1923, 7; BHCM, 10 December 1923, 58.

63 PRO, HLG 49/122, Report of Interview with Bristol Housing Committee, 6, 24; *BTM*, 9 October 1923, 6; 11 October 1923, 9; 18 October 1923, 6–7; 19 October 1923, 6; *BO*, 2 June 1923, 7.

64 *BTM*, 31 October 1923; 4, 19 October 1923, 6; 18 October 1923, 6; *Report of the (Bristol) City Engineer* (1922–3), 9–10; *Report on the Present Position of the Building Trade* (1924), 14.

65 BHCM, 17 January 1923, 72–3; 21 January 1924, 93.

66 Richardson and Aldcroft, *op. cit.*, 129; Bowley, *op. cit.*; *The Times*, 31 January 1924, 14; *Builder*, 8 April 1927, 588; BHCM, 16 February 1925, 37; BCM, 31 March 1925, 123.

67 *BTM*, 2 January 1924, 7; 2 January 1925, 7; *BO*, 2 June 1923, 7.

68 BHCM, 5 May 1924, 141; 7 July 1924, 174; 15 September 1924, 211.

69 *Builder*, 4 March 1927, 377; 9 March 1928, 430; BHCM, 26 January 1928, 685, 7 May 1928, 728; *WDP*, 20 March 1928, 5.

70 BCM, 9 July 1929, 241.

71 BCM, 9 December 1919, 43–4; 24 March 1920, 150; BHCM, 19 July 1920, 350.

72 R. Postgate, *The Builders' History* (1923), 444–6; *International Labour Review*, July 1922; L. Orbach, *Homes for Heroes* (1977), 120–5; *BO*, 22 January 1921, 8.

73 Orbach, *op. cit.*, 120–5; *BO*, 22 January 1921, 8.
74 BHCM, 5 September 1921, 116; *BO*, 15 October 1921, 11; *Hansard*, 28 May 1924, 409; 18 June 1924, 2114.
75 *Report on the High Cost of Building Working-Class Dwellings* (1921), 50; BHCM, 4 December 1921, 284.
76 BHCM, 24 June 1918, 40–1; 20 January 1919, 82–3; 20 October 1919, 193; 3 January 1921, 3; 23 May 1921, 22; 6 February 1922, 191–2; Marriner, *op. cit.*, 153; Richardson and Aldcroft, *op. cit.*, 137; *BO*, 24 May 1919, 6; *Builder*, 27 January 1922, 135; *Interim Report on the Prices, Costs and Profits of the Brick Trade* (1920), 5.
77 BHCM, 10 February 1919, 86; 16 June 1919, 128–9; 20 October 1919, 195; 27 October 1919, 198; 3 November 1919, 202; 18 April 1921, 72.
78 Richardson and Aldcroft, *op. cit.*, 34; BHCM, 3 March 1919, 94; 20 October 1919, 193; 30 August 1920, 373; 3 January 1921, 3; 23 May 1921, 22; 6 February 1922, 191–2; *Report on the High Cost of Building Working-Class Dwellings* (1921), 20.
79 BHCM, 31 June 1919, 138; 28 July 1919, 147; 11 August 1919, 153; 22 December 1919, 20; 12 April 1920, 329; 5 July 1920, 336; 19 August 1920, 365; 13 September 1920, 380; Marriner, *op. cit.*, 178ff.; *Bristol Chamber of Commerce Journal*, 1921–7; *WDP*, 19 July 1921, 20 July 1921, 21 July 1921, 28 October 1921; *BO*, 13 December 1919, 10; 31 October 1929, 9; *Interim Report on the Brick Trade* (1920), 6; *Builder*, 29 July 1921, 144.
80 Richardson and Aldcroft, *op. cit.*, 75, 135–6; *BTM*, 14 March 1923, 10, 13 February 1924, 9; 6 October 1924, 5; BHCM, 17 January 1924, 72–3; *Report of the Interdepartmental Committee Appointed to Survey Building Materials*, June 1924.
81 *BTM*, 20 February 1924; *Report on the Present Position of the Building Trade* (1924), Appendix B.
82 BHCM, 22 February 1924, 100; 3 March 1924, 102; *BTM*, 6 June 1924, 16; 6 October 1924, 7; BCM, 20 June 1924.
83 *Reports of the Interdepartmental Committee Appointed to Survey the Prices of Building Materials*, 1924, 1926 and 1927; *WDP*, 4 June 1924, 7; *Hansard*, 3 June 1924, 174, 1042; 25 July 1929, *230*, 1481; *BO*, 11 December 1926, 9; *The Times*, 24 February 1927, 19.
84 *Builder*, 17 June 1927, 990; BHCM, 15 July 1929, 921; 25 November 1929, 3 December 1929, 993.
85 H. Ashworth, *Housing (Housing Standards)* (1947), 11.
86 Wm Cowlin and Son Ltd, *A Record of Building* (1928), 24.
87 See my entry on F. N. Cowlin in forthcoming *Dictionary of Business Biography*. *Builder*, 28 May 1920, 642; 11 June 1920, 694; BHCM, 21 August 1919, 159; 10 May 1920, 308; 5 July 1920, 341; 19 July 1920, 352; 29 November 1920, 433; 31 May 1921, 321.
88 *BTM*, 18 October 1923, 7; 15 December 1923, 5.
89 BCM, 9 November 1923, 41; *Builder*, 30 April 1923, 367; 2 November 1923, 694; *The Times*, 6 October 1924, 8.
90 *BTM*, 16 October 1923, 3; 30 October 1923, 6; 15 December 1923, 5; *WDP*, 13 October 1923, n.p.; 27 October 1923, 5 and 10; BCM, 9 November 1923, 39–40; BHCM, 22 October 1922, 30; 10 December 1923, 58; 17 December 1923, 62; 2 June 1924, 157; *BO*, 18 September 1926, 7.
91 *BTM*, 18 October 1923, 7; PRO, HLG 49/123, memorandum, 10 May 1924; notes on interview, 12 December 1923; HLG 49/122/751/1, 6 November 1924.
92 *The Times*, 24 September 1924 and 7 April 1925, 'Housing and building supplement', viii–ix.
93 BCM, 31 March 1925, 123; 15 June 1925, 7; 14 July 1925, 199–200; BHCM, 16 February 1925, 37; Fremantle, *op. cit.*, 128; *Annual Report of the Ministry of Health 1924–25*, 49; *Report of the Bristol City Engineers 1925–26*; PRO, HLG 49/122; *BTM*, 30 September 1925, 10; *BO*, 18 September 1926, 7.

94 BCM, 11 May 1926, 196; BHCM, 29 September 1927, 606; *BO*, 18 September 1926, 7.
95 'Bristol housing 1919–1930', 38, 43.
96 This term was used by Manning Robertson (a Deputy Architect to the Ministry of Health in the days of Addison) to describe the Chamberlain houses; *Builder*, 30 April 1923, 367, and 9 November 1923, 727.
97 *BTM*, 11 April 1923, 9; *BO*, 12 February 1927, 7; 8 December 1928, 7; *WDP*, 11 April 1923, 7; BHCM, 7 December 1925, 263, 4603; A. Ravetz, 'From working class tenements to modern flats' in *Multi-Storey Living*, ed. A. Sutcliffe (1974), 126–31.
98 BHCM, 10 June 1918, 34; 21 October 1918, 63; 4 November 1918, 66 and 70; 2 December 1918, 74–5, no. 1205; 17 February 1919, 89–90; H. Jennings, *Sixty Years of Change* (1971). The Tudor Walters Report (1918) noted that 'the desire for the parlour was remarkably widespread': cited in N. Branson, *Britain in the 1920s* (1975), 138; *BO*, 15 February 1919, 3, 5.
   For a definition of 'welfare feminism' see Banks, *op. cit.* In Bristol, the local women's co-operative guild, Hilda Cashmore and other Liberal and Labour Party women involved in campaigning for high-standard council housing, had been suffragists before the war.
99 BHCM, 30 September 1918, 58; 21 October 1918, 63; Jevons and Madge, *op. cit.*, 73. Members of the Conservative and Liberal Parties (and later members of the Citizens Party) were not opposed to the notion of the parlour house *per se*; what they objected to was the cost of a parlour house on the rates: *WDP*, 7 April 1923, 5. For local Labour opposition to the erection of non-parlour houses, see BHCM, 18 June 1923, 385; *BO*, 2 June 1923, 7.
100 BHCM, 19 May 1919, 122; 16 June 1919, 128; 23 June 1919, 134 and 136; *BO*, 21 June 1919, 10; C. Powell, 'Fifty years of progress', *Built Environment* (October 1974), 532–5; J. H. Jennings, 'Geographical implications of the municipal housing programme in England and Wales, 1919–1930', *Urban Studies*, VIII (1971), 122.
101 The Bristol Women's Housing Advisory Committee was set up in 1920, with the approval of the Housing Committee and Council, by Miss Hilda Cashmore (the warden of the Barton Hill University Settlement and the founder of the local branch of the Garden Cities and Town Planning Association). The committee wrote a detailed report of recommendations for the new council houses, inspected new corporation houses throughout the decade, and conferred with the Housing Committee. Its function was to advise on housing standards, particularly internal fittings, with an eye to keeping up high standards. Despite its request it was never allowed any formal power, and when its decisions ran counter to Housing Committee objectives, they were politely ignored. Jennings, *op. cit.*, 19; BHCM, 9 February 1920, 240; 25 July 1921, 106–7.
102 *Builder*, 11 June 1920, 694; 'Bristol housing 1919–1930', 68; *WDP*, 21 July 1921; BHCM, 24 January 1921, 27–8; 24 October 1921, 29–51; BCM, 14 February 1922.
103 *BO*, 23 September 1922; *WDP*, 10 November 1922.
104 *WDP*, 10 November 1922; BHCM, 3 July 1922, 237; 4 September 1922, 259; 22 January 1923, 314; 5, 19 February 1923, 327; *BO*, 23 September 1922; BCM, 11 July 1922, 219; 13 February 1923, 97; Jennings, *op. cit.*
105 BHCM, 21 January 1924, 93; 18 February 1924, 97.
106 BHCM, 19 February 1923, 332; BCM, 13 February 1923, 102; *BTM*, 11 November 1924, 9.
107 BCM, 9 March 1926, 151–2.
108 *BTM*, 10 March 1926, 9; *The Times*, 24 February 1926, 14.
109 *BTM*, 7 September 1926, 8; 15 October 1926, 7–8; 19 October 1926, 8; 11 May 1927, 7; *BO*, 9 October 1926, 9.
110 *BTM*, 24 January 1926, 8; 15 December 1926, 8; 1 August 1928, 8; *Builder*, 11 February 1927, 255; *BO*, 16 July 1927, 4; *The Times*, 13 January 1927, 12ff.; BHCM, 16 November 1927, 631ff.
111 *BTM*, 18 October 1927, 9; 21 October 1927, 8–9; *BO*, 22 October 1927, 8.

112 BHCM, 13 June 1928, 7; 31 July 1929, 9; BCM, 16 November 1927, 631ff.

113 BHCM, 16 November 1927, 631ff.: 'Memorandum upon the preparation of a comprehensive housing scheme'.

114 *Ibid.*, BCM, 31 July 1928, 311.

115 BHCM, 21 November 1927, 652; BCM, 31 July 1928, 311; *BO*, 4 August 1928, 7.

116 *BTM*, 1 August 1928, 8; 26 October 1928, 8; *BO*, 10 March 1928, 7; 4 August 1928, 7; BCM, 31 July 1928, 311–12; BHCM, 26 July 1928, 728; 'Bristol housing 1919–1930', 28–9.

117 P. Hall, *Great Planning Disasters* (1980); 'Bristol housing 1919–1930', 28–9.

118 BHCM, 12 April 1920, 286; 5 July 1920, 3; BCM, 24 March 1920, 18ff.

119 BHCM, 8 December 1919, 216, 22 December 1919, 220; 12 April 1920, 284; 21 June 1926, 395; *BO*, 24 April 1926, 7; 7 July 1928, 9; BCM, 9 October 1928, 369.

120 BHCM, 16 November 1927, 631ff.; *BTM*, 24 April 1929, 6; 9 October 1929, 5; 17 October 1929, 8.

121 Jevons and Madge, *op. cit.*, 35–43; A. Jackson, *Semi-detached London* (1973), 129ff.

122 Jevons and Madge, *op. cit.*; BHCM, 10 May 1920, 222; 3 October 1921, 135, 3 July 1922; 8 May 1922, 222; Bristol Housing Department, *Report*, 1955, 55.

123 S. Humphries with S. Mullen (eds), *The Bristol Oral Interviews (Tapes and Transcripts)* (1981), Avon Central Reference Library.

124 'Bristol Housing 1919–1930', refers to the small and irregular incomes of tenants and their inability to pay economic rents.

125 Jevons and Madge, *op. cit.*, 55–6; Bowley, *op. cit.*, 17–20.

126 *WDP*, 29 July 1919, 3; *BTM*, 24 July 1918, 2; BHCM, 30 September 1919, 58.

127 *WDP*, 12 March 1919, 3; *BO*, 17 May 1919, 3.

128 BCM, 9 December 1919, 43–4; BHCM, 26 May 1920, 315; 19 July 1920, 350; 31 May 1921, 320.

129 BHCM, 26 May 1920, 1315; 12 July 1920, 346–7; 13 September 1920, 379; 5 September 1921 (A. W. Smith's report).

130 *BO*, 1 March 1922, 7; BHCM, 5 December 1921, 172; 24 April 1922, 214–15; 12 June 1922, 232–3, 691–2.

131 *BO*, 11 March 1922, 7.

132 A. Sayle, *The Houses of the Workers* (1924), 163–4; BHCM, 12 June 1922, 232, 190; 3 July 1922, 238, 700, 241, 707; 24 July 1922, 249, 746; 4 September 1922, 259, 763–7; *BO*, 15 July 1922, 8.

133 BHCM, 8 January 1923, 311; 5 February 1923, 323; *BTM*, 11 April 1923, 7.

134 *Bristol Housing Department Report* (1925), 8.

135 BCM, 29 May 1923, 199; *WDP*, 11 October 1923, 6.

136 Bowley, *op. cit.*, 42–3; E. Simon, *How to Abolish the Slums* (1929), 118.

137 BCM, 10 November 1924, 109; 9 December 1924, 54.

138 *BO*, 21 May 1927, 9.

139 *BTM*, 19 October 1926, 8; 23 October 1926, 9; BHCM, 22 March 1926, 9.

140 'Bristol housing 1919–1930', 4; *Bristol Housing Department Report* (1925), 8; *BTM*, 13 April 1927, 8; *WDP*, 7 February 1928, 5; BHCM, 7 March 1927, 522.

141 BHCM, 16 November 1929, 631ff. (Smith's memorandum to Housing Committee); *BTM*, 12 June 1929, 8.

142 BHCM, 23 March 1925, 62; 30 April 1925, 83; 18 October 1926, 549; 22 October 1928, 811; 23 December 1929, 1001.

143 *BTM*, 15 May 1929, 9; H. R. Burrows, 'The housing problem in Bristol' (*c.*1931; typed MS, University of Bristol Library).

144 Jevons and Madge, *op. cit.*, 98–9.

145 *Annual Report of the Bristol City Engineer, 1919–21*; City Treasurer's comments, *Abstract of Accounts for 1921–2*, i.

146 BHCM, 27 March 1920, 282; 26 April 1920, 289; 5 July 1920, 338.

147 BHCM, 6 June 1921, 96, 306; 4 August 1920, 357; 31 January 1921, 31; 7 February 1920,

34; interview with Mr Harris, a former member of Bristol's Housing Department, 16 January 1979.

In his report of September 1921, A. W. Smith divides his discussion of the 'management of Housing Estates' into the following categories: deposits, collection of rents etc., arrears, houses vacated, defective houses, repairs, temporary dwellings, care of houses, cultivation of gardens and forecourts, Shirehampton . . . Communal Bath House, undeveloped sites: BHCM, 5 September 1921. See also F. Gray, 'Consumption: council house management', in *State Housing in Britain*, ed. S. Merrett (1979), 209–16.

148 'Bristol housing 1919–1930'.

149 B. S. Townroe, *The Slum Problem* (1928), 186–7; *BO*, 16 April 1927, 4; 21 May 1927, 9; BHCM, 30 May 1927, 565; 26 January 1928, 685; 4 June 1928, 742; 15 July 1929, 921.

150 Sayle, *op. cit.* (1924), 189; Chamberlain's remarks are in his foreword to Fremantle, *op. cit.*; BHCM, 30 May 1927, 565.

151 See Jevons and Madge, *op. cit.*, 94. Although critical of the 'slumming mentality' of some housing welfare officers, the authors saw them as necessary, if inadequately trained.

152 Mr H. Harris, interviews January 1979 and June 1980.

153 See A. W. Smith's report in BHCM, 5 September 1921; *BTM*, 11 April 1923, 7; 'Bristol housing 1919–1930', 53; Jevons and Madge, *op. cit.*, 23ff.; *Report of the Bristol Housing Department* (1928), 6.

154 *BTM*, 13 April 1927, 8; 'Bristol housing 1919–1930', 59.

155 BHCM, 27 March 1920, 282; 5 September 1921; BCM, 17 June 1930, 293. For a brief overview of the development of allocation procedures and a discussion of their implications, see Gray, *op. cit.*, 216–17.

156 BHCM, 5 September 1921; 3 July 1922, 245.

157 BCM, 17 June 1930; Jevons and Madge, *op. cit.*, 95, 97, 24; *BTM*, 9 October 1929, 5; *Annual Report of the University Settlement at Barton Hill, Bristol, 1929–1930*.

158 Jevons and Madge, *op. cit.*, 77. Sheppard, who favoured the 'home life' of the cottage, also advocated some centrally-located dwellings for poorer families so that women and girls could go home to get the dinner ready: *BTM*, 12 April 1920; L. Davidoff *et al.*, 'Landscape with figures', in *The Rights and Wrongs of Women*, eds A. Oakley and J. Mitchell (1976); A. Oakley, *Housewife* (1977).

159 A. Griffith's report on housing in *Report of the Medical Officer of Health for 1919*, 14; BHCM, 5 September 1921; 'Bristol housing 1919–1930', 59; *BTM*, 15 July 1925, 8; 24 January 1927, 8; Jevons and Madge, *op. cit.*, 78; Humphries with Mullen (eds), *op. cit.*

160 BHCM, 4 September 1922, 259, 737; 24 June 1924, 168–9; *BO*, 16 February 1929, 9; 9 March 1929, 9; Jevons and Madge, *op. cit.*, 86.

161 BHCM, 5 July 1926, 401; *BO*, 12 March 1927, 5; 22 October 1927, 8; *BTM*, 18 October 1927, 9.

162 BHCM, 16 November 1927, 632ff.: 'Memorandum upon the preparation of a comprehensive housing scheme'; *Report of the Bristol Medical Officer of Health 1930*: J. H. Burrows, 'The housing problem in Bristol' (MS, *c.*1931). The housing stock had risen by 15.3 per cent to 83,584 occupied dwellings from 1921–31 whilst the population over this same period increased only by 4.5 per cent: *Housing Report, Census of England and Wales, 1931*.

163 'Bristol housing 1919–1930', 62–5; H. Tout, *The Standard of Living in Bristol* (1938); Jevons and Madge, *op. cit.*

Index

Leeds, Municipal Tenants Association, 118, 120
Leeds Permanent Building Society, 103
Leeds suburbs:
 Beckett Park, 146
 Headingley, 145, 146
 Kirkstall, 146
 Lawnswood, 145
 Moortown, 145, 146
 Oakwood, 144
 Roundhay, 144, 145
Leeds, Tenants Defence League, 104
Leeds, Trades Council, 105
Leeds and District Property Owners and Ratepayers Association, 110
Liberal Land Enquiry Committee, 5, 7, 44
Liverpool, 111, 112, 159
Livett, R. A. H. (Housing Director, Leeds City Council), 128, 134, 139, 140, 141, 142
Lloyd George, D., 4
Local Government Board, 60, 104, 123
local government finance,
 pre-1914, 4, 6, 8
 and parties, 4–5, 6
 rates, 10, 21, 22, 23, 24, 51, 52, 53, 54, 56, 57, 58, 65, 75, 80, 81, 83, 84, 85, 86, 115, 172–3, 192, 201
 weakness 20
local politics:
 Co. Durham, 25, 45, 46, 50, 51, 68, 74
 Leeds, 105–6, 111, 118–19
 Bristol, 165, 168
London 3, 4, 7, 8, 9, 28, 32, 112, 156, 195
Londonderry, marquis of (Durham landowner), 59
Lupton, C. A. (chairman, Improvements Committee, Leeds), 144
Lupton, Alderman F. M. (chairman, Unhealthy Areas Committee, Leeds City Council), 144, 146

Madge, J., 32, 195, 197, 206, 207
Manchester, 111, 112, 128, 139, 163, 200
Marriner, S., 10, 178
means tests, 23, 117, 118
Melling, J., 10
Middlesbrough, 43
Miles, Sir Napier, 174
miners, 24, 44, 45
mining subsidence, 58, 59, 63
Ministry of Health, 13, 22, 27, 46, 51, 53, 54, 55, 56, 58, 60, 61, 62, 63, 64, 65, 66, 67, 69, 70, 71, 73, 75, 77, 78, 80, 81, 82, 83,

85, 89, 108–13, 115, 116, 126–8, 144, 178, 199, 200, 206
Ministry of Labour, 180
Ministry of Munitions, 126
Ministry of Reconstruction, 184
Morris, R. J., 25
mortages, 8, 9, 13

National Association of Conservative and Unionist Associations, 192
National Bonds Campaign, 169
National Federation of Building Trades Employers, 66, 176, 180
National Federation of Building Trade Operatives, 180, 181, 183
National Federation of House Builders, 180
National Federation of Property Owners and Ratepayers, 21
national income, distribution of, 8
National Labour Housing Association, 14
National Smelting Company, 183
National Union of Women Workers, 158
Nettlefold, J. S. (Birmingham politican and housing reformer), 2
New Earswick (York), 126
North Eastern Housing Association, 20, 46, 50, 52, 53, 64
Northern Guild of Commerce and Trade Protection Society, 88
Nottingham, 180

Offer, A., 7
Office of Works, 11, 64
old peoples' homes, 45, 61, 70, 131
Oldham, 23
Onslow Committee 1923, 12
overcrowding, level of, 26–7, 42, 43, 44, 47, 50, 78, 79, 80, 104, 114, 115, 158, 208
owner-occupation, 6, 9, 15, 33, 50, 90, 109, 113, 114, 143, 146, 164, 167, 199

Pheysey, Lilian (Bristol Labour councillor), 167
philanthropic housing, 4, 33
Pigou, A. C. (economist), 2
population, 43, 47
 Leeds, 103, 104, 106
 Bristol, 164
Port Sunlight, 159
property management, 8
public utility societies, 5
Public Works Loans Board, 54, 55, 56, 169
pubs, 25, 138, 195, 207–8

221